John Stoughton

Recollections of a Long Life

John Stoughton

Recollections of a Long Life

ISBN/EAN: 9783744661140

Printed in Europe, USA, Canada, Australia, Japan

Cover: Foto ©Thomas Meinert / pixelio.de

More available books at **www.hansebooks.com**

RECOLLECTIONS OF A LONG LIFE

BY
JOHN STOUGHTON, D.D

AUTHOR OF "ECCLESIASTICAL HISTORY OF ENGLAND," "STARS OF THE EAST,"
ETC., ETC.

London
HODDER AND STOUGHTON
27, PATERNOSTER ROW

MDCCCXCIV

THIS VOLUME OF RECOLLECTIONS

IS DEDICATED

TO MY LIFE-LONG FRIEND

THE REV. JOSHUA CLARKSON HARRISON,

WHOSE WISDOM HAS AIDED ME IN PERPLEXITY,

WHOSE SYMPATHY HAS CHEERED MY SORROWS

AND ENHANCED MY JOYS,

AND WHOSE CONSTANT FRIENDSHIP HAS BEEN

THE PRIVILEGE OF MY FAMILY

AS WELL AS MYSELF.

J. S.

ADVERTISEMENT

MORE than forty years ago I edited the autobiography of the Rev. W. Walford. This book, which fully answers to its name, is a remarkable production, entering into the secrets of the author's soul, unveiling the struggles and sorrows of a mysterious experience.

The work now published is of a very different kind. It really relates to others more than to myself, and brings within view some incidents of religious history and aspects of personal character more interesting than any confined to my own experience. It presents associations during a long period spent in various work, in distant journeys, and in friendly intercourse with many distinguished persons.

I enter into no theological discussion, or any relation of spiritual conflicts, the results of such introspection, as the autobiography of my departed friend describes. I only give recollections of what I have seen and heard, especially in relation to those whom it has been my privilege to regard as more or less intimate friends.

It was just after retirement from Kensington that I began to gather up the following reminiscences, with a permission that my family might publish them after my decease. They were then put aside, and not looked at for years.

Within the last few months it has struck me that so many likely to feel an interest in my Recollections have passed away, and others are so far advanced in life, that if the publication be longer delayed, few indeed will be left likely to feel any interest in my narrative.

Conscious of failures in memory at my advanced age, I have availed myself of memoranda made when travelling, long before any book of this kind was contemplated.

I have been greatly helped in this volume by my dear daughter, with whom I reside, who has frequently accompanied me in my travels, and been my valued secretary at home. Without her aid I could not have brought these Recollections through the press.

TUNBRIDGE WELLS,
 January, 1894.

CONTENTS

CHAPTER I

1807—1828

Birth and boyhood in Norwich—Education—My mother—Early tastes — First sight of the sea — Public events—Early studies — Roman Catholicism — Friendships — Religious change—The Christian ministry—College days . 1—18

CHAPTER II

1828—1832

Fellow-students—Public excitements—Old House of Commons—William IV.—Popular preachers in London : Daniel Wilson, Rowland Hill, James Parsons, Irving, Dr. Chalmers—Monthly lectures—Work amongst the poor—Political excitement 19—38

CHAPTER III

1832—1837

First sight of Windsor—Anecdotes of George III.—Rev. A. Redford—New chapel and ordination—Bishop Selwyn—Funeral of William IV.—Queen Victoria's coronation and wedding — Chaplainship to a Highland regiment — Eton Montem—Windsor Auxiliary to Bible Society—Queen's patronage—Windsor a century ago—Eton Institute—Early friendships . . . . . . 39—58

CONTENTS

CHAPTER IV
1837—1843

Sir Culling Eardley and tent preaching—Case of conscience—Public questions—Missionary tours—Newstead Abbey—Byron and Scott—Royal visit to Edinburgh—Up the Rhine—The Rev. W. Walford—Bagster, the publisher—Radicals a century, ago—John Bergne, of the Foreign Office—Tractarian controversy, and No. 90 . . . . 59—75

CHAPTER V
1843—1850

Removal to Kensington—Life of Dr. Arnold—Ladies' schools at Kensington—Kensington friends—Archdeacon Sinclair—British Schools and Duchess of Inverness—British and Foreign Bible Society; London Missionary Society—Young Men's Christian Association — Evangelical Alliance — Sub Rosâ—Tractarianism and Dr. Pusey—Political excitement —Visit to Geneva—Cæsar Malan—Notting Hill Chapel—Father of Rev. F. D. Maurice—Visit to Newport Pagnell and the haunts of the poet Cowper . . . . 76—100

CHAPTER VI
1850—1854

The papal aggression—Discourses on the Romanist controversy—Palace of glass—Evangelical lectures in Exeter Hall—Memorial of Dr. Doddridge—Visit to Germany and Switzerland; thence to Milan, Verona, and Venice—Intercourse at Kensington with remarkable people . . . . 101—119

CHAPTER VII
1854—1862

Visit to Rome: Holy Week, Pio Nono and the feet-washing, Catacombs—Naples—Vesuvius—New chapel at Kensington

—Commencement of the Congregational Union—Algernon Wells — The "Rivulet" controversy — Visit to Berlin, Dresden, Schandau, and Prague—Affecting sudden death at Kensington—Family bereavements—Tour in the Pyrenees—St. Sauveur, the Emperor Napoleon, and Empress Eugenie
120—137

CHAPTER VIII

1862—1865

Bicentenary of Bartholomew ejectment — Family bereavements —Commencement of friendship with Dean Stanley—His sermon on "The Feast of the Dedication"—His sermon when the American President was present—My Eastern tour: Alexandria, Cairo, the Desert, Approach to the Holy City, Communion in the Episcopal Church, Dr. Rosen, Story about the Sinaitic MS., Hebron, Eshcol, Solomon's Pools, Monastery of St. Saba, the Dead Sea, Jordan, Across Olivet to Jerusalem, Journey to Bethel and onwards to Damascus, Reflections crossing the Mediterranean, Rhodes, Storm, Smyrna, Ephesus, Constantinople—Home by the Danube, Germany, and Belgium—Reflections . . 138—161

CHAPTER IX

1865—1872

Church history—Visit to Dr. Hook, Dean of Chichester—Anecdotes of Wilberforce, Bishop of Oxford—The Dean's life at Leeds—Extracts from his letters—Acquaintance with Dr. Swainson — At Cambridge when the announcement of wranglers occurred—Disraeli's school-boy days — Social gatherings to promote union—The Archbishop of Syra at Westminster—Acquaintance with Matthew Arnold—Publication of "Ecclesia"—Friendly intercourse with Bible Revisionists—The Right Honourable Cowper Temple's bill for opening Church pulpits to Nonconformists—Extension of Oxford University—Debate in the House of Lords—Dinners at Mr. George Moore's house after the annual Bible meetings in Exeter Hall—Death of Dean Alford and of Sir Donald Macleod—Party at Lambeth Palace—Bishop Wilberforce's extemporary power—Dr. Guthrie's social habits—The education question—Athenæum Club—Academy Dinner—"Ecce Homo," and Lord Shaftesbury . . 162—200

CHAPTER X

1873

Voyage to America for the General Meeting of the Evangelical Alliance—Hospitality of the President, the Honourable Mr. Dodge—Visit to Sunnyside, where Washington Irving lived, and to the Mountain House overlooking the Hudson—The Niagara Falls—Four days spent on the banks—Description of scenery—Montreal, Boston, Andover, New Haven, and New Plymouth—New York—Proceedings at the Conference—Reception of 600 guests by Mr. Dodge—Meetings at Princeton, Philadelphia, and Washington—Note from the poet Longfellow—Letter of Abraham Lincoln to Mr. Gurney
201—229

CHAPTER XI

1874—1875

Death of Dr. Binney—His opinion respecting the exclusion of liturgical worship—Unveiling of Bunyan's statue at Bedford—Unveiling of Baxter's statue at Kidderminster—Anecdote of Fletcher's preaching at Madeley—Meeting at Kensington on my retirement—Dr. Stanley's speech—Kensington friendships—Results of visits to the poor—Methods of preaching
230—250

CHAPTER XII

1875—1879

Luther celebrations—Death of Lady Augusta Stanley—Her "At Homes"—Anecdotes of Lamartine, Guizot, and Lord Russell—Touching words—Funeral in Westminster Abbey—The three benedictions—The Dean's account of the Royal Marriage at St. Petersburg—Breakfast at Lambeth with Archbishop Tait, and conversation relative to a conference between Conformists and Nonconformists; The plan, The meeting, Subject discussed—Character of the Primate—Visit of the Queen to Mrs. Bagster, who was nearly 100 years old—My pilgrimages to Ban de la Roche and Broad Oak—Days at the Deanery with Dr. Stanley—My lectures at Edinburgh—Scottish society—Singular discovery of lost MSS.—Conference at Basle—Addresses of President M. D. Sarasin—Death of Mrs. Stoughton . 251—284

CHAPTER XIII

1879—1883

Conversation with a distinguished nobleman upon ideas of religion amongst the upper classes — Days at Spezzia, Pisa, and Florence—Introduction to Cardinal Howard, who sent an invitation to visit him—Conversation with a friend of his—The Cardinal's reception very cordial—Offers of a special introduction to the Vatican Library authorities—Successful day in consequence—Protestant brethren in Rome—Christian antiquities—Dr. Somerville's mission—Drive to Subiaco—Home through Venice—Revisit to Italy in 1881—Special work in library at Florence amongst memorials of Savonarola—Death of Dr. Stanley—Character and habits — Cromwell's skull — Tour in Germany — Sir William McArthur's mayoralty—Death of Archbishop Tait—Excursion to the Grande Chartreuse . . . . 285—313

CHAPTER XIV

1883—1885

Journey to Spain in preparation of book on Spanish Reformers: Through France to Figueras, Barcelona, Tarragona, Poblet, Valencia, Cordova, Granada, Seville, Madrid, Escorial, Toledo, Valladolid, Burgos . . . . . . 314—337

CHAPTER XV

1885

Third and last visit to Rome—Changes in the city and its surroundings—Where did Paul live during his captivity?—Evangelical Alliance meetings at Edinburgh and Glasgow—Death of Lord Chichester—Mr. Cheetham, M.P.—Visits to Dr. Magee, Bishop of Peterborough—Lord Ebury and Moor Park—Friends in Norfolk—Increase of Roman Catholics in Kensington—Chapel openings at Hastings—Autumnal meeting in 1886 at Norwich—Bishop's palace
338—360

CHAPTER XVI

I. Church of England—II. Presbyterians—III. Baptists—IV. The Friends—V. Methodists—VI. Congregationalists
361—391

CHAPTER I

1807—1828

I WAS born in the parish of St. Michaels-at-Plea, Norwich, November 18th, 1807. My father was in some respects a remarkable man. For his great integrity, he won the name of "the honest lawyer"; he would undertake no cause, if unconvinced of its justice, and declined the office of coroner because its duties would have shocked his feelings. Of strong understanding, and fond of reading, after living a thoughtless life, he became an earnest Christian, and worshipped with Methodists, chiefly from circumstances—still regarding himself as a member of the Established Church. Two elder sisters and an elder brother of mine were baptised by the parish clergyman; so was I, the Archdeacon of London being my godfather. I have been told that I "was intended for the Church," and some Episcopalian friends have amused themselves with speculations as to what might have been the result.

My mother before she married was a Quakeress, and used to tell of eminent "Friends" she knew in her girlhood, especially Edmund Gurney, who preached "with great power" in the Gildencroft Meeting House. She was brought up a Quakeress by her mother, but her father was, at least in later life, a staunch Methodist. She remembered John Wesley, and used to tell how he took her up as a child and kissed her.

My father died in my fifth year. Of him I have but a faint recollection. My grandfather, at a distance now of seventy-five years, visibly stands before me—a tall old gentleman with flaxen wig, large spectacles, a long, blue, bright-buttoned coat, and big buckled shoes. He was Master of Bethel Hospital, an institution for the insane, in my native city; and, as I spent much time with him for a year before his death, I saw and heard a good deal of the patients under his care. "Master," said one of them, "I want to propose a toast— may the devil never go abroad or receive visitors at home." "What brought you here?" somebody asked an inmate. "The loss of what you never had, or you would not ask such a question," was the prompt reply. A man who fancied himself King of England drew on his cell wall pictures of ships which he called his fleet, and would never speak unless he was addressed as "Your Majesty." I once narrowly escaped severe injury from a woman, who seized me as her child and squeezed me so hard, that no violence could induce her to relax her grasp; but gentle words, and a promise that I should be taken care of, secured my release. Alternate severity and indulgence, at that time, in the treatment of patients led to a sad tragedy in the case of my grandfather, who was killed by a man employed as gardener. He was thought to be harmless, and used to mow the lawn. One morning he drew the scythe across his master's body and nearly cut him in two.

My mother had a dream the night before, and saw in it her father lying on a bed, pale as ashes, which she interpreted as meaning something terrible would happen to him. When, at breakfast time, she was told by a gentleman of what had occurred, she coupled it with what she had seen in her sleep.

We were living at the time in a very old house with diamond-paned windows, a brick-paved entrance hall, and some rambling passages. I well remember the little bedroom in which I slept.

There resided with us an old lady, widow of a Norwich gentleman, who had been a friend of the famous George Whitefield. She used to tell anecdotes of the popular preacher—how he called himself Dr. Squintum, and, when supping off cowheel, a dish he liked, would say, he wondered what people would think of his being so employed.

My mother had a strong verbal memory which her son has not inherited; and it enabled her to instruct and entertain me by reciting long extracts in prose and poetry. She was a great reader and did much to instruct and cultivate my mind by her frequent recitations. My education owes more to this, and other circumstances, than to schoolmasters under whom I was placed. However, of course, rudiments of knowledge fell to my lot in the usual way; but my culture in chief resulted from devouring books, from instructive conversation, and from the delight I felt in observing nature, and looking on what was ancient. When other boys were at play, I liked to get by myself and read; biography and history having for me pre-eminent charms. Lord Nelson had been dead only a few years at the time I speak of, and what I learnt about him as a Norfolk man immensely gratified my curiosity. His aunt was a friend of my grandmother, and great was my delight to see and hear such a distinguished lady; the gratification being enhanced by a bright shilling she slipped into my hand. The river Wensum, old trees by the water-side, the picturesque village of Thorpe, Whitlingham White House and woods, the uplands of Mousehold, walled-in gardens all over the city, wild hedgerows, sheltered nooks and corners under weeping willows, cattle feeding in green meadows, and swans swimming on the river —these objects afforded me an æsthetic education.

From a child I took an interest in historical tales, and felt delight in listening to my mother's memories of early days. She recollected the American war, and spoke of a family dispute amongst her elders, which lasted just as long—ten years. Excitement in William Pitt's day she brought vividly before me; and she told how Thelwall, the orator, delivered revolutionary harangues, and being attacked by a mob, he was glad to escape by clambering over the roofs of houses. The trials of Horne Tooke, Hardy, and others, and Erskine's famous speeches in their defence, were in my boyhood modern incidents. Objects in the city excited archæological tastes. The Norman keep, Herbert de Lozinga's Cathedral, Erpingham Gate, the Grammar School, the Bishop's palace, with ruins in the garden, dilapidated towers on the edge of the river, Guild Hall, St. Andrew's Hall, and the Old Men's Hospital—these had for me a mighty charm, creating fancies by day and dreams by night. The East Anglian city had not old houses such as Prout found on the Continent, but it contained picturesque, tumble-down tenements, and other "bits," sketched in "Highways and Byeways of Old Norwich." The sight of these created a habit of looking after ancient quaint remains, which has never forsaken me.

Guild day, with its triumphal arches, carpets and flags hung out of windows, Darby and Joan sitting in a green arbour, the Mayor's coach attended by "Snap," and the "whifflers"; the rush-strewn cathedral pavement, as the Corporation marched up the nave—all this gave birth to boyish enthusiasm for the picturesque. Every Guild day, on a green baize platform near the west door of the cathedral, the head boy of the Grammar School delivered a Latin oration before his Worship. What envy that boy aroused in my bosom! Elections, too, were objects of intense interest to me as a childish politician, when Whig candidates were carried in blue-and-white satin chairs, on the shoulders of men who tossed them up, as the Goths did their heroes upon battle shields.

As to another part of my education, I loved to read the lives of eminent people, and devoured a good many memoirs of men and women in religious magazines. Norwich was at that time distinguished for literary, artistic, and benevolent celebrities; and I felt proud as a boy to think of them as pertaining to my own birthplace. The appearance of several amongst them I have still, after the lapse of seventy years, vividly before me—Mrs. Opie, the Taylors, the Martineaus, Joseph John Gurney, and Bishop Bathurst, with several beside.

May I add, the first sight of the sea at Yarmouth I can never forget. It was a November morning in my ninth year. The sky looked angry; the wind-swept waters and tall billows broke furiously on the beach; the hulk of a stranded vessel lay on the sands—emblem of life's shattered hopes.

Public excitements prevailed in my boyish days beyond what the present generation has witnessed. After the battle of Waterloo, and the consequent peace, which was coupled with an idea of plenty, large loaves were paraded on poles as symbols of abundant food, mistakenly supposed to come as a natural consequence now that Buonaparte was conquered. There arose, instead of this, much distress amongst the lower class, greatly owing to corn laws enacted for the protection of agricultural interests. Bread riots followed, and I now catch glimpses of a mob in 1816 marching to the New Mills to sack a granary, and shoot into the flushes of the river Wensum, loads of grain and flour. Such tumults were surpassed in breadth and depth of feeling, amongst the upper class, by the excitement attending the return to England of Queen Caroline after the accession of George IV. in 1820. Never have I known such agitation in private circles, as when society split from top to bottom on the question of her Majesty's character and wrongs. For months there were almost incessant processions from London to Hammersmith in honour of the lady, who was sojourning at Brandenburgh House. Unnumbered addresses were presented to her, and whenever her carriage appeared, it evoked rapturous shouts. During her trial things were done and said startling beyond parallel. Documents full of abominable details were deposited in a "green bag," which called to mind the words in Job xiv. 17 ; and when filthy evidence was furnished on the king's side against his wife, counsel on her side attacked him as a second Nero, and compared him to the infernal shadow in Milton, which "the likeness of a kingly crown had on." Round the hearthstone families and friends were divided on this absorbing subject; and such word battles as Home Rule now occasions were then far surpassed.

My school days over, I entered a lawyer's office. He put into my hands "Blackstone's Commentaries," which interested me less in what was said about real and personal property, the rights of things and the rights of persons, with the law of descent and entail, than in what appeared touching legislation, and the principles of government. De Lolme on "The Constitution," I read with avidity. Having to attend the Law Courts at times, I listened to forensic eloquence with great interest; a love for oratory being further gratified by hearing speeches at public meetings when Lord Suffield and Joseph John Gurney advocated negro emancipation and other reforms.

Theological discussions interested me immensely. The lawyer in whose office I was became a Roman Catholic, and, finding me an inquisitive youngster, talked on the subject, explaining the doctrines and ceremonies of his Church. Whilst the information he gave me was worth having, I determined to read Milner's "End of Religious Controversy," and other Catholic books; and beyond my interest respecting matters of an antiquarian flavour, I felt the importance of ascertaining true grounds for Protestant beliefs. My master took me once a week to North Walsham, and in cold winter nights, as the moon shone on the snow-sprinkled hedges, plied me with arguments for transubstantiation, purgatory, and the like. I ventured humbly to dispute his positions, and to contend for truths on the opposite side; though the match was unequal between a boy of fifteen and a man of forty, primed by the priest to whom he owed his conversion. Those night drives were useful, and led me to see some of the better aspects of Roman Catholic faith and character, whilst they aroused inquiry, and led to clearer convictions than I might otherwise have reached respecting principles in debate. Here let me observe that early intercourse with friends of different denominations has in the best sense broadened my habit of looking at questions, and inspired a tolerance, not of error itself, but of persons holding error, because they are often better than their creeds, and have in them a great deal that is good, as well as something of another quality. Quiet intercourse in early life with members of various denominations I find to have been a school for the culture of Christian charity.

Removed when about sixteen to another office, with the idea of entering the legal profession, I met with fellow-clerks of education and taste, who proved very helpful; one in particular became an intimate friend. He had been a favourite pupil of an eminent classical schoolmaster, and was well up in Horace. We had much talk on subjects of common interest. His temperament had a melancholy tinge, owing to his state of health, for he was in a slow consumption, but behind dark clouds there lay a sky full of humour, and his conversation often sparkled with unaffected wit. He could be a little satirical at the expense of juvenile follies, in which he did not share; whilst amiability kept him from giving pain to the most sensitive. Our friendship continued until his early death, when he passed away " in the faith and hope of the Gospel."

Amongst early educational influences which I enjoyed may be reckoned the opportunities I had of listening to public speakers of different kinds—lawyers at the bar, preachers in the pulpit, orators on the platform, and candidates during elections; for Norwich was contested most earnestly in my boyhood. Moreover, the city was remarkable for musical culture. It had weekly concerts. Festivals also occurred; these I attended again and again with much enjoyment. My friends who know my ignorance of music will smile at this.

It might be when I was about seventeen that on a Sunday morning I took a walk into the country with a volume of Chalmers' sermons under my arm. I read one of them on Rom. v. 10. The perusal deeply affected me, and on the evening of the same day, I heard a Methodist minister preach upon John iii. 16. These two impressions commenced a lifelong change in my experience and character—a change so great, that it led to the abandonment of my former occupation, and issued in the consecration of my after-days to the Gospel ministry.

About that time a journey to London on legal business gave me an opportunity of hearing distinguished preachers, Dr. Adam Clarke and Dr. Collyer amongst the rest—a privilege which deepened my religious convictions. I may observe in passing, as regards my visit to London, that the first sight of it, on a dull morning after a night in the Norwich mail, I have never forgotten—Bishopsgate-street, the Old Post Office, and all round the Mansion House—how different the neighbourhood appeared in 1826 from what it does now! In Waterloo-place, Pall Mall, I spent more than a month, and I can now see George IV. descending the steps of Carlton House (where the Duke of York's column stands), leaning on a page's shoulder on the way to his carriage.

On returning to Norwich, my thoughts fixed on the subject which had previously engaged my attention. A few years ago, when conversing with a friend in the coffee-room of the House of Commons, a report was mentioned of a certain Dissenting minister's intention to enter Parliament, if a seat could be obtained. My friend remarked emphatically, "That would be a come-down." He himself at that time held office, and was on the way to become a Right Honourable; and when I expressed my surprise to hear him talk so, he rejoined that he considered the Gospel ministry as the highest employment on earth when a man really "*was called to it.*" I felt, sixty years ago, exactly in that way, and only wished to know that such a call awaited me. I spent some months in coming to a conclusion, and at length felt convinced that it was my duty and privilege to spend life in Christian preaching and pastoral work.

Then arose the question, In what ecclesiastical connexion? My relation to Methodism had arisen from circumstances, but now some study of ecclesiastical principles was necessary. I began to read what I could on the subject, acquainting myself with different sides, and being open to conviction one way or another. I had no predilections, and was ready to be either a clergyman or a Dissenting minister. I arrived at the conclusion that Congregationalism, *on the whole*, as far as I understood it, came nearest to New Testament teaching; but that probably no existing connexion corresponded exactly with Churches of the first century. What I thought then has been confirmed by studies in after-years, devoted largely to the New Testament and the history of Christendom. I have learned to distinguish between principles lying at the basis of religious beliefs and existing organisations through which they are worked out. The former may be true and sound, whilst the latter are defective, and in some points mistaken.

It is curious that at the time I first made up my mind I knew socially next to nothing of Congregationalists as a body; my chief associations having been with Methodists, Quakers, Churchpeople, and a few Roman Catholics. I joined the venerable society of Christians assembling in the Old Meeting House, Norwich; its fathers and founders having been gathered into Church fellowship, during the seventeenth century, under the teaching and influence of William Bridge, who resided in Yarmouth; some of the members being Norwich folk. When I expressed my desire for the ministry to two Dissenting ministers—the pastor of the Old Meeting House and his friend who occupied Princes-street pulpit—I met with different opinions, the former advising me to pursue the study of law, the latter encouraging my desire for the ministry. In the end these two friends concurred in advice, the consequence being my introduction to Highbury College, London.

I had from the beginning cautions against forsaking in after-life the pulpit for any other post. William Godwin, the famous author of " Political Justice" and other works, also W. J. Fox, the Anti-Corn-law lecturer, a distinguished public character at that time, had been intended for the Dissenting ministry, and, indeed, entered it. By a remarkable coincidence, both these distinguished men were connected with the Old Meeting House, where I then was accustomed to worship. Their abandonment of an early faith and a sacred calling for the sake of literature and politics, was held up to me as a beacon, to warn me off dangerous rocks.

Before noticing my entrance into college, I may

be allowed to mention that the congregation which I joined contained some noteworthy people. Mr. William Youngman was a hard-headed, intelligent, and inquisitive man, much given to theological argument and incisive criticism of current opinions. He tried the patience of orthodox religionists, and was the terror of neophytes. Once, when I dined with him, he commenced talking about original sin as I was hanging up my hat, and went on in the same strain to the end of my visit. He found his match at book meetings in Mr. Thomas Brightwell, F.R.S., an eminent naturalist, whose name is perpetuated in a memoir of a plant called after him, to be found, if I correctly remember, in the Transactions of the Royal Society. He was a diligent student of the Bible, and published notes on the Old Testament, drawn chiefly from the Scholia of Rosenmuller and Michaelis.

In 1828 I entered Highbury College, afterwards merged in New College, St. John's Wood; the professors—or tutors as they were called in my time—being Dr. Henderson, Dr. Burder, and Dr. Halley. Dr. Henderson had been engaged in foreign missionary and Bible work, spending much time in St. Petersburg, Copenhagen, and Stockholm, where he became acquainted with the languages of

Northern Europe. He drilled us in the languages of the Old Testament, initiated some small study in Syriac, and delivered elaborate lectures on the evidences and doctrines of Christianity. He suggested essays to be written during the vacation on subjects demanding research, and he regularly required the careful preparation of comments on the original Scriptures, to be delivered *viva voce* in class. Dr. Burder was son of George Burder, once well known as the author of "Village Sermons." He lectured on mental and moral philosophy, and employed as text-books the works of Reid, Stewart, and Brown having himself graduated in a Scotch university. Exceedingly careful, conscientious, and precise, he opposed all bold speculations, and was incapable of sympathy with mystical thinkers. He had a clear apprehension of whatever he taught, and used to lay down as a canon of composition. "Express yourselves, not so that you *may*, but so that you *must* be understood." Dr. Halley was a good classical scholar, impulsive, unsystematic, and by no means a severe disciplinarian. He enthusiastically admired Demosthenes and Cicero, and to hear him give extempore versions of these orators was an immense treat. We read with him some Greek tragedians and Latin poets, and he delivered lectures on history and antiquities. Mathematics came within his department; but, certainly in my time, he never turned out a wrangler. His influence, however, was very stimulative, and he inspired when he did not instruct.

Defects in the Nonconformist educational system were apparent to me at that time, much more so have they become to me ever since; but, to a considerable extent, they arose from uncontrollable circumstances, so many students having had few advantages in their boyhood. I have lived to witness a great improvement in Nonconformist college methods.

It should not be omitted that during the latter part of our term a few of us attended the mental and moral philosophy class of Professor Hoppus in the London University College, Gower Street, that institution having been established by friends of unsectarian education, and numbering on its councils, and amongst its officers, several Nonconformists.

CHAPTER II

1828—1832

MY most distinguished fellow-student for intellectual power and literary attainment was Henry Rogers, afterwards a large contributor to the *Edinburgh Review*. Some of the articles he wrote for that periodical have been published as essays in three volumes. His feeble voice stood in the way of his being an effective preacher; but his learning and ability eminently fitted him for the duties of a professor. In that capacity he rendered high service at Spring Hill, Birmingham, and next, at Lancashire College, Manchester. He was highly esteemed by Lord Macaulay, and Archbishop Whately; excessive modesty alone prevented his introduction to the highest literary circles.

He was a clear-headed, acute thinker and reasoner, delighting in Socratic talk, trotting out an unsuspicious conversationalist, until he entangled him in inconsistency and contradictions, the remembrance of which might be afterwards useful. Rogers, to the end of life, was a humble and devout Christian. Our intercourse in after-days was pleasant, and to me most encouraging.

William Drew, who became a devoted Indian missionary, was another of my contemporaries, and, from sympathy with him, I caught a portion of his spirit; had I possessed the needful qualifications, I could have devoted myself to a similar enterprise.

Samuel Bergne, for many years an able and much-appreciated secretary of the British and Foreign Bible Society, was another of my fellow-students. With him I became extremely intimate, owing, in part, to an extraordinary family affair, which I have been requested to relate. My father, before he married, had living with him a sister, to whom he was strongly attached. After their separation, she went to reside in London, and dropped all correspondence with him; to the day of his death he could never ascertain what had become of her. Methods were adopted to find out her residence, but all in vain. More than thirty years had elapsed since she disappeared, when one day I met Bergne, who had been visiting his mother at Brompton. " Have not you a relative there ? " he asked. " Not that I know of," was my reply. Then he told me that an evening or two before, as he was sitting by the fire, it flashed upon him how he had heard that an old friend of his mother's, before her marriage, bore the same name as mine ; that she came from Norwich, and that her brother was a lawyer. I was taken aback by what my friend said, and then related what I had heard in childhood respecting my father's long-lost sister. " Depend upon it," he exclaimed, " I have found for you the lady your family have been seeking in vain." I soon received a request to meet the stranger at Mrs. Bergne's house, when something like a scene occurred, as the separated relatives stood face to face. Yet neither then nor afterwards did she shed any light upon the mystery. She had a husband who proved to be no less a mystery. We never could learn anything about his connections ; but, at the time of my introduction to him he was engaged on *The Morning Post*. We afterwards learned from himself, as well as others, that he had been employed in this country as an agent of the Imperial French Court ; certainly he had in his possession a key to the cipher-writing, used by the first Napoleon. He showed me relics of that extraordinary man, and had much to say of several notabilities at home and abroad. What of fact mingled with fiction in his strange disclosures I cannot say; but, after his death, I saw some of his papers, including an unintelligible correspondence between Mr. Canning and himself; also letters relating to private scandals of great people, only fit to be thrown into the fire. He lived in an imaginary world, and used to say that Napoleon Buonaparte was still living. To his influence, I suppose, the mystery which shrouded my aunt's life after her marriage, might be ascribed.

The four years I spent at Highbury were marked by much political excitement. In 1828 the Corporation and Test Acts were repealed. The Catholic Relief Bill was carried in 1829. In 1830 William IV. succeeded his brother. The "three days of July" the same year occurred in Paris: the abdication of Charles X., and the accession of Louis Philippe, swiftly followed each other; and a fresh impetus was thus given to the cause of English liberalism. The Duke of Wellington's protest against reform, the defeat of the Ministry on the Civil List, and the introduction of the Reform Bill the next year, produced an excitement which I do not think has been equalled since, though for passionate discussion in the homes of England, it has been surpassed by what occurred during the trial of Queen Caroline. Earl Grey, Lord Brougham, and Lord John Russell were popular idols, their names in everybody's mouth, their portraits looking down from innumerable shop windows, their busts set up in house after house, their likenesses printed on handkerchiefs and stamped on pipes and jugs, and all sorts of ware. They were mobbed and hurrahed wherever they went, and their carriages were dragged by the populace through streams knee-deep.

At that period the old House of Commons was standing, and went by the name of St. Stephen's Chapel. Within its walls the Reform battle was fought; and there still lingered round it memories of Pitt and Fox, Burke and Sheridan. I had a great curiosity to see this English forum, and when I obtained admission, with my tutor, Dr. Halley, who explained the building and what was going on, I seemed to be in an old Presbyterian meeting-house, with galleries on three sides, the Speaker's chair, with its wooden canopy, resembling a pulpit, at the farther end. Members were "cribbed, cabined, and confined." The forms of the House were interesting to me, and afforded a framework in which to insert images of men in the reign of George II. I had but to put Court dresses and cocked hats on the members, and forthwith the age of Walpole came back to view. A messenger from the Lords, the bowing of an officer as he approached the table, with its wigged clerks, and other matters of ceremony illustrated my readings of Parliament business in olden times.

One figure especially I now recall—that of Sir Charles Wetherall, a fierce opponent of reform. Up he rose, violently gesticulating, his shirt very visible between his black waistcoat and dark nether garment.

The coronation of William IV. and Queen Adelaide indicated a change in that august ceremonial, which showed how reform touched royal pageantry. Though an instance of a double coronation, it came short of the elaborate display when the previous monarch sat alone in Edward's chair. I saw the procession going down to Westminster, along a narrow street at Charing Cross—old-fashioned shabby shops standing where now you catch sight of palatial hotels—old Northumberland House, with its gardens, occupying the space now become a broad avenue. The beefeaters, the trumpeters, and the footmen in attendance upon the gaudy state-coach, with its royal occupants, were very picturesque. And what a crush there was to avoid the mob streaming down from the Haymarket!

All sorts of reports were afloat, tending to make the new king popular. It was said, that immediately after his accession, he came to town in the dickey of his carriage, and invited, after an unceremonious manner, his old naval friends to come and dine with him. A story went the round with rare applause that, after the defeat of the Reform Bill, when he wanted to dissolve Parliament, he said if the royal carriages could not be got ready, he would go in a hackney coach. How far such tales were true I do not know; but a nobleman, present at one of His Majesty's dinner-parties at the Brighton Pavilion, told me that, on that occasion, the king toasted some of his guests in sailor fashion, and remarked that his seafaring pursuits had scarcely fitted him for a throne. Then, pointing to the queen, he added that for any improvement in his ways he was indebted to that good lady. The story raised him in my estimation and that of many others.

I must now turn from politics and royalty to what was more in my own way.

The Rev. Daniel Wilson, afterwards Bishop of Calcutta, stood high amongst London Evangelicals as Vicar of Islington, and I sometimes heard him in his crowded church; but my great delight was to walk down to Camberwell to listen to Henry Melvill, then in the zenith of his popularity. His manner was peculiar—he had a curious shake of the head, and a strange inflection of voice at the end of a sentence, which kept up attention. As to style, he was artificial in the extreme; every paragraph seeming to be planned on the same model, ending with the words of his text as a well-turned climax. The preacher swept his auditors along with the force of a torrent from point to point. I heard him at Barnes, when he was advanced in life, deliver one of his old discourses, I should judge little, if at all, altered; but it lacked the fire of early days, and the congregation evinced little of the sympathy which seemed to quiver in London churches at the sound of his voice twenty or thirty years before.

Rowland Hill, though a very old man in 1830, continued to fill Surrey Chapel with a crowded audience. I listened to a sermon in which he recommended young people when they set up house-keeping to secure one piece of furniture especially—*i.e.*, the looking-glass of a good conscience, so that husband and wife, keeping it clean, might see themselves in it, with joy and thankfulness; "for a good man is satisfied from himself," and, he added, "so is a good woman." John Angell James, of Birmingham, was one of the most popular preachers at that time, and he occasionally occupied Surrey Chapel pulpit; but William Jay, of Bath, was a more regular "supply," and echoes of his sonorous voice I still catch as I read his pithy and impressive sermons. When he came to preach Rowland Hill's funeral sermon I had left college, and he honoured me with an invitation to preach for him at Bath the Sunday following. In 1886, when I occupied the same pulpit in my old age, a lady told me that she remembered my being there more than fifty years before, when the people wondered at their pastor's sending "such a boy to take his place." A similar occurrence had happened when Jay first preached for Rowland Hill.

James Parsons, of York, was a frequent visitor to London, and used to occupy for several Sundays in the year the pulpit of Moorfields Tabernacle, and that of Tottenham Court Chapel. Congregations gathered an hour before service to listen to this youthful preacher. He had been educated for the law, and, with a strong taste for rhetorical efforts, had cultivated, by the study of English authors, his own extraordinary gift for public speaking. Almost inaudible at first, his voice would gradually rise into tones shrill and penetrating; and after repeated pauses, when people relieved themselves by bursts of coughing, he would, during his peroration, wind them up to such a pitch of excitement as I have never witnessed since. He was thoroughly evangelical and devout, and did an immense deal of spiritual good. I became intimately acquainted with him in after-years, and found in his friendship a source of much enjoyment. His conversations in the parlour were as full of anecdote and humour as his sermons in the pulpit were of pathos and power. I have heard a member of Parliament, one of his deacons at York, say that Mr. Parsons' eloquence in early days was perfectly electrifying, and that, as he listened to him at that time, he felt as if he must lay hold on the top of his pew to prevent being swept away by the force of the preacher's appeals.

Edward Irving occupied the Caledonian Church in Hatton Garden, a retired and ugly-looking Presbyterian meeting-house; but the nobility flocked round him, and it was picturesque to see Scotch schoolboys in Highland kilts placed in front of the pulpit. As I was trying to get in at a side door, up walked the gigantic orator, with his black locks and broad-brimmed beaver, as if an old Covenanter had risen from the dead. An infant lying in the arms of that strong man added to the effect of the picture. His manner at that period was grand. His sermons were carefully prepared and read, every word, but with a blended majesty and pathos which no extempore utterance could exceed; and his reading of the twenty-third Psalm, Scotch version, was inimitable. His favourite word, "*Fatherhood*," quoted by Mr. Canning with admiration, and now so hackneyed, impressed religious people wonderfully by its freshness. A fellow-student took me some time afterwards to call on him at his house in the then New Road. He was unwell and sat by the fireside wrapped in a blue gown. He talked to me for some time on the subject of baptism, the right understanding of which, he said, was a key to many theological questions. I could not assent to all he said, nor indeed understand it, but did not dare, at my age, to make any reply. When he had ended he slowly rose from his chair. It seemed as if he would never finish rising, he was so tall. When erect, he waved his hand to a nursemaid, who was walking across the room with a babe in her arms, and then, placing his hand on my head, he offered a solemn intercession, suggesting the idea of a Hebrew prophet blessing a young Israelite.

At a later period he took up peculiar views on prophecy, and on some ecclesiastical points. Then he became wild and incoherent. I heard him preach outside Coldbath Prison to a few bystanders, very differently from what he had done in Hatton Garden. He seemed to have lost unction as well as thoughtfulness and eloquence. On a cold winter morning, before breakfast, several students and myself walked down to his new church in Regent Square to witness "the gift of tongues," which, amongst other imaginations, he believed had been miraculously bestowed. The building was dark, for the sun had not risen, and the mysterious gloom heightened the effect of the exhibition which followed. First arose inarticulate screams, then exclamations of "He is coming!" "He is co-m-i-ng!" drawn out in marvellous quavers. What appeared to me inarticulate and incomprehensible sounds, were regarded by him and many people as Divine utterances. They deemed them the return of Pentecost—a gift of tongues. At London Wall Church I saw him afterwards arraigned before the presbytery for heretical opinions touching the Lord's humanity. He fought his battle manfully; and whatever people might think of his sentiments, they could scarcely fail to be impressed with the sincerity and earnestness of the man. The trial issued in his expulsion from Regent Square—poor fellow! It is touching to think of his history; popularity was his snare. It turned his head; yet, after all, he sacrificed that very popularity to sincere convictions. His latest life was an instance of martyrdom for conscience' sake. Those who condemn his opinions must honour the man.

Dr. Chalmers came to preach at Regent Square After the benefit derived from his printed sermons, I might well desire to hear his voice. The pitch of excitement to which he wrought himself up surpassed everything of the kind I ever witnessed. His vehemence was terrific, yet all seemed natural. He was John Knox over again—John Knox in manner, more than John Knox in thought and eloquence of expression. He moved on "hinges," as Robert Hall said, or rather, "like a cloud, that moveth altogether, if it move at all." The fact is, he felt what he was saying. It went down to the depths of his own soul, and hence it reached the souls of others. The crowd in the church was immense, numbers standing all the time; yet it was curious to learn that the sermon was already in print—in print, I believe, years before. He often redelivered his discourses, even after publication; and Dr. Wardlaw of Glasgow told me his distinguished neighbour informed him, that he tried to lessen the crowds at church by announcing that next time he meant to deliver what they had heard already. "Yet," with a childlike simplicity the old man added, "they come in still larger numbers than before!" Not many preachers are troubled in that way.

At the time now referred to, religious services were not multiplied as at present; hence great interest was taken amongst London Congregationalists in what were called "Monthly Lectures," given by ministers who carefully prepared what they delivered. Three come back to my recollection now. The first, in Jewin Street, was delivered by Dr. Collyer, a popular divine, who attracted the notice of royalty, and had the Dukes of Kent and of Sussex to hear him. I knew him well in after-days, when he spoke of friendly intercourse with him, vouchsafed on the part of Queen Victoria's father. The subject of the doctor's lecture was

"Our Colonial Empire," and a felicitous text was selected from Ezek. xxviii. 14—16. He urged on his audience the claims of distant colonies, then much neglected; and he painted vivid pictures of England's commercial wealth and vast possessions, insisting strongly on our national responsibilities. The second I remember was in Claremont Chapel, from the lips of my tutor, Dr. Halley, on the importance of intercessory prayer, showing its place in Church history, as a pivot on which turned events of unutterable importance. A third, at Bermondsey, was delivered by a minister of great pulpit gifts, named Dobson, who discoursed on the topic of the final resurrection. I am not in the habit of saying the former days were better than these, yet I may be permitted to express my opinion that those three lectures would bear favourable comparison with the best productions in Nonconformist homiletics at the present day. Among venerable forms present at these lectures, to officiate or listen, were Dr. Winter, of New Court, now covered by buildings sacred to the law, a man of high repute, stout in figure, and strong in opinion; and Dr. Pye Smith, spare, attenuated, ethereal in presence, Melancthon-like in spirit, and as full of learning as Melancthon, with scientific knowledge which entitled him to the place he held by the side of accomplished geologists. I may also mention James Stratten, of Paddington, who had an eagle's eye, and a combination of face, voice, thought, and style which rendered him unique amongst preachers, —like Rembrandt amongst artists—rich in lights and shadows. Nor should Dr. Fletcher, of Stepney, be forgotten, whose purity of thought, felicity of diction, and depth of evangelical sentiment attracted large audiences. The Claytons were well-known members of this goodly fellowship. How these and other names are passing out of remembrance!

Looking back to " sixty years since," I am struck with the difference between certain aspects of Metropolitan Nonconformity presented then, and others familiar now. Indeed, a similar state of things is obvious when we turn to the religious history of other great cities. Citizens then for the most part *lived* in London. Westminster and the opposite side of the Thames saw, on Sundays and week days, in the same neighbourhood both the poor and rich. Thus pious families exerted an immediate and constant influence where they lived, and my remembrance of Metropolitan domestic life then is intensely gratifying. There were happy homes in London where now want and misery abound. Organised district work goes on, but it is a poor substitute for the presence of godly and philanthropic people in their own homesteads, coming in constant contact with those who needed sympathy and help.

Efforts were not wanting for the benefit of London on the part of Christian people in general. The City Mission had then been recently founded, and students in Highbury College lent a hand in work amongst the poor. I remember a district in existence, called Saffron Hill, full of old tenements now swept away. Some fellow-students went with me to the spot on a Sunday afternoon, and we preached from a doorstep, while women looked down from their windows, and perhaps men below were smoking their pipes. Drury Lane was a dirty, neglected neighbourhood; and, in a room hired there, we conducted a service on Sunday nights. Sometimes disturbances arose, but the work went on. Nor were certain districts in the country round London neglected. There we preached and visited the aged sick, praying by the bedside, and ministering such instruction and comfort as we were able.

Public religious meetings in those days were comparatively rare, and the style of speaking was different from what it is now—more ornate, with apostrophes and appeals of a kind which has vanished away. The annual Bible gathering was held in Freemasons' Hall, the floor covered with a closely-packed audience. A passage was partitioned off on the left hand side for the access of speakers to the platform, who were eagerly watched, and loudly applauded, as they approached, their heads amusingly bobbing up and down as they quickened their pace. The diminutive William Wilberforce, eye-glass in hand, his head on one side, came skipping along; Dr. Ryder, Bishop of Gloucester, with big wig, and smooth apron, followed at a more dignified pace; Cunningham, Noel, and other evangelical celebrities were sure to be present. Rowland Hill, by his quizzical look, and humorous tongue, could not fail to make a mark; and Burnet of Cork, who afterwards became pastor of the Independent Congregation, Camberwell, was a vast favourite, his rising to speak being a signal for loud cheers. There he would stand, calmly extemporising sentences which exactly hit the occasion, and the audience'—all eyes turned towards him— upturned faces seeming, as he said, to resemble "a tesselated pavement." He liked to compare North and South Ireland with one another, as showing the contrast between a Bible-reading and a Bible-ignoring population.

After Exeter Hall had been opened there arose a tremendous controversy about Unitarians and the Bible Society. Some well-known speakers could not get a hearing, and the scene on the platform was terribly confused, until Rowland Hill rose and put the assembly in good humour, by remarking that he "would accept the Bible from the hands of the devil; only he would keep him at a distance, and take his gift with a pair of tongs."

In the same place anti-slavery meetings were held. I remember one in particular when, besides Buxton and Mackintosh, O'Connell and Sheil were present. Mackintosh spoke with philosophical calmness. O'Connell was full of invective, satire, and pathos; one moment terrific in denunciation, then heart-melting in tones of sympathy; now stamping with his foot, and laying hold of his scratch wig, as if he would tear it in pieces; next, with gentle whispers, drawing tears, or creating laughter. Sheil, in a torrent of declamation, was carried off his legs, borne along by his own impetuosity, completely overmastered by himself; whilst his Irish friend never lost self-control amidst most violent storms of passion.

Some time afterwards, I listened to Lord Brougham in the same hall on the same subject. He was then past his best days, but flashes of oratory, full of satire and invective against the party he had left, burst forth in a long speech, which, as chairman, he delivered in the middle of the proceedings, to the interruption of previous arrangements. It was, I suppose, by no means equal to his earlier efforts, but enough remained of thunder and lightning to remind one of his eulogised resemblance to Demosthenes.

CHAPTER III

1832—1837

WHEN I first saw Windsor in the winter of 1830-31 how different the town appeared from what it did afterwards! All about Thames Street and Castle Hill was crowded with old houses and shops on both sides of the way, and the walls bounding Lower Ward were hidden from view, except where the Clock Tower, which stood in advance, looked down upon the passers-by. A large plain brick mansion, called the Queen's Lodge, long since removed, occupied the right hand of the road leading to York and Lancaster Gate, while old-fashioned tenements lined the approach to the royal precincts. On the night of my first arrival patches of snow covered the roofs, and dotted the pediments of doors and windows; over Henry VIII.'s gateway hung a gorgeous hatchment in memory of George IV., who had not long before left this life.

It was slow travelling from London to Windsor in those days, especially when the waters were out, and the roads were heavy, and thick fogs rendered the leaders invisible to the coachman; whilst deep ruts clogged the wheels and now and then an icy flood came up to the axles. In the town I heard a great deal about "Windsor of the olden time," when highway robbers were rife, and gentlemen who took to the road would lie in wait under cover of a plantation, and, galloping over a field, stop the traveller and lighten him of his purse. According to one informant, a tradesman in High Street, at the latter part of the eighteenth century, kept a swift-trotting nag, which he mounted after dark to do a little business on the road, and then returned richer than he went. People at that time, as I heard some of them say, did not think of riding or driving over Hounslow Heath alone; but, when approaching that ill-famed spot where gibbets lingered by the roadside, were careful to wait till a number was formed able to defend themselves against the attack of thieves. The sobriety of many inhabitants in the royal borough did not stand high, and at mayors' feasts the guests did not think they sufficiently honoured the hospitalities of the evening, unless they drank so much as made it difficult for them to find their way home.

Anecdotes of George III. were rife. I heard that he used to rise early, take a walk before breakfast, and sit down in a certain bookseller's shop, looking at publications on the counter. But one morning he saw a book by Tom Paine lying there; after that he paid no more visits. Sometimes he said very shrewd things. A Bow-street runner, named Townsend, liked to attend early prayers when His Majesty was present, and to make himself heard in loud responses. One day he was running about after service looking for something he could not find. "Townsend, Townsend, what are you after?" "I have lost my hat, please your Majesty." "You prayed well," was the monarch's rejoinder; "but you did not watch." The king had a wonderful memory; and once, as a troop of yeomanry rode past in review, he pointed out a man amongst them of whom he had bought a horse twenty years before, and whom he had not seen afterwards.

An old inhabitant, who became my father-in-law, vouched for the truth of some of these stories; and bore testimony, not only to the condescension and familiarity of George III., but to the kindness and consideration of George IV. One remark which my friend and relative used to make as he was walking through the apartments of the castle, produced a startling effect. Stopping before the picture of Charles I., he would say: "He looks just as he did when I last saw him." The fact was that my relative was present when Sir Henry Halford superintended the exhumation of the beheaded king; and he first caught a glimpse of the royal face, because he assisted in cutting open the coffin lid. The face was perfect, and exactly resembled Vandyke's famous portrait of Charles I. When exposed to the air the dust crumbled away.

After preaching at Windsor, as a student, several times, I received an invitation to become co-pastor of the Congregational church. The Rev. A. Redford, a man of singular consistency of character, who by his conduct as a Christian minister won the respect and confidence of the town generally, as well as of his own little flock, had been in office for many years, and needed assistance in his sacred calling. He won my heart; and as a son with a father I laboured with him in the gospel. George III., who had a domestic or two in his household attending on this good man's preaching, was heard to say: "The clergy are paid by the country to pray for me, but Mr. Redford's praying is without pay."

In the prospect of my becoming co-pastor, the congregation in 1832 determined to build a new chapel, the one in existence being not sufficiently large ; and as a sign of the honour in which the senior minister was held, I may mention, that Church-people, as well as Dissenters, contributed to the fund. The late Earl of Derby, then Mr. Stanley, who represented the borough, subscribed £50. The other member gave a like sum. The vicar and almost all the leading inhabitants were found on the list. The fact is now mentioned to indicate the good understanding between different classes of religionists which then existed in Windsor.

I was ordained the day after the new chapel was opened, at the beginning of May 1833. It was a service long to be remembered. Such services were thought more of in those days than they are now. Ministers and friends came from a great distance, and a large congregation was sure to assemble. Generally the spirit was devout. An introductory discourse illustrated the grounds of Nonconformity. After this several questions were answered by the candidate, as to his Christian experience, doctrinal sentiments, and reasons for believing he had a call to the ministry. A deacon of the Church related the steps which had led to the present choice, and, afterwards, the ordination prayer was offered with a solemn laying on of hands. In my case, my venerated co-pastor fulfilled this duty; and it was interesting to me that, in like manner, he had been ordained by Rowland Hill. A charge to the inducted minister followed; then came a sermon to the people, pointing out their duties. The holy influence of that day rests on me to this hour, after the lapse of more than fifty years.

The fresh impetus now given to our religious work served to stimulate friends in the Establishment, who had so helped us in our department of the one great cause. A Sunday evening service was commenced in the parish church, and a new Episcopal place of worship was erected in Eton, where it was much needed. In addition to the vicar of Windsor and his curates, some of the masters at Eton College came forward in parish work, rendering help by sermons at a third Sunday service then recently commenced. The Rev. T. Chapman, afterwards a Colonial bishop, took the lead, and did much to revive religion in the town. But the most distinguished labourer at the time was the Rev. G. A. Selwyn, then connected with

Eton, who was afterwards one of the most heroic missionary bishops of modern times; with him it was my privilege to co-operate in the establishment of the Windsor Infants' School.

He would fain have induced me to enter the Establishment, but though he did not succeed in that respect, he ever treated me with a brotherly regard, which I sincerely reciprocated. Before he embarked for his distant field of labour he wrote a farewell note in which he said: "On the few points in which we differ, I thank God we have been enabled to dwell, often at some length, without one particle of that acrimony which often discredits controversy, and proves it to proceed rather from human passions than from zeal for the truth of God. I cannot recollect, throughout all our intercourse, one single word which can be considered as a breach of charity between us. For this I am especially thankful, that when I go to offer up my gift upon far distant altars, I shall have left no brother at home, with whom I ought first to have been reconciled."

I had a ticket for St. George's Chapel when William IV. was interred. The interior of the building was dark, except as illumined by torches in the hands of soldiers who lined the nave, and by numerous lights within the choir. When the procession drew up about nine o'clock, at the south entrance, the blaze of outside torches was seen through the stained windows; then the appearance of heralds in their tabards followed: next the slow march of mourners close to the coffin, the Duke of Sussex being most conspicuous; afterwards a funeral dirge echoed from the fretted roof. The silence was further broken by the Burial Service and the repetition of royal titles. "Sic transit gloria mundi" came last, and left an ineffaceable impression.

I was further favoured with a ticket to see the coronation in Westminster Abbey. When the procession entered the nave, officers of state and foreign ambassadors appeared in rich costume. Diamond-decked coats and rich mantles made a grand show, yet they chiefly served to set off the simple dignity of the queen in her early girlhood, whilst a spell of loyalty touched spectators looking down from lofty galleries. The coronation shout of "God save the Queen" needed to be heard that it might be fully understood. Afterwards, a stream of dignified personages, with mantles and coronets, issued from the choir and covered the nave with a tesselated pattern of rich colours.

To the coronation succeeded the royal marriage,

honoured at Windsor by extraordinary festivities; and at night the cortége of the bride and bridegroom, on their way to the castle through decorated and illuminated streets, evoked a rapturous welcome from assembled thousands. But what above all other incidents of that occasion lives in my memory at the present moment is the sudden view which I caught a day or two afterwards of the wedded pair in a pony carriage, driven by the bridegroom as his bride nestled beside him, under his wing, with simplicity which gave exquisite finish to the chief pictures which passed before me that summer.

Another incident may be mentioned. At a town meeting it was proposed that an address of congratulation should be presented to Her Majesty by the mayor and others. The presentation followed at a levée. It was interesting to see notabilities assembled in St. James's Palace at the first public reception by Her Majesty after the royal marriage. Amongst a crowd of noblemen in the ante-room were pointed out, in particular, Dr. Phillpotts, Bishop of Exeter, with an eagle eye indicative of his intellect, and Joseph Hume, the sturdy economist; both of them much talked of at that period. Others I have forgotten. After waiting we were ushered into the presence, the Queen, with Prince Albert at her side, occupying a place near a window not far from the entrance door. Since that I have knelt before Her Majesty more than once, but how great the difference between the first and last occasions—the girl become a matron, the sparkling bride a sorrowful widow, and the newly-married wife a mother with sons and daughters standing round in reverence and affection.

If I may here anticipate a Windsor ceremonial of later date, let me mention the royal presentation of colours to a regiment of Highlanders to which I acted as chaplain. The colours were bestowed in the quadrangle of the castle on the day when the christening of the Prince of Wales took place. The Prince Consort, the King of Prussia, and the Duke of Wellington, with several other grandees, formed a group under the shadow of the castle porch. As chaplain to the regiment I was allowed to stand near, and was struck with the Prince's German accent, which he seemed to conquer in later life, when he spoke almost like a born Englishman. The Duke addressed the soldiers in his accustomed plain style, giving them very good advice. Preparations for the banquet in St. George's Hall, which a number of people were allowed to see, were very magnificent, tables being covered with gold and silver plate. Some antique pieces brought from the Tower were of special interest. In the evening I joined the non-commissioned officers, to whom a dinner was given, and I was glad of an opportunity to recall to their minds the Duke's address. This Highland regiment while in Windsor attended worship in our chapel, when the band accompanied the singing, and Highland bonnets hung round, outside the galleries. I visited the barracks, conversed and prayed with the sick, and baptised the children. My relations with the colonel and the officers were pleasant during the whole time that the Scotch remained in Windsor.

Going back a few years, let me notice "Eton Montem," then witnessed in all its splendour. Approaches to the college were guarded by boys in fancy costumes: coloured velvet coats, yellow boots, caps decorated with graceful plumes, appeared on the scene. The youngsters levied a tax on all comers, calling it "*salt*," which they deposited in bags suspended from their necks. As royal carriages swept across Windsor bridge, picturesque sentinels received handsome donations from royal hands. The gifts, together with a large number of others, formed a fund for the captain of the school to defray his expenses at Cambridge, whither he was sent in prospect of a fellowship. The procession of boys to Salt Hill, where the captain waved a flag after a prescribed fashion, excited immense interest, and was witnessed by multitudes. The sight in the college gardens as the day closed, afforded perhaps the best of the pageant, for these lads, attired in Turkish, Greek, Italian, and other showy garbs, mixed with their friends so as to form a picture of animated life, with old trees and old buildings for a background.

I had not been long in the town before I became intimately connected with the British and Foreign Bible Society, which laid a strong hold on my affections as a boy, and to which I firmly adhered, after I became a man. Our auxiliary was a flourishing one. Some relatives of Lord Bexley, president of the parent society, lived in our neighbourhood, and used to come over to our annual gatherings in the Town Hall. One of them, the Rev. Mr. Neal, of Taplow, was a constant visitor. He typified a class of men now almost extinct. They loved the Establishment, and, judging of it by its formularies, identified it with the cause of evangelical religion. They knew much less of

Anglo-Catholic theology than of Puritanical works. Owen and Baxter occupied a conspicuous place on their literary shelves, by the side of Latimer and Calvin. The Evangelicals were nevertheless faithful to their own ecclesiastical order, preferring episcopacy to any other form of government. Not on social or literary grounds had they sympathy with Dissenters, or from what is now recognised as "breadth of opinion," but they cultivated union, on purely evangelical grounds.

At our Bible Meeting, with good old Mr. Neale, other evangelical clergymen were present, also one of our borough members, Mr. Ramsbottom, M.P. (who always took the chair), and Sir John Chapman, a strong conservative Churchman, was sure to be on the platform. I cannot say that the speeches were brilliant, though the deputation from London interested us much. First came Mr. Dudley, who had been a Quaker, but was then an Episcopalian; and, to the facts he detailed, there were added peculiarities of utterance, which gave a flavour to what he said. He slightly stuttered ; and once, as he described how the blind were taught to read with their fingers the pages of embossed Bibles, he said it reminded him of the words, " That they should seek the Lord, if haply, they might *feel after*

Him and find Him." Hesitation of speech made the quotation increasingly effective. After him came Mr. Bourne, who had, I believe, been formerly a stipendiary magistrate in the West Indies; and he had a singular *click* in his voice. He told a story of some ladies who had coloured their maps so as to distinguish, by a pink colour, the countries where the Bible was circulated—thus "*pinking* the world for Christ." The good man's click told curiously on his pronunciation of words; and I used, sometimes, to make my Bible Society friends smile, by inquiring whether they offered a premium for agents with a "*diversity of tongues.*" the Rev. Sydney Godolphin Osborne—the famous "S. G. O." of *The Times* newspaper—had at that period a living near Windsor, and took great interest in our auxiliary. He was a fine, tall, aristocratic young man, of straightforward character, strong common sense, and a racy style of utterance. He made capital speeches, and in many ways helped on our work; in one way especially, which deserves distinct mention. He thought it would be a good thing to obtain royal patronage for our auxiliary, though Her Majesty's name was not identified with the parent society. He wrote to Lord John Russell, then a Cabinet Minister (whose brother,

Lord Wriothesley Russell, after he became Canon of Windsor, lovingly supported our cause). When Lord John laid the request before Her Majesty, she graciously gave her name as local patroness, and sent a donation of twenty guineas. It is worth mentioning that this occurred at a time when party politics were running high. Two letters communicating the Queen's kindness may be here inserted.

The first was addressed to the Honourable Godolphin Osborne.

"Sir,

"I have the honour to acknowledge the receipt of your letter respecting 'The Windsor Auxiliary Bible Society,' on which the Queen was last year pleased to bestow her patronage, which I have submitted to the Queen, and though Her Majesty does not usually grant a donation to those institutions to which Her Majesty's patronage only has been given, yet, the Queen, taking into her consideration that the establishment in question is in the immediate neighbourhood of Windsor Castle, has been pleased to direct me to forward twenty guineas as a donation. I beg to enclose a draft for that sum, and request you will have the goodness to acknowledge its receipt.

"I have the honour to be,
"Your most obedient servant,
"H. WHEATLEY."

This letter was conveyed to me by the person addressed, who added the following note:—

"I wrote to Sir H. Wheatley about a donation from the Queen to the Bible Society. I have received a satisfactory answer, and a draft for twenty guineas. If it meets your approbation, I would wish that the fact should not be known to any but ourselves just now. At the present moment the country is so *party-mad*, and there is such a determination to catch at anything for party purposes, that I am anxious to avoid giving a handle of any sort to either side in a matter which has no real reference to politics. I only wrote last week from Wales, and got an immediate answer, which I have acknowledged, saying, at the same time, that at the anniversary meeting a more official acknowledgment will be sent.

"I remain,
"Yours truly,
"GODOLPHIN OSBORNE."

This letter sheds light on the state of public feeling existing at that day.

In connection with the town of Windsor, let me mention two or three traditions I received from the lips of my beloved wife, who became the light of my dwelling on May 12th, 1835. Her good old father, Mr. George Cooper, had long been a sort of Christian Gaius, receiving as guests under his hospitable roof several men and women of renown. Often would she speak of Rowland Hill, who repeatedly visited her home on his way to Wotton-under-Edge, where he spent the summer months. He delighted to preach in our little chapel in High Street, where the Eton boys would attend to see and hear the eccentric old clergyman, who in his youth had been one of their predecessors as a schoolboy. He would tell Mr. Cooper how he used sometimes to steal at eventide beyond Eton bounds, to attend a prayer-meeting in a cottage, which he could reach only by leaping over a ditch with the help of a long pole. He allowed the good woman who lived there an annuity, which Mr. Cooper used to convey as long as she lived. Rowland Hill liked to hear at High Street Chapel the Hundredth Psalm in Watts's Hymn-book, and the youngsters who came used to alter the last verse, shouting: "When *Rowland Hill* shall cease to move."

I remember hearing how Charles Wesley, the son of the great hymn-writer, visited the town, accompanied by his sister, and spent an evening in Mr. Cooper's house, greatly to the joy of my wife as a girl. They arrived in a sedan chair, dressed in Court costume. His execution on the piano was surprising; and those who watched his thick, short fingers, as they swept over the keys, said it was miraculous how he played.

Before I conclude what I have to say of my life in Windsor, let me advert to attempts I made to promote intellectual and literary improvement, according to methods then beginning to be popular. There was an Institute formed in the adjoining town of Eton for the encouragement of reading amongst such as had not enjoyed the advantages of early education. A room was opened, furnished with a few books, where inducements to what is termed mutual improvement were provided, and there the famous astronomer Sir J. F. W. Herschell delivered an inaugural lecture, which gave it at once a character of distinguished respectability. I was invited to join in the infant enterprise, which I did with pleasure and satisfaction, and felt it an honour to become one of its lecturers. The effort made at Eton was followed at Windsor. I threw myself into the enterprise, and worked on its behalf as long as I remained in the town. The committee honoured me with an invitation to lecture in the Town Hall, where my effort was kindly accepted by a large audience; a short course on the History of the Castle and Town followed. This, by request, was published in a volume dedicated, by permission, to the Prince Consort. In its preparation assistance had been furnished through books, documents, and advice, by residents in the town, and by officials in the castle.

In concluding this chapter, I am constrained to notice some friendships which were enjoyed by me during my Windsor residence. Poyle is a small hamlet on the Great Western road not far from Windsor, near Colnbrook. Sixty years ago a long line of mail coaches passed every night the turnpike-gate, as cottagers heard the blast of the guard's horn, and stepped out to see the coachmen, in like livery, handling the reins which guided their teams. Hard by the spot there was a paper mill, spanning a pretty little river, the Coln, which kept the machinery in motion. The whole formed a picture common in the early part of this century, not so common now. Close to the mill were two goodly residences, occupied by two brothers named Ibotson, of an old Nonconformist stock, who could trace back religious ancestors to Puritan days. What pleasant gatherings of congenial friends I met with at Poyle!—neighbouring pastors, and the Rev. Joshua Clarkson Harrison, born not far off, and at the time building up a goodly reputation in London and its environs, were of the number.

In contrast with these bright circumstances, I must notice incidents of a far different kind. My dear wife lost about that time two brothers in early life by what we call accidents; but, worse still, while I was from home one summer, my beloved mother, who lived with me, set fire to her muslin dress, while the servant was absent, and immediately became enveloped in flames. Some one passing by endeavoured to render assistance, but it was too late, and the next morning she expired. Bright summer weather was for a long time after that, to my eyes, covered with a pall of darkness; and to look on the blue sky and the gay summer flowers only made me more sad.

CHAPTER IV

1837—1843

BEING disposed beyond immediate pastoral duties to help in religious work outside, I found ample opportunities for doing it. Sir Culling Eardley was at that time zealous in the furtherance of village preaching. Coming to Windsor, he offered to help us in purchasing a tent for services in the neighbourhood. It was procured and employed, but with less success than had attended his enterprise of the same kind in Hertfordshire. I undertook, at his request, a fortnight's tour in that county, and one evening preached near a wood, where John Bunyan, in days of persecution, addressed the neglected peasantry.

Revivalism at the period now referred to, attracted attention in England, in part owing to the circulation of American books, and the preaching of American divines. A great awakening occurred at

Reading, Henley, Maidenhead, and Windsor. Streams of people might be seen on dark winter mornings, lantern in hand, on their way to the place of prayer. Chapels were thronged, ministers were in full sympathy with each other; all worked with a will. Looking back on the whole, I believe genuine good was done; yet in some instances the effect was transient. Conversion was insisted upon, and peace with God through Jesus Christ was offered; but whether moral improvement in the details of human life was proportionally emphasised, and practically carried out, I am not prepared to say. Certainly, appeals respecting holiness in general were not wanting. Rightly to adjust the balance, so as to guard against self-righteousness on one hand, and the neglect of personal responsibility on the other, requires vast wisdom. To induce people to look at themselves and to Christ also, cannot be accomplished without thought and discrimination in promiscuous gatherings. Whatever might be defects in the movement, assuredly they did not come from artificial arrangements. No one can be said to have "got up the thing."

At all times in the course of our ministry "cases of conscience" occur. One in particular I may mention. I was once sent for to visit a dying person. The home, the people, the surroundings, excited revulsion, as well as a determination to improve a strange opportunity. I found a young woman on her deathbed, and another sitting by, who used phraseology indicative of evangelical sentiment. She offered to leave the room that the patient might unburthen her mind to me. It was obvious some secret of guilt lay on the sufferer's conscience. I had no wish to be a father confessor, and pointed her to the *only One* who can pardon sin. At last the dying creature uttered a piercing exclamation, which seemed to me an acknowledgment of sin. What the secret was she did not disclose. Presently she entered "the silent land." When I called again, I intimated to her attendant my surprise at what she had said, for I could not doubt that she was leading an immoral life. She frankly confessed she had fallen into vice, after expressing a belief that she had been converted, and *had* been a "child of God." The incident was affecting, instructive, and admonitory.

Public questions interested me much, and I took part in those which belonged to philanthropy and religion. Amongst them at the time I speak of, negro emancipation stood foremost. From boyhood it laid hold on me. Speeches at

Norwich, by Joseph John Gurney and others, had left an abiding impression; and when the great controversy became ripe for settlement, I threw myself into the struggle. The excitement throughout the nation was intense, and it laid hold chiefly of the religious section of the British public. Missionaries had been at work amongst negroes, and had seen the horrors of the system. The persecution of Smith, a missionary in Demerara, who died in prison, evoked passionate sympathy; and the appeal of Knibb, another missionary, who came over as an advocate of emancipation, struck the nail on the head, and drove it into the centre of this colossal wrong. Nothing is more manifest, to those who witnessed what went on in England half a century ago for slave emancipation, than that, however manifold the arguments employed, however numerous the methods and agencies in motion, it was Christianity which lay at the heart of the movement. Quakers were amongst the most zealous co-operators in this advocacy for freedom, and I much enjoyed the fellowship into which I was brought with followers of George Fox, early family associations strengthening bonds of friendship between us. Deputations went up to London to wait upon Mr Stanley, Colonial Secretary, afterwards

Earl of Derby, and I well remember the crowd gathered in a large room in Downing Street, to strengthen the hands of that gentleman in his chivalrous enterprise. The history of steps which led to the final victory it is not for me to tell in these pages, but I may mention the third reading by the Lords of the Emancipation Bill in August 1833. It filled multitudes with joy; and on August 1st, 1834, the Act took effect, when a solemn celebration of the event occurred in England, as well as the West India Islands. That day I preached at Windsor from Jer. xl. 4:—"And now, behold, I loose thee this day from the chains which were upon thine hand."

In 1839 the Anti-Corn Law League took shape. I distinctly recollect the scene presented at a great bazaar in Covent Garden Theatre, in aid of Free Trade, when there was a wonderful gathering of notabilities and other folks. Stalls, articles, and ornaments, were varied and imposing; and as that exhibition appeared before the present age of bazaars was fully inaugurated, it had a more dazzling and bewildering effect than efforts of the kind can have now that they have become so common.

Dissenters' grievances, too, were exciting subjects in those days. Certain disabilities had an irritating effect on those who felt them, and legislation was sought for their removal. No doubt, in the heat of the conflict things were said on both sides which, on calm review, cannot be justified; and I am in my old age more than ever convinced that union of the *suaviter in modo* with the *fortiter in re*, is the best method of conducting controversy.

My holidays, whilst I was a Windsor pastor, were spent in preaching; but there were two exceptions, when I broke ground as a tourist. Travelling in Nottinghamshire and the neighbouring counties, I visited Newstead Abbey with a fresh remembrance of Washington Irving's description of the place. I had a gossip with an old domestic, who told me stories of Lord Byron, whom she knew as a boy, and used to carry on her back on account of his lameness. He pricked and otherwise tormented the patient creature, so as, on one occasion, to provoke her so much, that she boldly ventured on a rather amusing act of retaliation. Leaning over her shoulders to look into an old chest full of feathers, she, to use her own words, "copped him over, and he came out for all the world just like a young owlet." What I then heard of his early days gave me an unfavourable idea of that child of genius, so caressed and tormented, so flattered and persecuted, so early thrown into unfortunate circumstances, and altogether so badly brought up. What a contrast between two poets, whose memories came vividly before me during this tour!—Byron and Scott, both of them lame for life; one a stranger to the other's purity. Years afterwards I heard Dean Stanley preach a sermon to children, in which, with his characteristic felicity of thought, he spoke of the contrasted influences of physical deformity in these two instances—how the club foot of the first was an occasion of mortified pride and ill-nature, and the club foot of the second was borne with patience and contentment. The story of Byron's club foot is now treated by some I hear as a popular delusion; but, at all events, he had something the matter with his foot which irritated his temper and made him disagreeable. Therefore the Dean's moral lesson remains untouched. In connection with good humour and kindness, a physical defect may be only a foil to set off moral excellence.

After passing through Yorkshire, Durham, and Northumberland in company with my dear friend Harrison, we reached Edinburgh by coach at midnight to find ourselves in the morning amidst grand preparations for the Queen's first arrival in the Scottish capital. The view at noon from Calton

Hill, as the arrangements for receiving royalty had reached their acme, was most magnificent. Princes Street, from end to end, presented multitudes of people in holiday attire, military uniforms, tartan, kilts and feathered bonnets, gave rich plays of colour. The crowd waited and waited, but no Queen appeared. Night fell, and the expectants went to bed disappointed. Next morning every one was taken by surprise, for Her Majesty, having been detained at sea, landed at Leith, whilst the Lord Provost was still asleep. My friend and I afterwards went to Stirling, and identified historic points which dot the field of Bannockburn—then to Perth, Dunkeld, Killiecrankie, and Blair Atholl.

In the course of numerous journeys I had opportunities of seeing the real state of Nonconformity in rural districts. It was then much better than some people suppose. There were then families of influence identified with country places of worship, who have not left behind them sympathetic representatives. The revival of religion in the National Church has produced a considerable change in the relative position of ecclesiastical parties. Sunday evening services in cathedral and parish church, and the pastoral activity of incumbents and curates, with numerous missionary and other organisations, have produced effects very visible in the eyes of old people, who can look back on the religious condition of England during the first quarter of the present century.

My first Continental tour occurred before I left Windsor. I visited a family at Rotterdam into which a fellow-student had married, and had pleasant insights into Dutch life. After peeps at the Hague, Leyden, and Amsterdam, abounding in a gratification of antiquarian and historical taste, slowly proceeding up the Rhine, I felt all the enthusiasm incident to a young traveller as he first gazes on castle-crowned hills which line the river. Many and many a ramble since on those romantic banks have increased rather than diminished my admiration of the Rhine.

Friendships have through life been essential to my enjoyment, I might almost say to my existence. Intimate acquaintance with people of remarkable character in my Windsor days was a source of intense gratification.

The Rev. W. Walford, for some years minister of a Congregational Church at Yarmouth, then classical tutor at Homerton College, and finally pastor of the old Meeting House, Uxbridge, was one of the most remarkable men I ever knew. I see him now, with his handsome face, bald head, well-knit form, keen eyes, compressed lips, rather tottering in gait, and brusque in manner. What walks and talks we had! In conversation he expressed himself with singular accuracy on theological and metaphysical subjects. He had Butler and Jonathan Edwards at his fingers' ends, and could pack into a few words some of their most abstruse definitions and arguments. He had a habit of turning round when you walked with him, and standing face to face, when he would, in a most luminous style, state his propositions and adduce his proofs. He read Sir William Hamilton with immense admiration, though he did not in all respects adopt his views; and, at a period when looseness of religious thought was becoming prevalent, it was a treat to see him make a stand, figuratively as well as literally, for a distinct utterance of what people believe. From no man's conversation have I derived more instruction and advantage. I can never forget his reading to me, with tears in his eyes, a translation he had made of Plato's "Phaedo."

One day an old gentleman called to say he was about to reside at Old Windsor, and intended joining our worship at William Street Chapel. He had a cheerful, lively expression of countenance, with a few short grey locks on each side of his bald head, and showed in his gait signs of paralytic seizure. Full of humour and kindness, he made a pleasant impression. Thus began my friendship with Mr. Samuel Bagster of famous Polyglot memory. Notwithstanding his lameness, he could at that time walk from Old Windsor to our house with the aid of a stick, only asking a helping hand at the commencement of his pedestrian attempts. Thus started off he would steadily pursue his journey dressed in a short cloak and wearing a very broad-brimmed hat. He was one of the chattiest, most amusing friends I ever had. He possessed a large fund of anecdotes, which he knew I liked; and from time to time, as I visited his house, he doled them out with no niggard hand. He had lived on books, and books were his delight. Many choice editions in handsome bindings lined the walls in his rambling, quaint sort of residence, where also flowers, gathered in his little garden, formed conspicuous ornaments. There he would sit nursing his foot, complaining of pain in his great toe, and would launch out for a pleasant sail over the lake of memory, and take me from one point to another. The old books he had bought and sold, the circumstances connected with the origin of his Polyglot and Hexapla, the fire which occurred on his premises in Paternoster Row—these he would narrate in a characteristic way.

He often talked about the French Revolution and events connected with it in our own country. Clubs of a more than questionable description were established, and he told me that, invited by a person of his own age to attend a meeting held in an obscure street, he was surprised, on his entrance, to find a number of men ranged on either side of a room, sitting by long tables, with a cross one at the upper end. There sat the president for the evening. Several foaming tankards were brought in, when the president calling on the company to rise, took up one of the pots, and striking off the foam which crested the porter, gave as a toast: "So let all ... perish." The blank was left to be filled up as each drinker pleased. The avowed dislike to kings entertained by these boon companions suggested to Mr. Bagster the word "kings" or "tyrants"; and at once he gladly left the place, not a little alarmed, lest he should be suspected of treasonable designs. With characteristic caution, he took care not to observe the thoroughfare through which he passed on his way back, that he might be able conscientiously to declare he did not know the situation of the place. He also related that his father had a workman in his employ, whom he knew to be a disaffected subject. He expostulated with him on the horrors of a revolution as illustrated in France, and dwelt upon the confusion which would ensue upon outbreaks on established order. The man lifted up the skirt of his threadbare coat against the window, and significantly asked: " Pray, sir, what have I to lose?" My friend was no Radical, no Whig, but a Tory of the old-fashioned type, who approved of things as they were, without, however, any consciousness of wishing to tyrannise over other people. He was a great admirer of Izaak Walton, and had made a collection of drawings illustrative of his "Compleat Angler," of which he intended to publish a new edition, with a life of the author. When he had completed his "Comprehensive Bible," which, by permission, he dedicated to George IV., he was allowed personally to present it to His Majesty; and I have heard him say that on that occasion he was introduced to the royal presence by the Archbishop of Canterbury. The publisher was already paralysed, and could walk only with a tottering step; but the Primate gave him his arm, and led him up to the so-called first gentleman of Europe, who received him very graciously, and accepted at his hands the handsomely-bound volume.

There were other people I met with at Windsor whom I may mention. At the house of Dr. Ferguson, a Scotch physician of good birth and high culture, I met with his son-in-law, the Rev. Mr. Moultrie, Incumbent at Rugby, and friend of Dr. Arnold. He was a man of genius and piety, and gave a conviction of personal goodness, which made me value his volume of poems even more than I had done before. I like to look at authors through their books, and then again at books through their authors. In some cases the personal damages the literary judgment; but in many cases I have enjoyed works much more after knowing the worker.

Mr. Jesse, the naturalist, was another of my acquaintances. He held an office in connection with royal parks and palaces, and I spent pleasant hours as he drove me in his little pony gig from Windsor to Hampton Court, in the restoration of which he felt great delight. An amiable disposition, gentlemanly manners, and large information, made him an excellent companion. From the account he gave of his early life I found his father was a clergyman, a friend of Lady Huntingdon's, and an occasional preacher at Spafields Chapel. Mr. Stark, the eminent landscape artist, was one of my hearers, a man of decided religious convictions, and conscientious in art as in other things. He and Mr. Bristow, the animal painter, were amongst my friends; and in Windsor Forest they found subjects for their united skill, Stark putting in the trees, Bristow dogs and horses.

Amongst London friends at that time, and long afterwards was John Bergne, brother to my fellow-student Samuel Bergne, already mentioned. Clerk in the Foreign Office, he rose to the superintendence of the Treaty Department. Full of knowledge respecting European affairs, he often amused me by his taciturnity whenever they came on the carpet,—abstinence from communication of office secrets having become to him second nature. His mind was rich with information on various subjects; and in the science of numismatics he was well skilled. His collection of coins was of great value, including examples of English money from the earliest time, and valuable portions of "great finds" in Greek states. His affluent conversation, overflowing with humour, his rapid utterance and command of language surpassed what I have heard from many good talkers, whom it has been my fortune to meet with during a long life.

With other remarkable persons, I became intimately acquainted after my removal to Kensington. These I shall notice in their proper place.

In 1833 arose the Puseyite or Tractarian controversy as it was called. Of this a full account is given by Dr. Newman, in his "Apologia"—an account, of course, proceeding from his own point of view. The strife both inside and outside the University of Oxford, where the masters of the Tractarian movement lived and worked, was of the hottest kind; and those engaged in it on both sides, under the influence of party feeling, failed to appreciate each other's position, and to estimate correctly the tendencies involved. The Anglo-Catholics did not believe they were so near Rome; the staunch Protestants did not calculate on the wonderful effect which the controversy would have in stirring up the latent energies of the Church, and in modifying forms of worship, even amongst Evangelical parties. An amusing story I remember hearing when the famous Tract, "No. 90," was published. The then Bishop of Winchester (I think) wished to see it, and wrote to his bookseller to forward a copy, but from illegibility of penmanship "*No* 90" was mistaken for "*No go*"; and the poor bookseller, after inquiring in the Row for a pamphlet with that title, wrote to inform his Lordship, that there was no such tract in the market. The story ran its round, and the Evangelicals pronounced "*No.* 90" "*No go.*"

Dr. Newman condensed within the space of a few years the Romeward tendencies of Christendom during successive ages: starting with Tractarian doctrines, it was consistent for him to become a Roman Catholic in the sequel; and Dr. Pusey, in pausing where he did, never explained the grounds of his practical inconsistency. I felt it my duty to point out the unscriptural character of the Tractarian movement in a course of lectures, afterwards published under the title of " Tractarian Theology."

CHAPTER V

1843—1850

I WAS quite satisfied with my position at Windsor and had no thoughts of leaving it, when Dr. Vaughan of Kensington accepted the principalship of Lancashire College, and at the same time overtures were made by his Church to me that I should succeed him in the vacant pastorate. I can truly say that my desires were on the side of remaining where I was. I only wished to know the Divine Master's will. I felt unwilling to accept what looked like preferment; but after visiting Kensington and preaching there, the path before me appeared pretty plain. I accepted the call I received. "It seems like a dream," I wrote to my predecessor. "Yes," he replied; "but it is like Joseph's—a dream from the Lord."

It was a curious coincidence that the Church at Windsor and the Church at Kensington were both in their origin connected with a coachman in the service of George III. His name was Saunders, and he enjoyed his royal master's confidence. They used to talk together about religion, and, encouraged by the King's good opinion, the servant put tracts in the carriage pocket; and when His Majesty had read them he asked for more. As the royal residence was sometimes in town, and sometimes at Windsor, the home of Saunders varied accordingly, and he felt an interest in both neighbourhoods, especially as it regarded the humbler class. He probably caught the revivalist spirit prevalent a hundred years ago, and did what he could to gather people together for religious impression. In this way a room called "The Hole in the Wall" came to be the cradle of Windsor Congregationalism; and a "humble dwelling," mentioned by the Kensington historian, was birthplace to the congregation which afterwards assembled in Hornton Street. "When the faithful servant begged permission, on account of age, to retire from His Majesty's service, that he might reside at Kensington, it was not without an expression of regret on the part of the monarch; but the request was granted, and as often as the King afterwards passed through the place he took the most kind and condescending notice of his coachman." *

* Faulkener's "History and Antiquities of Kensington," p. 317.

In " Poems by John Moultrie," there occur these lines—

> " I have a son, a third sweet son, his age I cannot tell,
> For they reckon not by years and months where he is gone to dwell."

During the first three years of my Kensington residence, there were three little children taken from us, and translated to that mysterious world, where our time reckonings are lost in an incomprehensible eternity. Altogether six children were brought with us from Windsor ; and to these were added five more in the first few years after our removal—making the domestic flock at the time I speak of eleven. Of that number only four remain on earth at this time,*—a fact which tells of joy, and of much sorrow, at the hands of our Heavenly Father. Three were taken from us between 1843 and 1849.

During my Windsor life I began to take a deep interest in the writings of Dr. Arnold, and afterwards, when his Life appeared, written by his admiring pupil, Dr. Stanley, that interest increased. As I read these memoirs I little thought that I should share in the Biographer's friendship ; and my admiration of the two men was so deep that I attribute any improvement

* 1893.

in my mind and character since, greatly to their combined influence. Through life I have been more than ordinarily benefited by their works, and as to the Master of Rugby School, I have always been eager to learn what I could from any Rugby pupils I happened to know. At this moment there comes to my recollection an anecdote related by a friend who had been a Rugby boy. He told me that some accident happened at chapel in the upsetting of Bibles or prayer-books, and their fall from the gallery created much disturbance. Boys who were suspected of having a share in causing what happened were called up by the Master, and my informant was of the number. He told me that Dr. Arnold *trusted* a boy who denied any offence of which he was accused until clear proof appeared to the contrary. This was designed to keep up mutual confidence. In the instance under notice the boy accused felt sure that Dr. Arnold was not satisfied with the denial; yet he allowed the matter to pass, because he would promote confidence between master and pupil. The anecdote confirms what I have since read. He was never on the watch for boys, and he so encouraged straightforward and manly action, in trivial as in great things, that there grew up a general feeling, that " It was a shame to tell Arnold a lie, for he always believed one." *

Kensington, at the time of which I speak, was famous for its number of ladies' schools, and in them several daughters of Nonconformist parents were receiving their education. They formed an interesting part of my congregation, and my pastoral relation to them prepared for lifelong friendships. Of this group of families were the Dawsons of Lancaster, the Rawsons of Leeds, the Cheethams of Staleybridge, and the Sharmans of Wellingborough. With all of them I became intimate, and their friendships have proved no small comfort to me in later life. Parents of these families were distinguished by usefulness in many ways. Mr. Rawson was the well-known gifted hymn-writer; and Mr. Cheetham was M.P., and took an active part in the repeal of the Corn Laws. Daughters of these gentlemen were under my ministerial care while pupils at Kensington, and afterwards became earnest Christian workers in different ways, and their continued affection is a comfort to me in my old age. A son of Mr. Dawson married a daughter of Mr. Rawson, and immediately they went to China for mission work; but the broken-

---

* " Christian Workers of the Nineteenth Century," S.P.C.K., p. 216.

down health of the husband compelled his speedy return to England. He is now doing good work as one of the London City Mission secretaries.

In connection with Kensington, I would further mention other helpers: Mr. and Mrs. Coombs of Clapham were so. Mr. Coombs helped me especially by a large donation to the fund for building my new chapel. In other ways I was brought into relation with him. He was Treasurer of New College, and an active member of the British and Foreign Bible Society, the Religious Tract Society, and the London Missionary Society. His intelligence, aptitude for conversation, and kind-hearted intercourse made his friendship a privilege of more than ordinary value. It was intensified by his family relationship to some of my Kensington flock, the Salters and the Talfourds, whom I shall mention elsewhere in these reminiscences. Amidst preaching and pastoral work, it was a relief to spend a short holiday under Mr. Coombs' hospitable roof at Clapham, where I found a large collection of books. He died before I left Kensington, but my friendship with his wife and daughter continued till they died.

Archdeacon Sinclair, who had accepted the vicarage just before I removed to Kensington, paid me a visit of welcome, and thus laid a foundation for subsequent intercourse. He was son of the well-known Sir John Sinclair, and brother of the authoress, Catherine Sinclair. All the family were remarkably tall. The Archdeacon was a man of eminent culture, and of extensive aristocratic connections. His great-grandmother, though a loyalist, was the noted lady who aided in the escape of Prince Charlie, after the battle of Culloden. This same ancestress lay buried in Kensington Church, in front of the pulpit. Archdeacon Sinclair was well read in theology, widely acquainted with the controversies of the day, and a thoroughly orthodox Churchman; also rich in family and Scotch traditions. He told me the MSS. of David Hume came into his hands, and from perusal of them he was confirmed in his suspicion, that the celebrated historian and philosopher had no deep convictions of any kind, but only played with subjects he handled, doubtful about his own doubts.

Returning to the notice of my ministerial life, it comes in chronological order to mention that we had at Kensington, in 1843, British schools, which, being undenominational, received help from Church-people and Dissenters. They had long been patronised by distinguished personages, and not long after I had become resident in the neighbourhood application was made by the committee to the Duchess of Inverness, widow of the Duke of Sussex, to become patroness of the schools. This circumstance led her Grace to invite me to call on her, which I did. I was shown into an old-fashioned drawing-room, furnished in the style of the last century, the walls being decorated with portraits of George III. and members of his family. Entering the apartment was stepping back, as it were, to "sixty years since." An old lady of diminutive stature, in black silk and a small cap, presently appeared, who entered into pleasant conversation about her late husband, and Mr. Ramsbottom, M.P. for Windsor, whom I knew very well. Both of them were zealous Freemasons. Her Grace had caught their spirit, as far as a lady could do it, and inquired of me whether I was a Mason. No doubt, could I have answered in the affirmative, I should have risen in her estimation. My visit was fruitful in reference to our schools, for she sent a donation of £20, apologising for not doing more at that time. Kensington Palace was then inhabited by other distinguished persons; and one of the secretaries of the Propagation Society, I think, at that time performed the duties of a chaplain to those resident within the walls.

It is appropriate in connection with the early part of my Kensington life to mention religious societies with which I closely associated myself. There is no doubt some truth in the lines that,

> "Distance lends enchantment to the view,
> And clothes the mountain with an azure hue."

In looking at benevolent work, remote in time or place, we are apt to paint it in fairest colours; but of the great importance of the religious work going on fifty years ago in London and the neighbourhood, there can be no question whatever.

The *British and Foreign Bible Society* I always regarded as lying at the very foundation of our religious activity. It had a comprehensive Auxiliary in the West End from the commencement of the society's operations, and annual meetings were held in the Haymarket, under the presidency of royal dukes. This Auxiliary was broken into parts, and Kensington had a leading place amongst them. Traditions of earlier days were cherished when I began to live in the royal suburb, and they invested our local gatherings with some dignity, as families when divided derive honours from their common ancestry.

The Missionary Society, as it was originally called—the *London Missionary Society*, as it was afterwards named—had from the beginning been supported by our Church; indeed, fathers and founders of the one appear amongst early workers in the other, and through the ministry of Mr. Clayton, Dr. Leifchild, and Dr. Vaughan, foreign missions found zealous supporters at Kensington. The London City Mission, then in its early age, had engaged my sympathies at Windsor. There we had a town missionary, who brought us into connection with work going on in the Metropolis. Consequently, when I came to Kensington, I took much interest in the annual meetings of the society, and was brought into intimate relations with its officers and supporters. Annual gatherings were held in Freemasons' Hall, Queen Street, where signs of the Zodiac, and portraits of Grand Masters, adorned the ceiling and walls, suggesting to speakers allusions, obvious or far-fetched, till they became rather threadbare and wearisome; but, from the beginning, narratives by the missionaries formed a chief source of interest.

The Young Men's Christian Association was formed soon after I came to my new charge, and with it I had connection from the beginning, being first on the list of lecturers in the City, before the annual courses at Exeter Hall commenced.

The Evangelical Alliance was founded in 1843, and as a desire for union has ever been with me a "passion," I joined the Alliance from the beginning. There was great simplicity in the earliest gatherings, and an air of novelty gave additional charms. However, some members professing catholic sympathies on the platform pursued an exclusive line of conduct on other occasions, and this circumstance provoked unfavourable comments. Plausible objections, moreover, were made to the society's constitution—the platform, too wide for some, being too narrow for others. I could have desired a wider basis and the furtherance of Christian unity apart from all controversy with those who differed from us. On the whole, however, it was a move in the right direction, and the gatherings of its early friends in town and in other parts of the country were of an eminently joyous description. Sir Culling Eardley and others, in private as well as public, promoted the interests of the Alliance. At that time several influential clergymen and leading Dissenters used to meet, not only on the platform, but in the homes of distinguished lay members, who threw themselves very heartily into the movement.

Brought into the neighbourhood of London, and already known by some brethren there, I soon found myself surrounded by many friends. For more than a century there had been in existence an association of Dissenting ministers, who took the title of *Sub Rosa*, from the confidential character of their intercourse. There were some of the most distinguished London Congregational ministers in the brotherhood at the time now referred to; and they discussed points of importance, and for the most part, as to denominational matters, acted in harmony. Some of the departed were men of great ability, conspicuous in the pulpit and on the platform; but the remembrance of them by the public is being gradually crowded out by new names and new questions of religious interest.

To turn to a very different subject, which synchronises with the period under review; let me notice that the month of October 1845 witnessed the stirring event of Newman's secession to the Church of Rome. It was an event of singular importance. I have noticed on a previous page that the Tractarian Movement was regarded by many as distinctly tending in the direction of Romanism. For a considerable time such a tendency was denied on the part of its abettors generally; yet, even as early as November, 1835, Dr. Pusey, who had such confidence in Newman, wrote to his wife : " I almost see elements of disunion, in that John Newman will scare people " ;* and, in 1836, Newman himself incidentally wrote : " As to the sacrificial view of the Eucharist, I do not see that you can find fault with the formal wording of the Tridentine decree. Does not the Article on the sacrifice of the Mass supply the doctrine, or notion, to be opposed? What that is, is to be learnt historically, I suppose." Besides the question of Eucharistic doctrine, Pusey's correspondence at this time gives clear evidence of other questions, more or less difficult, in respect to doctrine, practice, or terminology, arising out of a more general appreciation of Church principles and order. † That which was called Puseyism prepared for Popery; and this was obvious to most people, though Pusey himself could not see it. Inconsistently, as I think, he remained where he was; and, now that he declined to follow his friend, it is surprising he took no steps to satisfy the public as to grounds on which he himself remained in the Church of England. His attachment to what he deemed the Church of his fathers, however, was

* " Life of E. B. Pusey," i. 336.
† *Ibid.*, ii. 33.

very strong, and he thought well of those who remained in that Church, though holding opinions different from his own. For instance, he wrote:

Ever since I knew them, which was not in my earliest years," "I have loved those who are called *Evangelicals*. I loved them because they loved our Lord. I loved them for their zeal for souls. I often thought them narrow, yet I was often drawn to individuals among them, more than to others who held truths in common with myself, which the Evangelicals did not hold, at least not explicitly." * There is a ring in these words which shows the sympathy which Pusey retained for those who loved the Saviour, though, in ecclesiastical matters, widely differing from High Churchmen. It appears to me that, if Pusey had been as *consistent* with his Tractarian principles as Newman was, Pusey would have followed Newman to Rome, but, happily, his loving spirit for Christian *goodness* kept him in communion with a Church where he saw piety beautifully manifested by some who differed from him in ecclesiastical opinion. I cannot make this reference to Dr. Pusey without saying that, with all my repugnance to his

---

" Life of Pusey," ii. 8.

ecclesiastical opinions, and the conviction I have, that while he never became a Romanist, he greatly helped on the movement which carried many in the popish direction, the perusal of his memoirs has given me a high estimate of his personal piety. His devoutness, his love to Christ, his unworldly habits, his affectionate disposition, and his self-denial in the ordering of his domestic affairs, so as to enlarge his pecuniary contributions to religious purposes, are worthy of their imitation who regard with sorrow his High-Church peculiarities. Might not domestic and social ties, as well as strong attachment to the Church of England from his childhood, have had something to do with his final course?

The Revolutions of 1848 brought with them an immense amount of excitement in this country, as in others. The month of April in that year can never be forgotten. An outbreak was feared in London. Special constables were sworn in. On the Sunday before the 10th of the month my friend, Mr. Walford, preached a remarkable sermon in Kensington Chapel. His text was Isa. xii. 2—"Behold, God is my salvation; I will trust, and not be afraid." Having unfolded the sentiment of the passage, he applied the principle to passing events,

and spoke of the political excitement in this
country at the time of the French Revolution,
which he well remembered. He assured us that the
excitement then surpassed anything which existed
at the time when he spoke, and expressed his
confidence in the rectitude and love of the Almighty,
who maketh the wrath of man to praise Him. The
preacher's age, and his vivid recollection of what
he had witnessed, gave force to his exhortations, as
tears were falling from his eyes.

Trust in Providence, touchingly enforced by
personal recollections, was honoured by what
occurred on the following day. The meeting on
Kensington Common, so much dreaded, broke up
in confusion. Ringleaders were alarmed, the mob
was scattered without the interference of soldiers
who had been provided against an outbreak, but
were concealed in public buildings, through the Duke
of Wellington's wisdom. A day which opened in
fear was spent in peace and confidence.

During a visit abroad in that year, 1848, I
reached Geneva, with letters of introduction to
Cæsar Malan, Gaussen, and M. St. George. Merle
D'Aubigne was from home. In company with
friends, on the Sunday afternoon, I attended at
Cæsar Malan's little chapel. We had mistaken the

hour, and, on our entering, he recapitulated the early portions of his sermon. Then, in his own pleasant parlour, he engaged in fervent discourse on his favourite tenet of Christian assurance. On parting he singled me out for the privilege of a double French kiss, and on my expressing a hope that we should meet in the Father's House, he rebuked me for using the word *hope*. With him it was a matter of assurance. Then I reminded him of the difference between present and future, and quoted St. Paul : " For we are saved *by hope* : but hope that is seen is not hope : for what a man seeth, why doth he yet hope for? But if we hope for that we see not, then do we with patience wait for it."

I parted from relatives, who had been my fellow-travellers, and made my way next morning alone by boat to Vevay, thence travelling to Basle and Strasburg. Traffic was interrupted, and relics of revolution were seen in marching troops and handcuffed prisoners.

In 1849 a movement occurred for meeting religious needs in Kensington. A chapel was much needed on Notting Hill, and one of my deacons, who lived there, promised a large donation for the purpose. A few friends met in Hornton Street vestry, and opened a subscription list, which at once secured £1500. With that we went to work.

At first, there was some notion of incorporating members of the two congregations in one Church, with a copastorate; and Dr. Vaughan, I think, indicated willingness to become my colleague. I should not have objected to such union, but feared lest the moral effect of our movement should be thereby impaired. The scheme might have been looked upon as one of self-aggrandisement, while it was meant as an act of self-sacrifice. The latter it proved to be, for we drafted off about fifty members, as the nucleus of a new Church. Also we missed about two hundred seat-holders, who took pews in the new edifice, and, of course, there arose a certain *éclat* around Notting Hill which left Hornton Street a little in the shade. But soon things revived; our chapel became as full as ever. Funds recovered, liberal things were devised, and one morning I found a handsome cheque on my library table Everybody seemed to be growing in kindness, and Hornton Street rose to more than its previous prosperity. It was an illustration of the principle—true of communities as well as of individuals—" There is that scattereth and yet increaseth."

In connection with my early residence at Kensington I may mention a circumstance which interested me. I observed several times, sitting near my pulpit, an old gentleman. Upon inquiry, I found it was the Rev. Michael Maurice, father to the Rev. F. D. Maurice, then at the height of his influence as author and preacher. I never had the pleasure of conversing with my venerable hearer, but I learned from different sources much relative to his character and career. Though descended from a thoroughly orthodox family, he was educated for the ministry under Dr. Abraham Rees, Dr. Kippis and Dr. Savage—the first two being Arian divines, and the last a moderate Calvinist. He became afternoon preacher at Dr. Priestley's Meeting House; and after officiating in other Unitarian places of worship, retired from pulpit work altogether. But he habitually associated with orthodox Nonconformists during the time he lived at Southampton. He also joined the British and Foreign Bible Society, and spoke for it on the platform. I wondered he should worship in Hornton Street, but information subsequently obtained served to explain the circumstance. He appears to have been a devout man with a large measure of Evangelical feeling.

I mention him as a type of no inconsiderable class of sincerely religious people.

I knew but little of his distinguished son, only having met him a few times at Dean Stanley's, and at Baldwin Brown's. I used sometimes, on a Sunday afternoon, to hear Mr. Maurice preach at Lincoln's Inn, and was much struck with the earnestness with which he repeated the Lord's Prayer. The difficulty he felt in making himself understood is amusing. Some of the principles, he said, which his friends attacked, were those he strongly objected to himself, and those which they held as against him, were just those on which he rested his own faith and hope. " I could not make them the least understand what I meant," he went on to say ; "and if I did they would only dislike me for it." It was not obscurity of style, as many thought, which made him unintelligible ; but obscurity or confusion of thought arising from complexity of perception. He saw so much that it puzzled him how to express it. I respected him greatly as an honest thinker, more anxious to commend himself to the Searcher of hearts than to his fellow-men.

It must have been, I think, in 1846 or 1847 that I received an invitation to preach the annual sermon on behalf of Newport Pagnell College, and thither I went in the month of June. The Rev. Thos. Palmer Bull, president, and his son, the Rev. Josiah Bull, were living under the same roof, their house and garden full of comfort and convenience, beauty and fragrance. The old gentleman had a good library, and in nooks and corners were MSS. and relics of Cowper and Newton, friends of his father, the Rev. William Bull. The father was the " Taurus," and his son the " Tommy," immortalised in Newton and Cowper's letters. When I had fulfilled my public duty I intensely enjoyed conversation with my elder host, as he showed me letters written, and relics possessed by the two celebrities so closely connected with his father's name. He told me how he used, when a boy, to accompany his father to Olney, where he dined with the poet ; that when grace was said, Cowper would play with his knife and fork, to indicate he had no share in acts of worship; that he would cheerfully converse on a variety of topics, but shunned all reference to religion. Notwithstanding, he would sometimes join in an Olney hymn ; and then check himself as one who had neither part nor lot in the matter. He would kindly talk with little Tom, who accompanied his father on those visits, and they, on their way to and from the now world-known town, would join in singing a psalm or hymn, to a familiar tune. The old gentleman, I was informed, sometimes indulged in the use of a pipe, as he drove along the accustomed road. Full of such memories, I made an excursion to Olney, stopped at the house near the park of the Throgmortons, saw the room in which the poet slept, traced his writing on a pane of glass, and thought of the despair to which, in that chamber, he was so pitiable a victim. Then I was taken to the unpretentious abode in the main street of Olney, where he cultivated a close intimacy with John Newton, and kept rabbits in his little garden,—which garden, at the time I think of, remained much in its former state. The summer-house, described by the bard, was still in existence. Here, pausing for a moment to gather up another memento of Cowper, I may mention, that a relative of mine pointed out a house in East Dereham, which was Cowper's residence; and told me that he remembered when a boy peeping through the keyhole of a door, and seeing him sitting in his chair. Cowper died at the residence of his kinsman, the Rev. Mr. Johnson. A friend of his gave me a leaf, in the poet's handwriting, from the translation of Homer.

Soon after my return from this excursion I was chosen to fill up a vacancy in the important Nonconformist Trust of William Coward, a London merchant, who appointed Dr. Watts, Dr. Guyse, and Mr. Neal, author of the "History of the Puritans,"—with another person who was a layman,—administrators of property which he bequeathed for charitable purposes. Much of it consisted of Bank stock; that having risen, the revenue had become very considerable.

Dr. Doddridge was a special friend of Mr. Coward's, and had under his care several ministerial candidates, supported by that gentleman. According to tradition, the merchant was very punctual, the minister less so; and when the former invited the latter to dinner, if he did not come exactly at the hour, the footman was ordered not to admit him. A gentleman who lived opposite was aware of this peculiarity, and his footman arranged with Mr. Coward's footman, that when Dr. Doddridge had been invited to dinner, mention should be made of it to the servant on the other side the road, that a dinner might be prepared for his reverence there. Other curious stories were told of our founder, which I have forgotten. The perpetuation of Dr. Doddridge's academy in different places, and under different forms, led to a transfer of the institution from Wymondley in Hertfordshire to Torrington Square, London, where, in association with London University College, it existed at the time of my accession to the trusteeship. For about two years I assisted in conducting the business of Coward College, as a separate institution. Then came a change. There were at the time three independent academies, as they were then called, in London and the neighbourhood—Homerton, Highbury and Coward. There were three sets of tutors, three boards of administration, three distinct buildings, and three distinct sources of expense. Previous attempts to accomplish the union of these institutions had failed; but at the time to which I now refer, an opportunity arrived for accomplishing the union. After conferences between "Heads of Houses" for some months, it was determined to sell the three buildings, then occupied by the students, and to erect one large new edifice, where they might be instructed together. The erection of New College, St. John's Wood, was the result. In the negotiations connected with this change, Dr., afterwards Sir William, Smith zealously co-operated with the Coward trustees. My dear old friend, the Rev. William Walford, took a great interest in the accomplishment of this business, but he died before it was completely effected.

He spent his last days in writing an autobiography, and after his death I found it was written in letters addressed to myself, with a request that I would edit the publication. This I did with a melancholy satisfaction. He had suffered acutely from mental depression, and the malady returned with violence shortly before his death. My last visits were most painful. He refused all consolation, and passed away under a cloud, like that which attended the sunset of Cowper. There were gleams of light, followed by dense darkness. Then he sank into silence, if not torpor. Days and nights rolled on, so different from their "tranquil gliding" which he described in his letters; but it was the happy confidence of his friends, notwithstanding his own fears, that the angry billow, no less than the gentle wave, was bearing the weather-beaten barque to the celestial shore. He died on June 22nd, 1850. The poor body looked like a wreck, but faith could see at rest the soul which had such hard work to pilot the vessel beyond reach of storms. A post-mortem examination proved that his depression arose from the condition of the brain. He was a good Greek scholar, and delighted in reading Plato.

CHAPTER VI

1850—1854

THE year 1850 opened with a storm of religious excitement, owing to a division of England by Papal authority into Roman dioceses, at the suggestion of Dr. Wiseman. It came to be called "The Papal Aggression." Some thought more was made of it, at the time, than circumstances warranted; but, looked at through the medium of history, it seemed to aim at a territorial authority over England, inconsistent with our repudiation of Papal supremacy. The way in which it was taken up by some good people was not wise, and there was an anti-popish commotion amongst some of my friends—a few only. The commotion was unreasonable, but was overruled for good, as the incident led some Protestants to look into their professed principles, which doubtless, in our country, lie at the basis of civil and religious liberty.

From one end of the island to the other, Nonconformists as well as Churchmen took an opportunity for expressing attachment to the Reformation. In two ways I became connected with what went on. The Presbyterian, Congregational, and Baptist ministers of London, representing the three denominations, resolved, in common with other ecclesiastical bodies, to approach Her Majesty with a protest against "Papal Aggression." The three denominations—like Convocation and certain English corporations—have a right of presenting addresses to the Sovereign; and on this occasion, the audience for accepting the addresses, was appointed to be at Windsor Castle. When the ceremony in the Royal Closet for receiving representatives of the three denominations was over, we were invited to lunch in the equerry's apartment. Covers were laid for two or three gentlemen, in addition to our party. "Pray, can you tell me their names?" I whispered to one of the servants, who, from my previous residence in the town, happened to know me. He could not say, and at the same moment the strangers, who proved to be Roman Catholic noblemen, felt a like curiosity to know who we were. I proceeded to explain the origin of the three denominations, which was quite a revelation to the gentlemen; who informed us that they had just presented a loyal address from 250,000 Catholics. They proceeded to say, that English Protestants had quite misapprehended the meaning of recent arrangements; and, after receiving a courteous explanation, we sat down with them, and had a pleasant chat.

At that time I delivered at Kensington a short series of discourses on the Roman Catholic controversy. I went over some of the main points in that controversy, avoiding misrepresentation and uncharitableness. I was not violent enough to please some ultra-Protestants, but I had the gratification of hearing, that two young Catholics ultimately became Protestants, and were helped by the lectures. I have met in the course of my life with several members of the Romish Church, who have appeared to me estimable characters. I had in my congregation a young lady, one of a family which ranked a Cardinal amongst its members, and whose mother remained a Catholic; in her dying illness she clung to Christ as her Saviour, saying, in the words of Solomon's Song: "I held Him, and would not let Him go."

In the same year, as I have said, the Palace of Glass was opened; and, being a Kensington resident,

I had opportunities of watching the edifice rising out of the earth as a beautiful exhalation. On moonlight nights, in the previous winter, how often, on my way home, it revealed itself, amidst floating mists, as a kind of ethereal structure!

There was a moral atmosphere created by the enterprise, which those who do not recollect it are unable to appreciate. It inspired thousands of people with expressions of charity and goodwill. The opening day can never be forgotten by those who witnessed it. The *Times* newspaper had a leader, which made one feel that a new era in history had arrived; that war and strife were approaching an end, and a millennial age of goodwill had dawned upon mankind. When, that day, we saw crowds, not jostling and pushing against each other; for almost every unit of the mass seemed willing to make way for a neighbour; when we witnessed the opening service, and beheld the royal procession moving through the stupendous aisles,—representatives of "all people that on earth do dwell,"—those present seemed to feel as they never did before. As the poet Montgomery conversed with me on the subject, he remarked that, looking down from the galleries upon the throng which passed before his eyes, it "reminded him of flowing waters gently gurgling through some broad channel." The people, thronging here and there round corners, seemed like eddies in a river with lofty banks.

In the Exhibition year efforts were made for the religious improvement of the people. The Press was in different ways employed for this purpose; and amongst other methods there appeared, as distinctively characteristic, a series of evangelical discourses in Exeter Hall. They attracted crowded audiences. The sermons were carefully reported and widely circulated. About the same time several similar methods were employed for the promotion of religion; services were held in theatres and other places of amusement. Having been engaged in these efforts, I can testify to the crowds gathered together, and the general decorum of their behaviour. Some to whom these buildings belonged took an interest in the proceedings, as I knew from conversation with dramatic managers, who expressed interest in the addresses delivered. Afterwards, services were planned to be conducted by Episcopal clergymen in Exeter Hall, but the plan was frustrated by opposition of parochial authority. After this, Dissenters undertook to supply the lack of service, and the first Sunday night, an Independent minister officiated, reading parts of the Liturgy in the Book of Common Prayer, and an

English nobleman acted as clerk, leading the responses.

The same year (1851) it fell to my lot at the autumnal meeting of the Congregational Union to read a memorial paper on Dr. Doddridge, who had died just a hundred years before, and had been pastor and Divinity Professor in Northampton, where the assembly met. We occupied the old meeting-house in which he preached; there in the vestry stood the chair in which he sat. From the pulpit which had been his, the centenary tribute to his memory was delivered. Mr. Bull, of Newport Pagnell, presented the original MS. of a funeral sermon which the doctor preached for his little daughter, partly written upon her coffin. A common sympathy, amidst deathlike silence, pervaded the audience, as if the divine who was commemorated had only just left the world, and we had assembled to honour his remains. The *genius loci* of the place, and traditions of the good man, passed away so long before, contributed to the occasion more impressiveness than it derived from other circumstances.

In 1852 my beloved wife travelled with me to Elberfeld to see our eldest daughter. We had, from an early period, formed the plan of sending our children abroad for part of their education, in order that they might learn a foreign language and see other forms of society besides our own. Therefore we placed our firstborn under the care of Pastor and Madame Schröder,- two very excellent persons, whose character and influence answered the high expectations we had been led to form. Pastor Schröder succeeded Dr. Krummacher as one of the pastors of the Evangelical communion. We enjoyed his society and that of his excellent wife, and saw something of German habits, which interested me much; they presented aspects unfamiliar to us. For instance, one Sunday afternoon we took a walk in the woods with our friend the pastor, and, on the way, he gathered into a large company one after another of his people, until it formed quite a procession; and, finally, we rested in a pleasant nook encompassed by trees, where the people drank coffee, and sang hymns.

After we had spent some days at Elberfeld we started for Switzerland, where I planned my wife and daughter should spend two or three weeks, whilst accompanied by a Kensington friend, I proceeded on a journey to Italy. We started from Zurich, crossed the lake, reached Coire and the Via Mala, and over the Alps, came down to the Lake of Como; thence we reached Milan, where we stayed three days. I then became acquainted for the first time with the Duomo and other churches. We spent a Sunday in the city, and felt deeply interested in schools founded by Cardinal Borromeo, carried on at the time with exemplary care; and we found at eventide, in a church, groups of worshippers, led by a layman, who knelt in front as they chanted responses. I was struck then, and have been oftentimes since, with the adaptation of Scripture passages on church walls, pointing to salvation through our Lord Jesus Christ. One thought, too, of Ambrose, who forbade the approach of Theodosius, wet with the blood he had shed at Thessalonica. Speaking of the adaptation of Scripture in foreign churches, I may mention other passages inscribed on their walls in other places, for example, at Treves, where under a picture of "The Nativity" we read "Verily Thou art a God that hidest Thyself," as applied to the Incarnation. Again, at Nismes, if I recollect aright, under the fresco of a captive rejoicing in his freedom, the words "Thou hast loosed my bonds"; and under another, representing martyrs and virgins at the portals of heaven, "With joy and rejoicing shall they be brought: they shall enter into the King's palace." After all, the kernel of the Gospel continues in Roman Catholic Christendom, though too often concealed under manifold innovations. Still there it is, if you look for it.

My reference to Milan brings before me other recollections of that wonderful city, as revisited again and again since 1852. Amidst manifold associations of art, archæology, history, and religion, one image, indelibly impressed on my mind, is that of Augustine under the fig tree in a garden, listening to a voice which cried, " Tolle lege "; at the hearing of which he sat down, took the Testament in his hand, and read Rom. xiii., and thus became a new creature in Christ Jesus. Wandering in quiet old streets, I have paused near some fig tree in a little enclosure of grass and flowers, to think of him who became the grandest father of the Latin Church.

From Milan we proceeded to Verona, and thence to Venice, where I felt " one of the greatest emotions of life." I have seen it again and again, but the first charm was greatest of all. Then Titian's " Peter Martyr " adorned the walls of SS. Giovanni e Paulo. Wonderful picture that! but it does not, to my mind, eclipse his S. Jerome in the Brera at Milan.

Let me return to Kensington. Perhaps this is as good a place as any, for saying a few words about people there, and others with whom I was brought into contact, during my pastorate.

Under the ministry of my predecessor, Dr. Leifchild, there lived in one of the stately houses in the neighbourhood, a gentleman—commanding in person and polished in manners—who was drawn towards the Dissenting pastor, though he had no affection for Dissent; if he smiled at the system, he liked some of the people. He lost largely on the Stock Exchange, but he bore it with much magnanimity. I was acquainted with some of the family, who were in prosperous circumstances, and who became my kind friends. I once met at their house with an old general—uncle to the Duchess of Gordon—who related a singular anecdote. He had been at the Eglinton Tournament, and, as the castle was crowded with guests, he and another person shared the same bedroom. That person was no other than the future Napoleon II. He kept his companion awake with talk about the French Empire and his uncle, declaring, that he was sure one day of sitting on his uncle's throne. The ambitious dream filled his mind, and overflowed in his abundant chat; though then it seemed a most improbable imagination. The incident was related some time after the tournament, and before the Republic was established; and when I afterwards heard of Napoleon's election to the presidentship, I saw it was by no means unlikely that the daring prophecy he had ventured, would come to pass. I have heard from other people that he often, when residing in London, talked in society of his coming elevation, as imperial ruler of the French. The uncle had seen beforehand the dazzling star of his destiny. His nephew did the same. There were people who fancied something supernatural in this, but it may be accounted for on natural principles.

Another story, of an amusing kind, I heard at a Chiswick garden party, to which I was taken by the kind friends at whose house I met the old Scotch soldier. Amongst personages of rank present at Chiswick were certain bishops, who had not dropped the old episcopal costume of a big wig, a most decidedly broad-brimmed clerical hat, and a conspicuous apron. Right Reverend brethren are still somewhat distinguished from other people, though some of them reduce the distinction within very restricted limits; forty or fifty years ago it was quite otherwise. They appeared then commonly—to use an undignified expression—in *full fig*, and as some occupants of the Bench passed by, in unmistakable array of the kind just noticed, a clergyman at the garden party now mentioned, told me of a prime minister, who used to remark, he thought, "Bishops well deserved all they got" (and it was much more then than it is now), "for allowing themselves to be dressed up, as such regular guys."

Literature and art were pretty well represented in Kensington, at the period I speak of. Contributors to *Punch*—Mark Lemon, Gilbert a Becket, and others—were my neighbours, and with one of them I spent a pleasant evening. Gilbert a Becket during a few weeks, when the parish church underwent repairs, used pretty regularly to attend our chapel, and I was struck by his attentiveness and devotion. He expressed his readiness to spend a few hours with me, at a friend's residence, only he stipulated that it should not be on an opera night; and when it was proposed to me I stipulated that it should not be on one of my service nights. Preliminaries being settled we accordingly met, and got on exceedingly well. What amuses me, as I think of it, is that, though I am not at all given to pun-making, the presence of a brilliant punster so inspired me, that I perpetrated one or two hits, which Becket pronounced very fair. Perhaps I may be forgiven by those who achieve pleasant things in that way, if I remark that there is something contagious in the practice; and it is difficult not to catch it, when in company with those who are imbued with the habit.

With another celebrity I came in contact through intimacy with his family, and his early connection with our place of worship. I allude to Justice Talfourd. When a young man he used to attend on Dr. Leifchild's ministry, his father and mother being members of the Congregational Church at Kensington. His mother, whom I knew well, related anecdotes of his early days at home, and at Mill Hill School, where he had schoolfellows who afterwards distinguished themselves in the walks of Dissent. He wrote home about his companions and told his mother of prayer-meetings amongst the boys; and of one boy in particular, very imaginative, and florid on such occasions. This schoolfellow became afterwards an eloquent minister, well known as Dr. Hamilton of Leeds. The Judge told me of his early attachment to that gentleman, and how, during the doctor's last visit to London, he went to hear him preach, and stepped into the vestry afterwards, to talk of old times; but the preacher had left, which was a great disappointment.

There was a strong religious side to Judge Talfourd's character, and he used to speak with much enthusiasm of my predecessor, Dr. Leifchild, whose preaching he said came up to his idea of the Apostle Paul's ministry.

Amongst artists living in Kensington were two Academicians, Uwins and Philip, who both belonged to our congregation—the first a regular, the second an occasional, attendant. Philip's wife—a beautiful woman, whom he introduced into some of his pictures—was a communicant with us at the Lord's table. I often visited the artist's studio, and listened to his picturesque description of Spain, and also to his accounts of family afflictions which elicited my sympathy.

From my boyhood I had taken an interest in art, and the friendship of several men distinguished in its cultivation was exceedingly instructive and pleasant. My travels on the Continent, which enabled me to visit most of the principal picture galleries,—rich in specimens by great masters,—educated and purified what little taste I had; and prompted me to somewhat extensive studies in artistic literature. These, blended with other habits of reading, I find an immense enjoyment in the leisure of my old age.

Mr. Theed, the sculptor, and his family, who attended Kensington Chapel, were our intimate friends; and he told me much about Gibson, his companion in art, and intimate acquaintance for many years, when they resided at Rome. With the latter gentleman I became acquainted slightly when I was in Italy, and had a long talk with him once about tinting sculpture,—which he advocated with zeal, and practised with skill. I felt there was force in what he said. Another Kensington name,—that of Edward Corbould, the water-colourist,—may be coupled with my friend Theed's. Each was connected with the other in artistic service to Her Majesty and family. I remember on the Sunday morning after the Prince Consort's lamented death, missing both these gentlemen at Divine worship, in consequence of their being summoned to Windsor—one to take a cast, and the other to make a drawing of the good Prince's face.

There was another group of hearers during the latter part of my Kensington ministry, to whom I was much attached. One of them, Cozens Hardy, M.P., who has won eminence in the legal profession, is son to the oldest friend I have. All now referred to are distinguished, not only by professional position, but by continued study in classical learning.

I must not pass by "annals of the poor." When I first went to Kensington, I was requested to visit an old shoemaker, crippled, and in humble circumstances, but with a good deal of natural politeness, the more striking from its surroundings. He had been a wild young fellow, daring to the last degree, and this was the cause of his incurable lameness. He was converted under the ministry of Dr. Leifchild. The preacher, in the course of a sermon, related an anecdote of Mr. Cecil, who previous to his becoming decidedly religious narrowly escaped with life, when thrown by his horse across the track of a waggon, which in passing only crushed his hat. The incident struck the listener. It resembled his own experience, and riveted his attention, preparing him to listen to the preacher's appeals. He became an exemplary Christian; and I often sat by his bedside to hear him describe the wondrous change wrought in his character, by Divine grace. "I am a wonder unto many," he used to say; and then, with faltering voice, would sing the old hymn—

> "Amazing grace, how sweet the sound,
> That saved a wretch like me!
> I once was lost, but now am found;
> Was blind, but now I see."

This was not the only case in which the humbler

members of the Church were a comfort to me. Often my heart was cheered by communications made by them, touching spiritual life. Such communications were perfectly artless, and arose from the absence of that reserve which, in the upper class, is the result of educational refinement. This circumstance often prevents a free revelation of what cultured people think and feel on the subject of religion. I have frequently noticed it, and never inferred, from delicacy touching soul secrets, any want of that which rises to the surface, and overflows in ready words, when uneducated people speak of their Christian experience.

I cannot omit a reference to the Gurney family, with some of whom I came into pleasant connection during my Kensington residence. As a boy, I had some knowledge of their ancestral relatives; and now I came into close friendship with Mr. Bell, brother to Mrs. John Gurney, who was mother to Samuel Gurney, the renowned London Quaker, and also to Joseph John Gurney, of Earlham, near Norwich—an equally renowned banker, and also a *Public Friend*, as preachers of that denomination, then were wont to be called. Mr. Bell had become one of my hearers and a communicant, much to his spiritual benefit, as he and his family informed me. He was a chatty old gentleman, and used to talk of his sister, Priscilla Wakefield, of Miss Schemmelpenninck, and of Samuel Taylor Coleridge—whom he met at the house of his friend Gilman, resident in Highgate. Through frequent vivid references to these celebrities, whom I knew by their writings and by report, I came to have a sort of personal acquaintance with them. Thus they became, more than ever, living realities. Besides this, I came to have a slight personal knowledge of Mr. Samuel Gurney, just mentioned, the well-known bill-broker, and also of Mrs. Fry, his sister, who did so much good as a prison visitor. Mr. Gurney was a stately person, with a benign countenance, and a musical voice rich in persuasive tones. The mental anxiety he felt during money panics, not only on his own account, but also from sympathy with others, was such, that he was known to spend sleepless nights pacing his chamber. Mrs. Fry was as dignified as her brother, and I now in imagination see her in her becoming Quaker garb, as she talked to me about her nephew Bell, and spoke gratefully of the benefit he had derived from my ministry. The younger Mr. Samuel Gurney came to live at Prince's Gate, Kensington, and used to worship with us occasionally. At his table I met with the Bunsens, and other remarkable friends and relatives of his. He told me that at any time when I needed, in Christian work, pecuniary help, I might apply to him without hesitation. The crash on "Black Friday" was a terrible trial, as it made him, after being one of the richest of London citizens, dependent on his relatives. I wrote to him words of condolence, to which he beautifully replied, saying that he trusted the tribulation which had befallen him would be for his spiritual welfare. His excellent wife bore up nobly, and the two afforded admirable instances of Christian patience and resignation.

CHAPTER VII

1854—1862

ON April 4th, 1854, I started the first time for Rome, provided with letters of introduction to Gibson, the sculptor, Penry Williams, the landscape painter, and two Roman Catholic dignitaries, one a Monseignor, the other president of the English College. All these gentlemen were polite and helpful to me.

My companions were Dr. Raffles, Dr. Halley, the Rev. Spencer Edwards, and another friend. The first of them was wonderful for relating stories, which he always told *secundum artem*. He kept us awake one whole night with his amusing anecdotes; but, as we were travelling through France at a time when espionage was prevalent, he would not allow us to make any political allusions. I was surprised at the retentiveness of his verbal memory; whilst he repeated long pieces, in which the amusement consisted of odd words, connected with no rational meaning, when put together.

It was Holy Week when we reached Rome. On Thursday there was the feet-washing at St. Peter's, and the supper afterwards: the Pope, as "servant of servants," ministering to the poor, but with great pomp on both occasions. We arranged to see the former, and found a transept on the right hand, fitted up for the occasion. Rank, fashion, beauty, arrayed in mourning, found accommodation in galleries commanding a good view. Ladies were veiled, gentlemen wore evening dress. Admission to that part of the edifice could be obtained on no other conditions. Pio Nono, a pleasant, genial-looking old man, who won a good opinion as soon as you looked at him, did his part well. He read the Gospel (John xiii.) in tones wonderfully musical and distinct, and then washed the pilgrims' feet with grace and reverence. The whole was artistically and solemnly done. "One can laugh at these things, as described in books," said Dr. Raffles—a staunch Nonconformist—"but *not* when witnessed, as now, in this magnificent place." Still, on a calm review, nothing like *worship* appears in any part of the ceremony. Then the *Miserere* in the afternoon! Those who did not witness it years ago can have no idea of it now; or of the gorgeous procession, amidst a blaze of light, to the altar of S. Paulo, and the prostration of the Pontiff and his Cardinals on the floor, in the midst of darkness, candles having been extinguished, one by one. The scene on the grand staircase was striking as the dignitaries returned, varying in appearance and character—an ascetic monk, a man of the world, another looking studious and reflective, a fourth keen and statesmanlike. Nobody could deny the Italian scenic skill in such matters. I have been at Rome in Easter, since then, much struck with subsequent changes. When all was over on my first Easter in Rome, I went to the English Episcopal Church, where the Lord's Supper was administered according to Protestant rites, and I could not but be impressed by the contrast between the two services. It illustrated the change effected by the Reformation. I mentioned this once to the Rev. Frederic Denison Maurice, who, of course, agreed with me; and, talking of Rome, he happened to relate an anecdote which I do not remember having seen in print. Pio Nono, after the suppression of Latin nunneries in Poland, received a visit from the Emperor of Russia. "You are a great king," said the former to the latter, "one of the mightiest in the world. I am a poor feeble man, servant of servants; but I cite you to meet me before the Judge of all, and to answer for your treatment of helpless women." There was the old assumption of authority; but there was a touch of grandeur in the words.

I saw the catacombs, following my guide, taper in hand; and in one of the strange passages was accosted by name. "Who could have expected to be recognised in this dark underworld?" I exclaimed. It turned out to be a person who had lived at Eton, and been a hearer of mine at Windsor. Other recognitions have occurred to me of an odd kind, when visiting several places.

I became so attracted by what I saw in Rome, and drank so deeply into the spirit of Arnold's letters, written there, that my last day was spent in pensive leave-takings of ruin after ruin, church after church. I have been there twice since, each for a longer time than the first; but not with quite the impression which I felt in the first instance.

We proceeded to Naples, stopped at Cisterna, at Terracinia, at Gaeta, and at S. Agata. Whoever has travelled the same road must long remember the fragrance of the orange-groves and the coloured dresses of the peasantry.

We had no trouble at custom-houses on the way, for my two companions and myself travelled in humble fashion. Otherwise did the two doctors, already mentioned, fare. Large sums were demanded of them on the Neapolitan frontier; and when they refused to pay, their luggage was searched, and a coloured pen-wiper being found, the officials declared it was a *revolutionary cockade*, and that books in their portmanteaus were no doubt full of treason and heresy. There was no alternative but to stay where they were, or to allow a soldier to accompany them in charge of the suspected articles. All this trouble was followed by apologies on reaching Naples, after an appeal had been made to the English Consul.

We saw the picture galleries and museums in Naples, and explored the city as well as we could during our short stay. Religious services of a special kind were being held in one of the churches; and I remember entering it on an evening when it was crowded with people, listening to a friar, who was earnestly preaching. Next morning, on revisiting the place, it was crowded as the night before, and the same priest occupied the pulpit. We drove along the old coast road, by the so-called Tomb of Virgil to Castellamare, Sorrento,

Posilipo and Pozzuoli (the Puteoli of the Acts), and had dreams of the luxurious life once spent on these shores, and of Paul's disembarkation on his way to Rome. We also spent a day at Vesuvius, where clouds of vapour were rolling upward; and I, with one of our party, crawled down to the crater, as near as we could, much to the dismay of our senior companions. On our way back to Naples we tarried as long as possible at Pompeii, looking at the wonders of that memorable spot.

An important step was taken at Kensington on my return from Italy. The "swarm" sent to Notting Hill did not permanently reduce the numbers of our congregation. On the contrary, they considerably advanced. The old chapel became more than ever inconvenient, and we resolved to build a new and much larger one.

I must now pass from local and personal affairs to notice a movement in Congregationalism at large. Independency leads to isolated action on the part of local Churches. It is unfriendly to cohesion and co-operation. It provides for freedom, and nothing else. Old Independents saw this, and checked the evil by maintaining local fellowships between Church and Church, by the employment of "messengers" one to another.*

About 1830 the wiser heads amongst us had clearly seen the evil, and endeavoured to overcome it. They concluded that centrifugal tendencies should be met by a centripetal force. Mr. Binney used to say, we were a collection of limbs—legs, arms, feet, and hands—all in motion, but not an organised body. To frame a body out of so many members, was the design of the Congregational Union. Algernon Wells may be regarded as its founder. He was one of the most beautiful characters I have ever known—intelligent, well read, sagacious, with extensive knowledge of men and things, and a profound attachment to evangelical truth. He had a rare order of eloquence, and wove pleasant tissues of thought in his sermons and speeches. If his speeches were not always sermons, his sermons were almost always speeches. There was a great charm in his conversation, and it often overflowed with wit. Though a decided Congregationalist, he was full of charity, and cultivated harmonious intercourse with other denominations. His policy

---

* Early Independent Churches had been particular in their relations to one another; and they would not recognise new communities without satisfactory evidence of character, principles, and conduct. They became more isolated afterwards.

as to the newly-formed organisation, was to make the meetings fraternal rather than controversial—a brotherly society to promote edification rather than an ecclesiastical army to fight with soldiers outside, or a council to settle disputes inside. The early meetings were held in the Congregational Library, and did not muster more than a hundred members. " Business " received at times a look askance : spiritual edification excited desire, and stimulated expression. Now and then came touches of humour, as when after talking about the state of the denomination till we were hungry, one brother rose and gravely asked " whether any intelligence had arrived from the Sandwich Islands."

Good Algernon Wells died in 1851, and soon afterwards I was requested by a sub-committee to meet them in conference on an important matter. It was to propose my election as Mr. Wells' successor. Now, secretaryships have always been my aversion—from an instinct, I suppose, such as guides inferior animals to shun what they were never made for. The secretaryship of the City Mission had been pressed upon me soon after my arrival in London, but I steadily refused it, from a conviction of utter incompetence ; and, for the same reason, I declined to entertain the proposal just mentioned. He who proposed the office for me accepted it for himself, and we worked together pleasantly through several years. I was elected chairman of the Union in May 1856, amidst much excitement. There have been strains on its strength more than once, but this first was the greatest.

Dr. Campbell had been for some time a prominent member. Hard-headed and hard-handed, of a bold, open countenance, and with a habit of planting his foot pretty firmly on the ground,—the outer man well indicated the inner; kind-hearted and affectionate at home, but not the same on a platform, or with an editorial pen in hand. He then gave no quarter to anybody who opposed him. "You are a good fellow," it was once said to him by a loving spirit; "but I don't like that great club you carry." That great club he swung about, much to the terror of many, and consequently he exercised a despotic sway, to which they were indisposed to submit. He held the doctrines of Calvinistic theology with a firm grasp, and looked with alarm upon certain opinions springing up amongst his brethren. He considered that there was looseness of sentiment, and a range of thought too free, existing amongst younger men, which imperilled the evangelical soundness of the Churches. He gave it the name of

Negative Theology. The name took, and was bandied about to the annoyance of persons to whom it was applied, many of them holding positive truths as firmly as Dr. Campbell himself. It happened that in 1856 Mr. Lynch, a man of genius and sensibility, with a mind cast in a mould the opposite of Dr. Campbell's, published a small volume of poetry entitled " The Rivulet." Some of the hymns it contained excited admiration, and are now extensively used; but the book, as a whole, aroused Dr. Campbell's wrath beyond measure. He wrote a criticism upon it, which awakened indignation in those who had read " The Rivulet " with approval. Fifteen brethren drew up and signed a protest against this style of review.

There existed, no doubt, a tendency on the part of a few brethren to give up certain theological expressions long held sacred, and also to throw into the background, if not to question, points of doctrine deemed perfectly Congregational. In the opposite quarter there appeared a tenacity of diction and an emphasis of opinion on old lines, accompanied by ungenerous reflections respecting those whom they deemed innovators. Very naturally, personal feeling was thus stirred up, and the Union seemed threatened with disaster.

" We men are a mysterious sort of creatures," said

John Howe to Richard Baxter. No doubt we are, and that in more ways than one: in this especially, that whilst discussing theories of God, Christ, and the Holy Spirit—all fountains of love—we are apt to be found drawing water from the wells of Marah.

The controversy, now spoken of, related to old and new aspects of theological thought. Looking back, I can but say, the balance sheet of past and present, in respect to what is now noticed, shows both gain and loss. All the gain, it strikes me, might have been secured without incurring loss at all; and, in making up the whole account, there should have been more charity in judging individuals, and more justice in discussing principles.

I wished, in my address, to combine the two, and so render the whole a sort of Irenicon.

A personal correspondence followed between two good men, which is now, I hope, buried in oblivion; but no secession of members from the Union took place, that I know of. The two tendencies still exist, but they call for no criticism in these pages. My views on the subject I have often expressed.

Before the close of my Windsor ministry I had begun to indulge in foreign travel, and in 1854, when I had spent some time in my Kensington pastorate, I ventured on a trip to Rome, which I have described already. After that, visits abroad were numerous, and from amongst them I select one paid in 1856, when I spent a few weeks with my two sons, who were then being educated in Berlin. My dear wife accompanied me through the greater part of the tour, as she was anxious to see how the lads were getting on. We made our way to the Prussian capital through Hanover, and, on reaching our destination, found all well. After spending a little while in Berlin, seeing the sights and becoming acquainted with some excellent people, we made an excursion to the South, and spent a few days at Dresden, where antiquities, pictures, and drives in the neighbourhood greatly delighted us. We proceeded to Schandau, a pretty little village, and there took lodgings, initiating ourselves into amusing details of German life. We attended the parish church on Sunday, taking interest in the clergyman, who was expounding to his people the history of David. We witnessed some of life's joys and sorrows, especially a funeral, which was very picturesque— bright flowers, red roses and green leaves, relieving the darkness of death, the hope of Heaven shedding light on the sorrow of bereavement. Excursions in the neighbourhood added to our family enjoyments of this sojourn, and one day we came in contact with royalty. The King of Saxony, the Queen, and a few of the Court, climbed up a hill which we had selected as a resting-place, commanding views of the Elbe. Their Majesties' servants in livery (who, by the way, were very civil to us) paid the royal reckoning to a humble châlet-keeper, as any of his subjects might do. We watched the King and attendants as they embarked in a boat for their Dresden home. My boys and I pushed on to Prague, where the bridge and St. John Nepomuk, the Hradschin, and the thirty years' war, John Huss and his house in the Bethlehem platz, the Jews' town on the banks of the Moldau, the Jewish burial ground, and the old synagogue, inspired historical memories of deep interest. We joined mamma and returned to Dresden the way we came; and there, after long gazings on the picture gallery, especially at Raphael's "Madonna and Child"—opposite to which people sat reverently, as if engaged in devotion—father and mother parted from the dear boys, and we wended our way homewards; not without lingering in Lutherland to look at homes and haunts of the great Reformer.

To return to my Kensington flock. In the year 1857, one Sunday night, after I had retired to rest,

I heard a loud ringing at the door-bell, and immediately rose. On opening the window, there stood a carriage; and the coachman, as soon as by gas-light he saw my face, cried out, "Oh, sir, my mistress is dead!" His mistress was Mrs. Jacomb, residing with her husband and family at Notting Hill. They had all been at Divine worship that morning in their usual health. The carriage had been sent to take me back to the mourners. I immediately rose and went. On reaching the house I witnessed a scene of domestic distress such as I never witnessed before. My deceased friend had in the morning worshipped with us, in her usual delicate health, and, as I learned, in more than her usual cheerfulness. She was preparing for evening service, when she was suddenly seized with illness, and in a short time expired. The husband and family were in deep distress, but they had a blessed knowledge of Him who brought life and immortality to light. She was a woman rich in spiritual sympathy, and had been no ordinary friend to me and mine, in our early married life. We had a large family, and, though favoured above many, had our domestic trials. How often I thought of what Paul said of "Phœbe, our sister": "She has been a succourer of many, and of myself also." I never knew any one who had more tender sympathy in trouble than Mrs. Jacomb, or was more swift in expressing it. Her husband was worthy of her, and her children "rise up to call her blessed." Those who survive are cherished friends. He was of an old Puritan stock, descendant of Dr. Jacomb, a renowned ejected clergyman after the Commonwealth; and the family genealogy is rich in noted names and memories.

In this chapter I cannot refrain from recording my own domestic sorrows. In 1853 a sweet child had died—little Catherine, born shortly after we left Windsor; and in 1858 another, more advanced in life, a boy named Arnold, full of energy and promise, was taken from us by our Heavenly Father. His illness was brief; but beforehand my dear wife had been anxious for his spiritual welfare, and her conversations were followed by the Divine blessing. His joyous, winning ways had won the hearts of visitors, and his death widely affected my congregation, awakening sympathy to a degree which inspired my liveliest gratitude. Our friend Joshua Harrison preached a funeral sermon for the dear boy, full of pathos and power.

In 1859 a friend accompanied me to the Pyrenees. Travelling by French railways, we reached Bayonne at the end of August, and then crossed the Spanish frontier in a Spanish diligence, which had all the lumber and shabby trappings of French ones. We reached San Sebastian at night, and next morning took a walk on the promenade, where the ladies in mantillas and veils flourished their fans with grace and dignity; and if there be something gay in French solemnity, there is something grave in the gaiety of Spaniards. We again climbed up a diligence, and travelled through the Lower Pyrenees to Pau, where, from the Grand Terrace, we saw peering out from the haze of a hot summer sky the mountain range—not near, as many imagine, but many miles off. Of course we saw the old palace where Henri IV. was born and wrapped up in his shell cradle. Along roads bordered by woods and hills, reminding one of Wharfedale, we reached an elevation at Sevignac, overlooking the valley of the Gave, with magnificent mountains in front, Pic du Midi coming into full view. Eaux Bonnes, with all the luxuries of a French watering-place, was then reached, whence we proceeded to Eaux Chaudes, where the mountains become awfully precipitous. We looked down from zigzag roads, cut out of declivities buttressed by rocks and embankments, with boiling torrents at the foot, roaring like thunder.

The Pic du Midi, streaked with snow, rises up so as to remind one of an Egyptian pyramid.

We determined to visit Pantacosa, and passed through a romantic defile, crossed the Spanish frontier again, and halted at a village, where the houses seemed walls without windows, the outlook being altogether from the back. Glimpses of Aragon's broad plain were caught, as we looked south, and crowds of Spanish muleteers passed us, laden with merchandise. The baths of Pantacosa occupy a gloomy region, shut in by rocks, and there I spent the Sunday as an invalid, my strength being overtaxed; but next day I rose in the enjoyment of health and vigour. Then we made our way to Luz. The church of the Templars built there is half fortress and half sanctuary. You enter through a machicolated gateway, into a church, the gloomiest I ever saw. Through a little door, the *Cagots*, a proverbial race weak both in body and mind, used to enter for worship.

Near to Luz is St. Sauveur, a narrow valley, richly wooded, with a tiny village jammed in among the rocks. At the time of our visit, the Emperor Napoleon and the Empress Eugenie were staying there. The house they occupied was small and plain; nothing distinguished it but the two sentinels at the door. All was silent and solitary, and nobody seemed to notice the royal residence, besides ourselves. In the afternoon, we saw their Majesties returning from a drive in open carriages with outriders. Napoleon sat on the box, Eugenie was chatting with her lady attendants. On alighting she remained at the door of the house, playing with her walking stick, and receiving a letter-bag. The Emperor came out, lighted a cigar, smoked and then walked on to inspect some men at work on a new road.

We made an excursion to Gavarnie—a shady defile with precipitous rocks, overhanging woods, and a river foaming and roaring four hundred feet below. Beyond is the Cirque, a basin-shaped valley of semi-circular rocks, with steps and stages, whilst a drapery of water fringes them all round. We ascended the Pic de Bergons, tarried a day at Bagnères de Bigorre, a central spot for tourists, with the usual appurtenances of such places. We proceeded to Bagnères de Luchon, by a romantic drive, commanding a view of the Maladetta with its snows and glaciers.

In the course of our rambles in the Pyrenees we were struck with Eastern customs. An unmuzzled ox went round a heap of corn. Sheep were not driven but led, and wine was kept in leathern bottles

CHAPTER VIII

1862—1865

THE year 1862, being the Bicentenary of the Bartholomew ejectment, was largely given by English Nonconformists to a remembrance of the confessorship and heroism which marked the ejectment of ministers in 1662. A meeting was held in the spring at St. James's Hall, Piccadilly, when papers were read, bearing on the commemoration. The preparation of one of them fell to my lot; but I was taken ill at the time for its delivery, and it had to be read by my friend, the Rev. Joshua Clarkson Harrison. A story is told of Garrick's reading a poem of Hannah More's, before a party of friends, when the effect produced was by Garrick attributed to the lady's composition, and by the lady to the reader's elocution. Whatever might be the impression made at St. James's Hall on the reading of the paper, it was divided between my friend and me, after the same fashion. In this address I advocated a Bartholomew celebration, on the ground, that it was good to remember sacrifices made for conscience' sake, and therefore professed my readiness to honour Jeremy Taylor as well as Richard Baxter. This brought a letter from the Bishop of Down and Connor testing my sincerity by an appeal on behalf of an Irish cathedral restoration in memory of Jeremy Taylor. I sent a small contribution, which brought back a pleasant response, such as I highly valued. Afterwards I met him at the Athenæum, when he invited me to visit him, with a view to Christian union in Ireland. I should add that the Bishop's scheme for the cathedral restoration failed, and he politely returned my small contribution.

In the autumn of 1862, I read a paper to the Congregational Assembly, in which I advocated certain methods of improvement. This subject I took up afterwards, with no result, however, that I could discover. The faults of other systems are always more welcome than the reformation of our own.

In 1863 we were visited by a family bereavement which was one of the heaviest sorrows of my life. John Howard Stoughton, born at Windsor in 1842, was a lad of extraordinary character, witty and artistic beyond his brothers and sisters, who loved him with no ordinary love. His love of art led us to place the youth under Mr. Thomas, a distinguished sculptor and decorator, largely employed in works at Windsor Castle. Our boy devoted himself to his pursuits with an assiduity which created much anxiety in his mother and in me, for it evidently injured his health. In the spring of 1861 we took him to Hastings, and Dr. Moore, an eminent physician there, carefully studied his case, and, as the result, advised that his artistic pursuits should be for awhile suspended, and that he should travel abroad, where he would see and learn much, without tasking his physical power. Accordingly, in the summer of 1861, he visited the Continent with his elder brother and me, went up and down the Rhine, and saw pictures, statues, and decorations, which interested his mind without overtasking his bodily strength. In the following autumn he was better, and under medical advice we arranged that, in company with one of his sisters, he should spend the winter in Rome. They did so accordingly, and our hopes were raised; but in the spring he had an attack, which rendered it advisable that he should remove from Rome to some other part of Italy. He did so, and paid a visit to friends in Leghorn. I left home with another of my daughters and two nieces, joining my children where they were staying; thence I accompanied them, on a pleasant tour through Florence, over the Apennines, and, by way of Bologna, Milan, and the Alps, to Geneva. Thence we came home through France. We returned in good spirits; but, as winter approached, fears reawakened. Gradually the invalid became weaker; but faith in the Invisible and Divine Father grew stronger and stronger. The youth spent with us a cheerful Christmas; but in spring it was obvious he was not long for this world. As the end approached he talked calmly on the subject with his beloved brother, the two being united in bonds of Christian faith, as well as natural affection. I can never forget the Holy Communion we—mother, father, brother, and sisters—enjoyed in a room overlooking our garden, when bursting buds told of nature's returning life, and the dear sufferer bore unmistakable signs of approaching death. But he was calm and cheerful, and took deep interest in the gracious ordinance. It was administered with solemnity by our dear friend Harrison, who loved Howard as though he had been his own son. He expired on March 31st, 1863, and on the following

Sunday evening my brother just named preached a memorable funeral sermon in Kensington Chapel.

In 1864 Dr. Stanley became Dean of Westminster, and on his expressing a wish to be introduced to some Nonconformist brethren, Dr. William Smith—editor of so many valuable dictionaries, and with whom I was then associated in the business of New College—kindly gave a dinner party to which he invited me. The Dean afterwards finding there was between us some similarity of taste in literature, and sympathy in desires for union, invited me to the Deanery; and so began a friendship with him and Lady Augusta, which lasted as long as they lived, and proved one of the most precious privileges vouchsafed to me, by the providence of our Heavenly Father. On December 28th, 1865, "the Feast of the Holy Innocents"—the Dean preached a sermon in Westminster Abbey. The sermon was in commemoration of the Abbey's foundation by Edward the Confessor eight hundred years before. The text was felicitously chosen from John x. 22, 23,—" It was the feast of the *Dedication*, and it was *winter*, and Jesus walked in the temple in *Solomon's porch*." " Feast of the Dedication " corresponded with the character of the service; " winter " was the season of both celebrations; the

northern porch a main entrance to the Abbey—
is called "Solomon's porch." The sermon was not
less appropriate than the text. It sketched the
history of the venerable edifice, and contained
marked allusions to Nonconformist ministrations
within its walls during the Commonwealth. Being
present on the occasion, I wrote to the Dean afterwards in reference to his allusions, when, in reply,
he said, "It gave me additional pleasure to deliver
them, from the reflection that there was at least
one person present capable of entering into them."
In the sermon, as delivered, he spoke of the Westminster Confession as the only one ever *imposed*
in the *whole Island*, and on my calling his attention
to this statement, and pointing out the distinction
between the *doctrinal* and ecclesiastical part of the
Confession, he answered, "I was not ignorant of
the distinction, nor did I mean to say it was
imposed in any offensive sense. For I was anxious
not to say a word that could be offensive to any
of my brethren, and merely wished to call attention
to the fact, that a document, which had received
in part a wider legal recognition than any other
since the Reformation, came from Westminster
Abbey." In the sermon, as *printed*, are the words
"*sanctioned by law* for the whole Island," and in

a note, "The doctrinal Articles of the Westminster Confession of Faith (were) sanctioned by the English Parliament in 1647, and the whole Confession by the Scottish Parliament in 1648."

In further illustration of the Dean's ingenuity when turning Scripture to account in the improvement of events, I may here repeat what he once related to me. He happened on a Saturday to be preparing a sermon for the Abbey, on some occasion when he was to plead for *two* objects, and had chosen for his text Gen. xxvii. 38—"And Esau said unto his father, hast thou but one blessing my father? Bless me, even me also, O my father." As the Dean was writing his discourse, some one stepped in and told him, the American President, General Grant, intended to be at the Abbey the next day, and suggested that it would be gratifying to Americans if some allusion was made to the incident. Immediately it was turned to account by the Dean in this way—that God had many blessings which He distributed amongst his children; that bounty to one did not mean denial to another; that Great Britain, for instance, had been blessed, but God had rich benefactions for America as well.

For years I felt an earnest desire to visit the East, and thus to become personally acquainted with Bible lands. A meeting was held in 1865 to present me with a purse of £400, and a pledge that expenses incurred through my absence from Kensington should be met, without any pecuniary responsibilities on my part. The friends who accompanied me were Dr. Allon, of Union Chapel, Islington, Dr. Spence, of the Poultry Chapel, London, Dr. Bright, minister of the Independent Chapel, Dorking, and two young lay friends—Stanley Kemp-Welch and Thomas Wilson. The Dean of Westminster gave me introductions to people he knew in Palestine, and afforded valuable assistance in other ways.

We started in February 1865. I kept a journal and sent home long letters. We visited Alexandria and Cairo, and then proceeded through the desert of Sinai to the monastery at the foot of Jebel Mousa. Turning north, we made our way to Gaza, thence to Ramleh, and so onwards to Jerusalem. The members of our little party, as we approached the city on horseback, rode at a considerable distance from each other. I knew that we should cross some ridges, before we caught sight of the city, and I happened to be in the rear of my fellow-travellers. I watched the foremost of them till I saw him pull up his horse, pause awhile, then take off his hat. I knew what that meant, and the feelings awakened I can never forget while I live. I eagerly, and I may say reverently, followed the foremost horseman, and as soon as I caught sight of the walls and the gate, I am not ashamed to say, my eyes were full of tears.

As we entered the Holy City the bustle was very great. Bedouins with yellow scarves round their heads, and striped robes on their shoulders; Syrians with snowy turbans, short jackets, and flowing trousers; Turks wearing the crimson fez; a rich man "clothed in purple and fine linen," mounted on a smartly caparisoned white ass, and a poor man on foot, ragged and tattered; camels and donkeys carrying loads of timber and brushwood, to the peril of wayfarers; Egyptian, Copt, Armenian, Greek, the black Nubian, the white Circassian, with groups of veiled women, shuffling over the stones in gay slippers—all these made a motley picture, which dazzled the attention of pilgrims from England. At length we reached our hotel, and had to make ladder-like ascents, and mount on roofs, story after story, before we could get to our apartments, whence we caught our first view of Mount Olivet.

We met with Christian friends in the Holy City, and were kindly invited by Dr. Gobat, Bishop of

Jerusalem, to spend an evening at his house, when he gathered together a party consisting of the principal foreign visitors at the time, most of whom were English. For two Sunday mornings we worshipped at the church on Mount Zion, near the Episcopal residence, and were glad of an opportunity to partake of the Communion. I have always delighted in fellowship at the Lord's table with Christian brethren of different churches, who, under different forms of administration, worship and adore the same Lord. Not only when travelling on the Continent have I received the Lord's Supper at the hands of Episcopalian brethren, but in England, on a few occasions I have availed myself of a similar catholic privilege.

Before proceeding further, let me relate a story I heard from Dr. Rosen, the German consul, respecting the famous Sinaitic MS. Tischendorf had reason to believe a precious treasure was hid in the monastery at Sinai. He obtained letters which he thought would assist him, but, on further consideration, declined to employ them. He found in the library part of his coveted prize; and, it happened at that moment, the office of Okonomos was vacant, and a keen contest for it was going on between two monks. He joined one party, and promised to use influence with the Russian Emperor in favour of their candidate, hinting that the present of a valuable MS. would promote their object. After a good deal of diplomacy this plan prospered. The MS. coveted by the scholar was secured, and the once hopeless candidate was installed in office. This was not all. The MS. was incomplete, and the missing part was found by Tischendorf in the possession of a Greek merchant. The promise of a Russian title proved more effectual than gold, and Tischendorf carried off his prize to St. Petersburg in triumph. I jotted down the story the evening Dr. Rosen related it, and here in a few words have I given the substance.

Of course we explored Jerusalem as far as our limited time allowed; and, under the guidance of Dr. Rosen, I had the privilege of visiting certain spots where recent discoveries had been made. I remember seeing what looked like indications of a well, from which, it was easy to imagine, people, in our Lord's time, used to draw water. Nor can I forget rambles on the line of walls commanding views of the city and neighbourhood. I can now distinctly recall my visit to a sepulchre outside the city, where a stone, like a large millstone, was lying at the door, as if recently "rolled away." I studied (as well as time, and what I had read on the subject, would allow), the question as to the place of crucifixion, and where our blessed Lord rose from the dead. Points still remain to be settled, as to the direction in which the city wall ran in the time of Christ. I cannot adopt any modern theories on the whole subject, which have made way in America and in England. It appears to me after long study, that grounds can still be maintained in support of the old tradition in favour of the spot where the Church of the Holy Sepulchre stands. We made a memorable excursion to Bethlehem, by way of Rachel's sepulchre, and descended the cave where, it is said, our Lord was born. We next proceeded to Hebron, where I stood by a flight of steps leading to the tombs within, longing to ascend and explore those hallowed resting places. Returning northwards, we stopped at the traditional oak, by which Abraham sat in the heat of the day—and at the vineyards of Eschol where old stocks are thriving still—and at Solomon's pool and gardens, not far from David's hiding-places. Then, after a long and exciting day, we found rest in the old monastery of S. Saba, from the terrace of which, we caught a view of the Dead Sea. We rambled on its melancholy shores, dipped in the Jordan, and then spent a night by the ruins of Jericho.

The order of our journey followed Dr. Stanley's directions, that we might have the advantage of crossing Olivet, so as to come suddenly on the point where our Lord "beheld the city and wept over it." From Jerusalem we proceeded northwards by Bethel, Sychar, Samaria, Esdraelon, and Nazareth, to Tiberias and the Lake. Thence by Safed we travelled over the hills of Galilee to Banias ("the Syrian Tivoli"), Damascus, and Beyrout. Banias is a charming spot. With the scenery from a hill overlooking Damascus I was charmed beyond measure, and was intensely interested in the antiquities of that grand old city. Dr. Allon, Dr. Bright and Mr. Wilson visited the ruins at Baalbec, but Mr. Kemp-Welch remained with me in Damascus to take care of Dr. Spence, who was very ill. He had to be leisurely taken over the mountains to Beyrout, approaching which we had never-to-be-forgotten views of the beautiful Mediterranean.

After leaving Palestine I wrote in my notes the following impression as to the Bible, which had been a constant companion and guide in our travels:—It is the Book of the Holy Land—the gospel of Palestine.

It is Oriental; it is Syrian; it is Samaritan; it is Galilean; it is Jewish. It paints the scenery of the Land of Promise from end to end, and the wilderness too. It echoes the voices of the people. We hear in it the murmur of towns and villages, we pass through; it breathes the pure, fresh, bracing air of the desert; everywhere as I opened the Divine pages I found them reflecting surrounding scenes. Even the brilliant Frenchman, who has tasked his genius to demolish the authentic life of Jesus and to build out of the ruins an imagination of his own, virtually admits the truth of what I have now advanced, for he points out the minute accuracy of the Volume; which shows how true in detail are the Gospels, how faithful to rock and stream, river and lake, tree and wild flower, is the entire narrative. Thus, after all he says to the contrary, he really raises in the reader's mind a fair presumption of its fidelity in higher matters.

One circumstance struck me as very noticeable—that is, the compression, within a small compass, of a number of stirring incidents related in Holy Writ. Dothan, where Joseph sought his brethren and their flocks; the plain of Megiddo, the battle-field of Israel; the river Kishon, "that ancient river," so fatal to Sisera's army; the valley of Jezreel, with its wide panorama, where Ahab had a palace; the heights of Gilboa, where fell Saul and his sons, with the well of Harod at the foot, where Gideon's three hundred men stooped and lapped the water; the garden of the Shunamite, opposite to Mount Carmel; the city of Nain and the cave of Endor; Tabor and Nazareth—all these spots come within a few hours' ride. Well might Issachar think "that rest was good, and the land that it was pleasant."

Our party began to separate at Beyrout. Dr. Spence, accompanied by Mr. Wilson, returned direct to England; the rest of us came home through Europe.

In crossing the Mediterranean with Dr. Allon and Kemp-Welch we touched at Cyprus. The coast looked flat and uninteresting, but the bright morning, the sparkling sea, and the manifold associations attaching to the islands inspired great curiosity and deep interest, though I felt by no means well. I began to be conscious that my appetite for travelling had somewhat palled, if not become almost dead. We landed at Larnaca, and found it a very poor place. The Greek churches were somewhat curious, from the circumstance of old columns with characteristic capitals being built into the walls. I noticed Greek priests sitting in wine shops, and some of them occupying places of traffic, selling different articles in huckster-like hovels. These men indicated the social degradation of inferior orders in the Eastern Church. However it may be with the dignified clergy in Russia, certainly priests in Palestine, Syria and the Mediterranean Isles afford low types of civilisation. After dwelling on what is related about Cyprus in the Acts of the Apostles, the conversion of Sergius Paulus, and the conduct of Elymas the sorcerer, became very real narratives; and with these memories in our minds we re-embarked and had a pleasant evening as we sat on deck. I fell asleep with the prospect of reaching Rhodes the next day.

The harbour, with its well-known mole and adjuncts, is very picturesque. We climbed up narrow streets, full of houses once occupied by the knights, and from the fortification, had an extensive view of the island and the Mediterranean. The Church of St. John, blown up by gunpowder, and shattered to fragments, seized on my imagination for a good while, as I wandered, and sat down on a spot, so rich in romantic story. We then returned to the interior of the town, and at the harbour watched the boatmen, busy at the seaside. As we were doing so, one of my companions exclaimed, "Stoughton, you've got the jaundice!"

and, sure enough, when we reached our steamer, the looking-glass proved this was true. When I rose next morning my limbs were of a saffron colour.

The weather changed. The sky was dark, and the views we caught of Asia were by no means inviting. At night there came a storm; and a storm in the Mediterranean is no trifling matter. Wind roared through the rigging; the vessel lurched and laboured, groaning as if the timbers would burst. Lying in my berth I could feel the dashing billows. Tables and stools were sliding about. The suspended lamps swayed to and fro, like the pendulum of a clock. Overhead confusion was terrible. Horses were kicking, and the sailors were swearing. We had a pasha with his harem on board, and, as might be expected, they were exceedingly terrified. Crowds of pilgrims returning from the Eastern celebration at Jerusalem, were lying on deck resembling herrings in a barrel, and the noise they made was terrific. Waves beat over our boat, till the poor creatures were almost drowned. Beside we had horses, bears and monkeys on board, and, of course, they added to the inharmonious concert. I rose from my hammock early, and with my companion, Mr. Welch, sought comfort from a cup of tea. Reaching the deck, I talked with one of the engineers, an Englishman, and asked what he thought of the storm. "Is there any danger?" I asked. He replied, "This has been a very queer night, and we have made no way. If it had lasted, that would have been serious." We safely reached Smyrna harbour in the afternoon.

Of course, I thought as we approached land:— There, on one of the hills yonder, the martyr, Polycarp, by death sealed the truths which he had proclaimed in life. As we landed, I thought myself in an Italian port, so European at a glance everything looked—houses, shops, and people—but, entering the town, the scene changed, for there the streets, bazaars, and costumes told of Oriental manners and customs. The next day a party was organised to visit the ruins of Ephesus. It can be reached by railway, and when we entered the station, we might have fancied ourselves at home; for there we met with English guards, and railway porters, like our own. We had a special train to convey us to the far-famed ruins. We visited what is left of the forum, the theatre, and the stadium, but it is difficult to identify anything; and it seemed to me, a definite idea of what Ephesus was in its glory is impossible. The view from the loftiest eminence is magnificent, including the vast plain, the winding river Cayster, and what, in Paul's day was the harbour of Miletus. At the time of our visit, Greek Christians were celebrating the Festival of St. John, on a lofty hill, the church there being a rude-looking structure. The cave of the seven sleepers was pointed out, on our way back to the railway station, and by the cave is a beautiful mosque of the fifteenth century.

On Saturday morning we embarked at Smyrna for Constantinople. We faintly discerned in the far distance, as we crossed those classic waters, point after point closely connected with ancient story. Of course, all the way, amidst Homeric scenes and associations, we called them to mind by Homer's help; but the thought of St. John's labours, his epistles, to the seven churches in the Apocalypse, more prominently occupied one's mind on the Lord's day, when we had worship in the saloon, and I preached, as well as I could, to a few sympathetic fellow-passengers.

On Monday morning early, we reached the Golden Horn, filled with shipping. Caiques were quietly gliding over still waters; but we were troubled at the Custom House by an ignorant soldier, who laid hold upon my "Homer" and detained it for two or three days.

Kemp-Welch was the only member of our party left, the rest proceeding homeward by another route. I made the most of what was possible during the four days spent at Constantinople. My friend and I followed the circuit of the city on horseback; through Stamboul, which appeared very Oriental, ruinous and dirty—through lines of cypresses, near cemeteries with turbaned headstones; and so, all round, till we reached the sweet waters. There we tarried a while, looking at the gardens, and their summer houses, called kiosks. The place is a resort like Hampton Court. Thence we returned to the city. Next day we crossed the Golden Horn, and saw the Sultan's seraglio, attached to which are more gardens and more kiosks. The place contains a library full of Arabic MSS., and a throne room, with the Sultan's divan, surmounted with a baldacchino. There His Majesty used to hold his court, attended by janissaries, and was screened from the view of subjects, except that his hands were visible. The Sublime Porte is the grand entrance to the room of audience for ambassadors from other courts.

We visited the arsenal with its ammunition, muskets, and swords. The building, it is said, was in the fourth century a church—the Church of S. Irene, where Chrysostom preached some of his wonderful sermons—and it has still in the apse an antique cross. But the grand ecclesiastical edifice of Constantinople is S. Sophia, with columns brought from Ephesus, and representations of four cherubim with their faces obliterated. A legend is preserved to this effect, that when Constantinople was taken by the Turks, a priest was saying mass—immediately a chasm opened in the wall and received him. There he still remains, chalice in hand, waiting to finish the service, when Christians recover the ancient edifice.

But I must not enter into further details of what I saw and heard during my short stay at Constantinople. I was now left alone, as my only remaining companion was obliged to return home by a different route.

Let me add in closing this part of my story, that the banks of the Bosphorus on which I gazed, as I left Constantinople, surpassed previous imagination. The gardens and kiosks by the waterside, looked paradisaical; and as we steamed along I was enchanted, one instant after another, by objects on the shore. All the way to the Black Sea was delightful. Then surroundings changed. Travellers, landed to find themselves amidst indescribable confusion. Thence we proceeded by rail across a dreary district, without trees, and abounding in shallow sheets of stagnant water, with plenty of storks, Egyptian geese, and other wild birds. Still, within the region crossed, there were fields of grain. We reached our steamer on the Danube, between six and seven o'clock on Friday evening.

We found the great river improve as we ascended it. At first we had low banks dotted with mosques and minarets, showing we were still in Turkey. On board the boat I was treated as an invalid, and the attention shown by captain, crew, and servants, was such as to inspire the warmest gratitude on my part.

The scenery on the banks of the Danube, in the earlier part of our voyage up the river, was very magnificent—rocks rising loftily from the water's edge on one bank, but low on the other. We passed richly wooded scenery, and caught glimpses of pleasant glens, with running streams and picturesque bridges. Further on were comfortable farm-houses and smiling villages. We reached Pesth on Tuesday, travelling by rail, and then proceeded, in the same way, to Vienna, where I tarried for a couple of days—seeing the magnificent cathedral, the vaults of the

Capuchin Church, the Prater, the Royal Palace, and the Picture Galleries. Travelling across Germany by rail I reached the Rhine, thence to Brussels, where I was entertained by my nieces then on a visit there. At last I found two dear daughters waiting at the Victoria Station, and at Fairlawn House, Hammersmith, there was a loving welcome.

At the conclusion of my narrative of Eastern travel, let me remark. What one sees in travelling through Palestine gives vividness to the narrative —makes what before were pale outlines, pictures of glowing colour and dazzling light. I do not forget the danger there is of being too much engaged with what is outward in Biblical studies— tarrying in the porch instead of worshipping in the temple—lingering by the hedge to gather flowers instead of pressing into the field to cut down corn —playing the geologist, instead of working as spiritual miners—finding out what is curious as to literature, instead of appropriating "the unsearchable riches of Christ." But still, what I gathered in the East is precious, and may minister to spiritual edification, as well as to mental enjoyment. How marvellous it is that whilst the Bible is so Eastern— while Oriental manners, customs, and scenery are photographed there, it is nevertheless an universal book! The Koran is not so Eastern as the Bible; at least, so it struck me, as I read it in the East; yet the Bible is the Englishman's book as the Koran could not be, even if we were all Mussulmans.

Specially forcible and beautiful were the impressions we derived touching the life of Christ; we felt how toilsome were his journeys as He *walked* along the rough and rugged pathways from Jericho to Jerusalem, over which we *rode*. How humiliating must have been his intercourse with the poor, who, no doubt, then lived in wretched mud hovels, such as we saw, not only in Palestine, but in Egypt; types of domestic habitation for the lower classes in ages past! We thought: Through such collections of "houses of clay" did He pass! Here did He tarry, and within such abodes! Not one of them was His own; He had not where to lay His head.

CHAPTER IX

1865—1872

IN the year 1867 I published the first volumes of my "Ecclesiastical History of England"; this calls for explanation of what preceded and prepared for it.

Immediately after I left college, and settled at Windsor, I commenced the study of Church history with much earnestness; and the first fruit was a course of lectures on the subject to my congregation, delivered on week evenings. When I had completed them they were sent by me to my revered tutor, Dr. Henderson, for criticism and advice. He encouraged me to pursue my studies in that direction, with the hope and intention of making use of them in after life. I followed his advice, and during the remainder of my Windsor ministry devoted all the time I could spare from pulpit and pastoral duties to researches into early annals of Christendom. In my investigations I was kindly allowed to use the Dean and Chapter's library. After I left Windsor, I turned attention to ecclesiastical affairs during the Puritan period. This happened just as I was about to pay a visit to my native county—Norfolk—where I commenced studying original records in Norwich. Proceedings *against Nonconformity* and other records there came within my reach, that part of England being somewhat rich in this department of history. "Spiritual Heroes" was the title of my first volume, which not long after was revised and enlarged in a second edition. The Congregational lecture on "The Ages of Christendom," was delivered and published in 1856. This led, in 1867, to the "Ecclesiastical History of England, from the Opening of the Long Parliament to the Death of Oliver Cromwell." "The Church of the Restoration," forming two volumes, appeared in 1870, and "The Church of the Revolution" in 1874. To complete the list of works on English Ecclesiasticism, there followed other volumes on the reigns of Queen Anne and the Three Georges. Afterwards came "Religion in England from 1800 to 1851." I state all this, because some confusion has arisen from a fragmentary publication of the original works and of successive editions.

In 1867 correspondence and personal intercourse

commenced between a distinguished Episcopalian and myself, of an interesting character. In that year I received an invitation to Chichester from Dean Hook. He was much talked of, on account of his High Churchmanship, and his pre-eminent activity as Vicar of Leeds. Dissenters counted him amongst their bitter foes; and I should have been much surprised, years earlier, had I been told I was to be a guest at his house. Yet so it was. Historical sympathies brought us together, and each found that the other wished to be fair in dealing with men who held opposite opinions. Both believed in a spiritual brotherhood reaching beyond denominational bounds. Soon after my arrival at Chichester he asked: "What shall we talk about? If I thought I could make you a Churchman, I would try to do so; and if you thought you could make a Dissenter of me, you would make the attempt." I replied: "Nothing of the kind; let us leave out ecclesiastical controversy, and talk of literary and religious matters, on which we are pretty well agreed; and when we have exhausted them we will take up points of difference." He went on to say, that his great friend Lord Hatherley, then High Chancellor, differed from him politically, and yet they had walked up together to the polling-booth to record opposite votes, without any breach of friendship. "And so," he said, "you and I can unite to a certain extent; and when we come to the parting of the way, we can each take our own course, with mutual good will." I entered into the compact. On historical and social subjects, and as to religion in its spiritual and experimental aspects, we were of one accord, and felt no inclination to unsheath swords.

We had pleasant drives in the country and cheerful chat at the dinner-table, when he included within his party members of the cathedral body. Plenty of anecdotes were related, some about Dr. Wilberforce, when Bishop of Oxford. The Bishop, I heard, used to tell a story, which showed how a man might, unconsciously, make a good pun. He had engaged to dine with somebody whose name was *Hunter*, a cattle grazier, and on his way, as was his wont, the Bishop bethought himself: "What topic of talk can we have together?" At the railway-station his eye caught an advertisement of "Thorley's Food for Cattle." That would suit very well. So the bishop asked the grazier his opinion of such provision for beasts of the field. The host replied: "It might do very well for *Oxen*, but not for a *Hunter*." He did not know he was quoting the diocesan name of his right-reverend guest (Oxon.), and forgot at the moment he was also repeating his own. The Dean gave a conundrum, invented by the Bishop, for the amusement of a young lady :—

"What part of your dress resembles two popular preachers in the Church of England?"

"Give it up?"

"Hook and I."

The Chancellor of the Cathedral, I think it was, spoke of Wilberforce's power of adapting himself to people whom he met. He liked to know beforehand who he was to see. Introduced to a Yorkshireman, he began to talk in the county dialect. Visiting a screw manufactory, he won the confidence of workmen by showing some knowledge of their business. Once at the Earl of Derby's (grandfather of the present Lord) he met gentlemen of the turf, and surprised them by giving the pedigree of a celebrated racehorse. On being asked how he came to be "well up" on such a subject, he said he had gleaned knowledge of that kind as a boy, in the stables of a trainer, near his father's house. He scarcely ever forgot anything he had heard.

The Dean was an early riser; and retired early to bed. We had family prayer in the library about nine o'clock, the family and the guests standing and kneeling together. He read the Psalms for the day, and used parts of the Morning and Evening Service. Once, about half-past ten in the evening, I said to Mrs. Hook—a charming woman, "light of the dwelling"—"I must bid the Dean good-night. Where is he?"

"In bed and asleep the last hour," she gently answered.

He told me that early rising had been his habit during his residence at Leeds, and was so still; that demands on his time, from forenoon to night, were such at Leeds as would have prevented all literary work, had he not secured hours for study before breakfast. Then it was he wrote his books. He worked hard all day when vicar, and adopted unusual methods of usefulness, holding something like Methodist class-meetings, which took strong hold on his Yorkshire parishioners. Familiar devotional gatherings he kept up at Chichester; and a poor old woman was so delighted with them, that, by an odd association of ideas, she compared them to feasting on "lamb and salad." These meetings he would humorously call by that name. I had a good deal of talk with my kind hostess about clerical incomes, and the demands made on them; and so I became disabused of false notions common amongst outsiders. From what I heard of large outgoings, payments on promotion, and so on, I am able to form a more correct estimate of pecuniary affairs in the Establishment, than I could before.

Considerable correspondence passed between us. A friendly intercourse was also maintained by subsequent visits. In a letter dated June 4th, 1867, he says :—

"I like a companion who will look out for points of agreement, and then coze upon them. I never court the society of those who love an argument, and look out for topics on which we disagree. You will, perhaps, infer from this, that I want vigour of mind; but I really believe that many minds are drawn out and strengthened by cozing instead of arguing, and I am sure that this conduces to brotherly affection. My wife and I after many years of hard work—and what is worse than work, worry—came here to retire from the world. We see little of general society, and confine ourselves to pleasant cozy intercourse, with our large and united family, and old friends. We cannot, therefore, offer you any gaiety when you come amongst us, but if you take us as we are, we shall hope to have some pleasant cozes."

In a letter, dated March 1868, he remarks:

"In the Peninsular War the pickets of the two armies were accustomed often to meet on the most friendly terms, and enjoy each other's conversation. But when the trumpet sounded each man was at his post, ready to do his duty. So it is with us. I have always acted on this principle of refusing to admit the assertion, that our differences are on non-essentials—and of offering, nevertheless, the right hand of friendship in private to those whom in public I might oppose, or rather by whom I was myself opposed. I was freely censured at one time for this; but when I left Leeds my Nonconformist friends rallied round me to bid me farewell, and several of them saw I had pursued the right course."

"The great thing which you and I have to do is to guard against the deadly sin of too many of our contemporaries—imputing motives. If we can discover a good motive, we may rejoice, even though we condemn the action to which it may have led. But no words can express, or thought conceive, the indignation I experience, when men seek to attribute good actions to bad motives."

The Dean was not one of your modern correspondents. The last of these extracts is from a letter on quarto sheets, which covers *sixteen* closely written pages.

Dr. Hook was a delightful talker, English to the backbone—"a thorough John Bull," as an Oxford don once said to me. There was a strong dash of humour in his constitution, and he was ready to tell amusing anecdotes of himself. He was no ritualist, no Puritan, certainly no Erastian; but a godly, warm-hearted, Christian man, whom it was a privilege to know.

During visits to Chichester I became acquainted with one of the canons, Dr. Swainson, then Norrisian Professor at Cambridge, afterwards Master of Christ's College in that University. He rendered me essential service whilst I was writing my volumes on "The Church of the Restoration." Some of the books and MSS. in the library of the cathedral were of great use; and when I visited him afterwards at Cambridge he rendered me further valuable aid. I had the pleasure of meeting some Cambridge dons at his dinner table, and I remember being interested and instructed by a long conversation on the rendering of names given in our version of the Bible to ancient instruments of music. In 1869 I was present at the announcement of wranglers for that year. I stood side by side with my friend in the gallery, close to the gentleman who held in his hand a paper big with the fates of university competitors. It was a dark morning, and at eight o'clock, amidst breathless silence, the personal secrets so many waited to learn, were publicly proclaimed. It was a grand piece of living mosaic which lay before me, as upturned eager countenances were fixed on the spot where I was standing; and the announcement of the new senior wrangler raised applause which seemed enough to lift the roof.

My friendly relations with Dr. Swainson continued through after-years; and his laborious investigations into Church creeds were frequent topics in our conversation. His inquiries into the date of the Utrecht MS. containing the " Quicunque vult," etc., were extraordinarily extensive, minute, and careful, as I can bear testimony from repeated accounts he gave of Continental journeys and inquiries. I apprehend that nobody ever spent so much time and labour on the inquiry, as he did; therefore his conclusions ought to carry much weight in the settlement of a controversy touching historical theology, as well as an archæological question.

On the occasion of my visit to Cambridge I went to see my friend, Mr. Fordham of Melbourne, who possessed a valuable collection of paintings; and I mention him here, for the sake of what he related respecting Lord Beaconsfield, who had been a schoolfellow with Mr. Fordham's brother-in-law, the Right Honourable Russell Gurney, Recorder of London.

They were educated at an academy in Walthamstow, kept by Mr. Cogan, a Presbyterian minister, whose son I knew well. Young Dizzy, as people called the politician, was famous at school for two things. He delighted in forming parties and getting up cabals—there was an embryo politician; next he excelled in telling stories, and would keep the boys awake at night by his romantic inventions—there was an embryo novelist. He had early dreams of future greatness, I think; and my friend informed me that he had talked to his schoolmates of being one day Prime Minister of England.

In the winter of 1867—68, Dr. Alford, Dean of Canterbury, delivered and printed a lecture on "The Christian Conscience," which was followed up, in *The Contemporary* by an article expressive of kindly feelings towards Nonconformists, and a desire for more friendly intercourse with them. I felt it a duty to respond to this overture, and did so, both privately and publicly. This prepared for a friendship which

I highly valued. About the same time, Archdeacon Sandford, father of the Bishop of Gibraltar, made a move in the same direction. I spoke to brethren in sympathy with myself, as regards union, and we thought of inviting a few clergymen to meet us— when, on my acquainting Dean Stanley with what we had in our minds, he expressed a wish to take the lead by getting several friends on both sides to dine with him at Westminster. Accordingly Dean Alford, Archdeacon Sandford, Prebendary Humphreys, and other clergymen, met my friends Binney, Allon, and others, at our good friend's hospitable board; and the party proved most agreeable. Other gatherings of the same kind followed, and at Fairlawn, where I lived, a long conversation took place, when, in addition to those just mentioned, Lord Ebury, Henry Winterbotham, M.P., Dr. Angus, Dr. Rigg, Dr. Roberts, and my intimate friend, Joshua Harrison, interchanged views in reference to Catholic intercourse. Dr. Alford, the Dean of Canterbury, afterwards invited Mr. Binney and myself to one of his garden parties, and soon afterwards he presided at the Cheshunt College Anniversary, when he uttered sentiments which were followed by a pleasant response from ministers of different denominations. On another occasion he met the Professors of New College, by invitation from the Coward Trustees; thus, and in other and similar ways, brotherly intercourse was considerably advanced.

If I may be permitted to trespass a little on what was at the time in futurity, I will, for the sake of preserving connection between incidents at that period, mention other circumstances which brought together, in a friendly way, members of different religious bodies. The first was of no great importance. I think it was in 1870, the Archbishop of Syra visited England, and made some little stir. Dr. Stanley entertained him in the Jerusalem Chamber, and invited a larger party to meet him afterwards. The host was not likely to lose such an opportunity for bringing together people of different opinions. Several were introduced to this stranger, who occupied during his visit, perhaps, a position above his usual one. The simple fact of this introduction was magnified, by newspapers, even the *Times*, into a sort of submission to Greek Archiepiscopal superiority; for the few whose names were mentioned were represented as receiving his formal benediction, and I wrote to explain the nature of the interview, which really amounted to nothing more than a respectful bow on the part of an Englishman to a foreigner, and the return on the foreigner's part of an accustomed Greek salutation. The intended effect of private civil reciprocities is often spoiled, by attributing to them meanings never intended and utterly absurd. Reports of them in quite a ridiculous way get into newspapers.

It was owing to the circumstance of my being "capped" in Edinburgh at the same time with Matthew Arnold, that I became acquainted with that remarkable man. He was by no means popular with Dissenters, owing to what, in some of his books, he said with reference to them. They appreciated his ability, but censured the spirit which appeared in some of his criticisms. My acquaintance with him convinced me that in some respects he was misjudged. When I came to know him pretty well, I playfully referred to some things he had written, which stung people whom I knew. "But I am not such a bad fellow," he rejoined, "as Dissenters think." "No," I replied, "but Dissenters look at you through your books; I look at your books through you—and that makes a great difference." I always found him kind, gentle, tender-hearted. He sympathised with me in domestic sorrows, and was pleased with some things I had written.

The publication of "Ecclesia," a volume by Dissenters, about the same time that another volume appeared written by Churchmen, was the means of bringing the editors and writers of the two works together at the house of a common friend, the Rev. H. S. Toms of Enfield. The Rev. W. D. Maclagan, editor of "The Church and the Age"—incumbent of a neighbouring parish (afterwards Vicar of Kensington, then Bishop of Lichfield*)—and Dr. Reynolds, of Cheshunt College, were present. Each editor proposed success to his brother editor on the other side.

This was an instance of mutual recognition and charity, worthy of being known; standing out, as it does, in pleasant contrast with bitter ways in which ecclesiastical controversies have been too often waged. Nor did that single interview end the intercourse thus begun, as I have had a few opportunities since of kindly intercourse with Dr. Maclagan, both as Kensington Vicar, and as a distinguished Bishop, earnestly doing his Episcopal work.

Another event occurred about the same time, in favour of union. The question of Bible Revision ripened to a practical issue in 1870.† A committee

* Now Archbishop of York.

† A very good account of this under the title of "Lectures on Bible Revision," has been published by my excellent friend and late colleague at New College, Principal Newth, D.D.

was formed by Convocation to carry out the project, and I had the privilege of being present during a part of the discussion. I heard the Dean of Canterbury, Dr. Alford, make an eloquent speech in favour of the design he had done so much to initiate, and for the accomplishment of which he laboured to the last. That speech was pronounced by some members as the most effective he ever delivered. In the evening of the same day, I came across Archdeacon Denison, at a clerical meeting, to which I was invited by an old Kensington neighbour, the Rev. J. E. Kempe, Rector of St. James', Piccadilly. There is nothing like private chat with men of pronounced opinions, who in public are accustomed to speak with vehemence. Judging from newspapers, one regards them as repulsive, whereas a little *tête-à-tête* in a quiet corner, makes a marvellously different impression. It was so in this instance, and the fiery Archdeacon, as I had thought him, proved a genial, humorous old clergyman, joking me on misconceptions of character formed by reading outside critics.

I must say, after all his antecedents, I found him a thoroughly hearty and kindly disposed Englishman and Christian. "The Revision," had a powerful and permanent effect in the relations of several distinguished Churchmen and Nonconformists. Some of my scholarly brethren, I need scarcely say, were chosen on the committee, and nothing could be more harmonious than their co-operation on both sides. Having enjoyed the friendship of some, and the acquaintance of more, I can testify to their mutual regard and affection. Some High Churchmen—as I know from having seen notes in their handwriting—expressed thankfulness to Almighty God for having brought them into this new relationship. It evidently removed prejudices, and inspired a feeling of religious oneness, where there had been before estrangement, if not alienation. At the same time Dissenting scholarship rose in estimation; and I found from conversation, that Churchmen held their fellow-revisers in high respect as critical students of the sacred volume. Some betrayed their possession of an idea, that Nonconformist learning in our day had risen far above what it was of old; an idea I endeavoured to correct, by maintaining that, whilst there has been a wider *diffusion* of knowledge amongst our ministers, it may be questioned whether the attainments of living men amongst us have not been exceeded by those of a past generation. Distinguished Hebrew scholars, such as Drs. Boothroyd, Pye-Smith, and Henderson, famous in the early years of the century, are dropping out of notice in the present day.

Social intercourse went on between the revisers and their friends. Reunions were held at New College, and Regent's Park College, and also in private residences.

An attempt on a bolder line to promote Christian union, came into prominence about the time now under review. I allude to a proposal for what has been called an "interchange of pulpits,"—more properly an interchange of preaching officers. A hundred years ago it was not altogether uncommon for Incumbents of the Establishment to preach in Dissenting chapels, especially those of the Countess of Huntingdon's Connexion; in a few instances a Nonconformist occupied a parish church pulpit. Such irregularities died out early in this century. But twenty years since there appeared a willingness on the part of several clergymen to revive the practice. Conferences were held with reference to the subject, and disscussions occurred as to what measures should be taken to secure legally, what seemed desirable to many. The Right Honourable Cowper Temple, afterwards Lord Mount Temple (now deceased), took an interest in the matter, and prepared a Bill to remove legal impediments out of the way. He sent me the following note :—

"My desire is to give power to the Bishop and Incumbent to allow any minister of any denomination, or any layman, to preach occasional sermons without requiring the person who preaches to do any of the things required of a Priest or Deacon.

"I shall not touch the Act of Uniformity, but provide for a case which is not included in its provisions—that of preaching sermons which are not part of the daily Church Service, though they may be delivered at the same time. All that is wanted is the admission that preaching in a church belonging to the Establishment is not exclusively a function of the Established Church."

I insert a copy of the Bill which he sent me.

"A Bill

"To enable Incumbents of Parishes, with the approval and consent of the Archbishop or Bishop of the Diocese, to admit to the Pulpits of their Parish Churches persons not in Holy Orders of the

Church of England, for the purpose of delivering occasional Sermons or Lectures.

"Whereas it is expedient that facilities should be given for the occasional delivery of Sermons in Churches of the Church of England by persons not in Holy Orders of the Church of England.

"May it therefore please Your Majesty,

"That it may be enacted, by the Queen's Most Excellent Majesty, by and with the advice and consent of the Lords Spiritual and Temporal, and Commons, in this present Parliament assembled, and by the authority of the same, as follows (that is to say) :—

"1. It shall be lawful for the Bishop of any Diocese in England, on the application of the Incumbent or Officiating Minister of any Church or Chapel belonging to the Church of England within his Diocese, or for the Ordinary of any Collegiate Church or Chapel, to grant, if he shall think fit, permission under his hand to any person, although he is not in Holy Orders and has not made or subscribed a Declaration of Assent in the terms set forth in 'The Clerical Subscription Act, 1865,' to preach occasional Sermons or Lectures in such Church or Chapel; and thereupon it shall be lawful for the person mentioned in such permission, on the invitation of the Incumbent or Officiating Minister, to preach an occasional Sermon or Lecture in such Church or Chapel without making any subscription or declaration before preaching.

" 2. The preaching of an occasional Sermon or Lecture, in pursuance of this Act, may take place in any Church or Chapel either, after any of the Services in the Book of Common Prayer, or at a time when no Service is used, as may seem best to the Incumbent or Officiating Minister of such Church or Chapel."

This Bill did not propose liberty for an Episcopalian incumbent to preach in a Nonconformist edifice—that object could be sought afterwards—and the limited freedom contemplated by the proposed measure failed to receive parliamentary support. The fact was, Members of Parliament, who were Dissenters, did not take up the question with any zeal, and some were decidedly against the proposal. They felt no more desire to see Nonconformists in Church pulpits than the Established clergy and laity did; though, of course, they took a different ground of objection. Lines of division remained strongly marked, and those who aimed at Disestablishment were bent on a more sweeping change. The time had not become ripe even for so small an alteration, and as there seemed no great willingness in any *party* to promote the proposal, it came to an unfortunate end. All kinds of means for promoting union have been suggested, and I have supported some very earnestly; but, in my old age, I am persuaded there is truth in the remark: " The more we grow in knowledge and advance in love, the more we should strive to preserve that simplicity, which is so peculiarly the characteristic of the Gospel, and the more we should guard against *the uncharitableness of supposing that every other view, except our own, must be useless or erroneous.*" *

The year 1871 was marked by an educational measure, opening Oxford to all denominations more fully than it had been. The Bill met with opposition from the Marquis of Salisbury and his friends. Some time before I had been requested by Lord Ebury to draw up for the Ritual Commission an account of Nonconformist modes of communion. The account is printed in the Report for 1870 (p. 139). Now I received a note from the Marquis, who had obtained a committee for collecting information, asking me to give evidence with regard to matters referred to them. Accordingly I attended. After listening to what Dr. Jowett, Master of Balliol,

* "Memorials of a Quiet Life." i. **237**.

had to say, I took my seat, to answer their Lordships' queries.* I had looked forward to examination as somewhat formidable, but found it far otherwise. It turned out to be a pleasant conversation.

When the Bill came under discussion in the House of Lords, I felt an interest in the debate, and consequently attended as a listener. After Lord Carnarvon had spoken, he stepped over to the spot where I stood, saying that his desire had been not to say anything discourteous to Dissenters. I received from him afterwards a note, written in the same spirit, and expressing a desire for the maintenance of friendly relations. About the same time it happened that a course of lectures was given on " Christian Evidences," in which bishops and other clergymen took part with Dissenting ministers.

The British and Foreign Bible Society is a bond of *social*, as well as *religious*, union. A dinner at Mr. George Moore's house, Palace Gardens, was, at that time, an annual institution, and after the Exeter Hall meeting in May, the committee, speakers, and other friends, met under his hospitable roof. The host appeared at his very best, frank, generous, and kind—no affectation, no assumption; only a rich vein of English geniality.

* Dr. Raleigh, Sir Charles Reed, and others, were examined.

On his right hand at such occasions, usually sat Lord Shaftesbury, on the left perhaps the Archbishop of Canterbury. Without flattery, but in homely ways of recognising service, the master of the table would call up one after another of his guests, and after we left the dining-room, we had family prayer together, a bishop and a Dissenter taking part in conducting the worship.

In 1871 the Dean of Canterbury was suddenly taken to his rest. The tidings gave great sorrow; and I felt it was due to his memory that some Dissenting brethren should attend the funeral. Harrison, Baldwin Brown, Newman Hall, and others did so; I was invited by the family to be one of the pall bearers. Dr. Stanley, Dr. Merivale, Dean of Ely, and others, met in the good man's library, where his picture of St. Michael's Mount,—on which he had spent some of his last hours—stood upon the easel, and Walton's Polyglot lay open at the Book of Exodus, where Dr. Alford had been reading just before his death. Slowly and sadly we walked into the cloisters, where places were assigned us, and the procession moved into the cathedral. There Mrs. Alford, with wonderful composure, joined in the solemn service. Shops were shut, and the streets lined with people, as we were conveyed to St. Martin's Churchyard, where we joined in singing one of his hymns, "Ten thousand times ten thousand," etc. He had expressed a wish to be interred there, and wrote the following memorandum: "When I am gone, and a tomb is to be put up, let there be, besides any indication of who is sleeping below, these words only: *Deversorium viatoris Hierosolymam proficiscentis*—*i.e.*, the inn of a traveller who is on his way to Jerusalem."

In a letter which I received from Canon Robertson, he said, in reference to this inscription: " Perhaps Mr. Bullock may be able to tell you, that some one has discovered the source of the words engraved at the bottom of the tombstone. My own inquiries have been fruitless." I have not been able to ascertain their origin.

A committee was formed to raise some testimonial to the Dean's worth, and they invited me to join them. They acted in correspondence with the Chapter, and it was determined that a painted window should be placed in the cathedral, and that it should contain symbols of the evangelists, and the scenes of our Lord's Temptation, in the larger circles; whilst the four smaller ones around, were to contain subjects showing that He exercised miraculous power of the same kinds, in which He refused to exert it, at the Tempter's suggestion.

In the following year I lost a valued friend, member of our Kensington church, Sir Donald F. Macleod, C.B., K.C.S.I. He had occupied the position of Lieutenant-Governor of the Punjaub, and met his death from a railway accident in December, 1872. He possessed a rare gift for putting himself into kindly fellowship with those he ruled, whether rich or poor, entering into their feelings and cultivating their regard so that he acquired a widespread influence in the Indian province, which might be called the country of his adoption. All the people loved him as a friend and father; hence it was said, that if the natives had to choose a prince, he would be their choice. In a leading journal, the remark of an Indian gentleman was preserved to the effect, that, "If all Christians were like Sir Donald, there would be no Mahomedans or Hindoos." His private life was of a piece with his public career. He had the power of making numerous friendships through the happy blending of religion with an affectionate disposition. "Wherever he went," said a relative, "his presence was like sunshine, and the sunshine was the reflection of another presence, even of Him of whom it is said, 'In Thy presence is fulness of joy.'" As he communed with us at Kensington, and was a personal friend, I can bear testimony to his cheerful manners in company. His tall, commanding figure attracted attention, and his calm, pleasant utterances won all hearts, especially those of the young, who would gather round him, attracted by the magic of his sympathy. This Indian gentleman visited the Cripples' Home; this Oriental scholar addressed a class in the East of London; this ruler, who might have died a rich nabob, gave away the surplus of his income in acts of charity.

In 1872 an incident occurred of an amusing description, which, as it has some significancy, is worthy of notice. A paragraph appeared in a religious newspaper to the following effect: "The Revs. Dr. Binney, Dr. Allon, and Dr. Stoughton have been, it seems, presented to His Grace the Archbishop of Canterbury at Lambeth Palace, by that consistent advocate of comprehension, Dr. Stanley, Dean of Westminster. It remains to be seen whether the Archbishop will invite either of the Doctors to preach in any of the Metropolitan churches, if not in the Abbey, or in the Cathedral. The Act of Uniformity will have to be repealed." If anybody who read this announcement had been acquainted with the circumstances, he would have seen its absurdity. The visit arose from an informal invitation to a party at Lambeth—from Dr. Tait, who was well acquainted with all the three persons. They needed no "presentation," such as the newspaper imagined. It is a curious fact, that, while some people complain of Dissenters being ignored or repulsed by the upper classes, when, instead of it, there is friendly recognition, the complainants imagine that, if the two classes do meet, there must be obsequiousness on the one side, and patronage on the other. It is supposed an impossible thing, for a Dignitary and a Dissenter to meet as gentlemen, without any professional design; on the occasion referred to, ecclesiastical objects no more entered the head of the host, as he welcomed us with cordiality, than it entered the heads of his guests. It was an affair of social courtesy, in which politeness on the one side, I hope, was returned on the other. By the way, at a Lambeth reception, after mingling with friends whom I had known for some years, I heard Mr. Binney say to Bishop Wilberforce: "Are you not surprised to see us here?"

"Surprised! Why, if you were not here, who should be here?"

This rejoinder puzzled my friend, when I ventured to add, "I understand your compliment, my lord, but at least you will acknowledge, it is something new."

"No, not new," he rejoined, and laying his hand on my shoulder, proceeded to say, "What is right is not new: is not righteousness as old as the creation?"

"Then you consider it is right for us to be here," I ventured to remark.

"Certainly; delighted to see you."

Some one overhearing this colloquy, observed in a whisper, "He will talk in a different way in different company." Possibly; but I believe there is force in what I have heard his friends say—he was a man of many-sided sympathy, thoroughly good-natured, fond of approbation, wishing to stand well with everybody, and for the moment *sincerely* meaning what he said. But he was changeful and inconsistent, saying one day, under an amiable impulse, what it was difficult to reconcile with his conversation another day in different company. I knew little of him personally as a man; but as a preacher, and author, I must say I have derived no small advantage from his sermons and addresses.

Further, in reference to Bishop Wilberforce, remarkable stories were current showing what a marvellous gift of extemporary eloquence he possessed. Archdeacon Sinclair told me that once the Bishop came to a meeting of the National School Society, totally unprepared, and whispered to him: "What points had I better take up?" The Archdeacon mentioned two or three. Wilberforce a few minutes afterwards rose, and delivered a speech on those very points, as if he had spent the morning in preparation. Dean Stanley told me that when the Bishop held a confirmation in the Abbey, he asked, as they walked together up the nave, whether there was any particular subject he would like to have introduced. One was mentioned. Forthwith the Bishop took it up in his address to the confirmed, in a way which led his hearers to suppose he had carefully prepared what he said.

Dr. Guthrie was one of the most genial men I ever knew; full of anecdote up to the brim. Indeed his conversation almost entirely took that form, and his racy way of telling a story gave what he said an irresistible charm. He was far more catholic than many of his brethren, and though he had respect for his ecclesiastical party, his sympathies went far beyond his own circle; and with reference to the Established Church of Scotland, though himself a *Free* Churchman, he cherished no animosity, and was not *indisposed* to preach occasionally in the old parish pulpits. His attachment to Evangelical truth was very strong, and for any deviations from it he would listen to no excuse. He visited some of my people at Kensington, and that brought me frequently into his society. How he used to talk of his visits to Mr. Disraeli and the Countess of Beaconsfield, of the wedding of the Marquis of Lorne, when he escorted the children of the family to Windsor Castle, and was especially noticed by Her Majesty, and was addressed as "My Lord" by somebody who thought him a bishop; and of a dinner-party at Argyle Lodge, when he met Mr Bright, and could hardly get in a word himself, because the great orator would talk so much! The last time I saw him was at breakfast with me at my house, when I think he was more brilliant and merry than usual. He knew I was entertaining thoughts of retirement, and he strongly urged me to relinquish pastoral duties and become an occasional preacher. Moreover he said, "It is better to be too early than too late in this respect. 'Why do you give up so soon?' one of Her Majesty's Ministers once asked me; 'you have all your wits about you.' 'Yes,' I replied, 'and if I were to wait, as some do, till my wits are gone, I should never give up at all.'"

An important crisis in the summer of 1872, had occurred in the history of New College. Dr. Halley from age and infirmities, retired from the principalship. Dr. Newth was chosen successor, and to fill up the chair, left vacant by my old friend and tutor, the services of three London ministers were called into requisition. Mr. Binney undertook the Homiletic Class, Dr. Kennedy became Theological Professor in the department of Apologetics, and I was invited to conduct instruction in Historical Theology. My hands were pretty full, but this was an engagement congenial to my taste, and for which I felt I was better qualified than I had been at the time when an invitation was given me to accept the office of principal.*

The question of my retirement from the pastorate occupied my thoughts at a later period, and I indicated this in a communication to the Church through my deacons. That communication was

* That was whilst I was in full work at Kensington, and not very long after our new chapel was built, while a debt of £1000 rested on it. I said I could not leave my charge whilst that debt remained. As soon as I had declined the New College principalship, my congregation swept off the debt as expressive of gratitude for my remaining amongst them.

met by a warm and earnest request that I would continue at Kensington Chapel a little while longer. I consented to tarry till the end of two years.

About the time just noticed, education in reference to public schools assisted by Government grants was keenly discussed. Those amongst Nonconformists who were disposed to accept State aid in support of schools in which religion was taught were regarded as acting inconsistently with their principles in opposition to State endowment of Christianity. Into that question it is unnecessary to enter here, but I repeat what I urged at the time referred to, that Government aid and Government inspection were co-extensive; that if Government assisted a school, and inquired *exclusively* into the *secular* instruction of pupils, the aid bestowed was to be regarded as in aid of that alone. The separation in a school of religious from secular instruction, appeared to me inconsistent with our duty *as Christians.* In guiding the intellect of the young, an infusion of Gospel truth is, I believe, of essential importance. A declaration to the effect that the Bible should be used in public schools was signed by several hundred Christian ministers, and in that declaration I most cordially joined. The severance of revelation from other fundamental grounds of youthful knowledge was, in my estimation, very mischievous.

Mr. Forster was condemned severely by a large number of Dissenters as being opposed to the interests of Nonconformity. I have good reason for believing that he wished to deal fairly between Church and Dissent. The opinions of all parties had to be consulted, and it was no easy thing for any man in his place to give universal satisfaction. I conversed with him at the time on the subject of his measure, and am persuaded he was honest throughout the whole business. When the strongest feeling against him existed, I know, from what he said to me, that he gave full credit to his opponents for good intentions. Of some friends we both knew, who differed from him widely, he spoke in the kindest terms. When he was regarded as an enemy by some Nonconformists, I was informed he attended a Nonconformist chapel in the country during a summer holiday; and I know he helped the pastor by pecuniary assistance,—that very pastor being my informant. Mr. Forster never lost sympathy with Quakerism. Our common friend, Mr. Braithwaite, a well-known member of that denomination, spoke at his funeral; and an eminent Baptist minister told me of his pleasant visits to Mr. Forster's residence.

Matthew Arnold proposed my name for election to the Athenæum Club. The usual mode is vote by ballot, which, on account of the number of candidates, occasions delay for many years. But the committee have power to choose annually nine members by special vote. I did not know fully until the secretary wrote to me, that I had been so elected—an honour to which I felt myself by no means entitled. The influence of Dr. Stanley, Mr. Matthew Arnold, and other kind friends, secured for me this great privilege, which has been a source of literary advantage and pleasure to me ever since. And I may here mention, from what occurred in the proceedings of the committee, as I was told, Nonconformity was, in my case, rather a help than hindrance; as the club, in a catholic spirit, desires to have representatives of different classes and opinions included on its rolls. On the same principle not long afterwards Dr. Martineau was introduced to the Athenæum.

I was surprised a few weeks after my election to receive an invitation to the Academy dinner, and was pleased to learn from one of the Academicians that this compliment, as well as the preceding, arose from the same spirit of *catholic* sociality. Nothing but presence at one of these banquets can give an adequate idea of their remarkable magnificence. A sudden burst of light, just before speeches commence, has a magical effect. Mr. Disraeli, then Prime Minister, delivered a highly finished oration, after sitting silent and sphinx-like for an hour before.

At an early part of the period to which this chapter belongs, the famous volume entitled " Ecce Homo " was published. It excited much controversy. I read it with interest and attention. It has long been my habit, in perusing works unfavourable to orthodoxy, to search in them for admitted principles which, by a fair application, may be employed in support of truths to which the author is regarded as being opposed. In the work just mentioned there is a chapter on what is called " Christ's Royalty ! "* Christ is represented as having established in the world a new theocracy in describing Himself as King of the kingdom of God ; in other words, as a King representing the Majesty of the Invisible Ruler of a theocracy. He claimed the character of Founder, of Legislator, and, in a certain high and peculiar sense, " of Judge of a new and

* " Ecce Homo," chap. iv.

Divine society." Whatever might be the views of the writer with regard to the nature of Jesus Christ, such a position as he reached, seems to me to involve Christ's true and proper Divinity. In other words, it is tantamount to saying that "Jesus Christ is Lord, to the glory of God the Father."

I remember that at the time, whatever might be the tendency of the work on the whole, I thought there were in it admissions of such a nature as to afford a basis for convincing arguments in favour of Evangelical Christianity.

One evening, at that time, I met Lord Shaftesbury at a friend's house, and had a conversation with him on the subject of the book. It is well known that, with the impetuosity which was so natural to that great and good man, he was swept along by a hurricane of indignation, which led him to pronounce "Ecce Homo" a work of most pernicious tendency. Of Lord Shaftesbury it might be said that he was like a cloud which moveth altogether, if it move at all. He could do or say nothing by halves; and however minds of a different order might judge of his acts and utterances, there can be no doubt that by the enthusiasm of his advocacy he carried beneficial measures which otherwise might not have succeeded. When I was talking with him after the manner just indicated and pointing out arguments which I conceived might be constructed out of some of the writer's admissions, he was evidently very restless, and expressed his strong conviction, that the book deserved to be strongly reprehended, in order to warn people against being led away by its contents. In the course of conversation he manifested, that he had not read what he so severely condemned. This habit of condemning books without reading them, it is to be feared, is too common in the present day.

Here let me add Lord Shaftesbury's manner was not always the same. At times he was gentle and exceedingly affable, of which I remember an amusing instance. We were travelling together from Peterborough, after a jubilee meeting of the British and Foreign Bible Society in that city. He was speaking of the profound ignorance of the upper classes respecting the character and habits of Nonconformists; and I ventured to relate to him, in illustration of what he had said himself, a story which I had heard respecting his father, who was Chairman of the Committee of the House of Lords. A solicitor waited upon him to confer respecting a Bill, which was coming before the Upper House, in reference to matters which affected the rights of Dissenters. The old Earl said to this gentleman, " I hear a good deal about these Dissenters, and some things very strange. I have been told they are people *who go about without clothes.*" The Earl laughed, and said, such a thing as I related was just like him.

CHAPTER X

1873

THE sixth General Meeting of the Evangelical Alliance had been fixed for the year 1870, in New York; but, owing to the war between France and Germany, it was postposed to the autumn of 1873. Canon Leathes, Mr. Harrison, and myself, received invitations from the American committee, to attend the assembly; and, accordingly, we started for our destination in one of the Cunard steamers at the close of the month of August. With the exception of rough weather in the earlier part, we had a fine passage. Going out we touched on the Irish coast, and, it being Sunday, we landed and spent the day on shore. We were on the coast of Waterford, and found the country very pleasant. We attended church in the forenoon, and afterwards took walks in the neighbourhood. I had spent a week or more in Ireland some few years previously, and had then seen spots in the Green Isle, which created a desire to see more. The city of Limerick on the Shannon had given me delight. Dublin is a magnificent city, and the object of my visit there had been to preach on a special occasion in Dr. Urwick's church. I saw at that time something of Irish society, and found controversy rife between Protestants and Papists. I took an opportunity of visiting the Killarney lakes, and found them all, and more than, I had imagined. Nor could I fail to be amused with the humour of carriage-drivers and other Irish people. Returning to our steamer on Sunday afternoon, we started for New York, and had, in the course of our voyage, rough weather and smooth. For sometime it was unfavourable—"four-fifths of a gale" somebody said; but in the latter part of our trip we had charming weather. Where the whistle at night had sounded like a wail of distress, it was now felt to be means of safety. Flag signals and rockets now and then relieved the tedium; so did the gambols of porpoises. Moonbeams in a mottled sky, were pleasant variations, as we steamed along at a rapid rate. The night before we landed in New York harbour, the sun went down like a ball of fire, the sea was intensely blue, whilst alive with little billows, like children at their sports; the bow of the steamer was crowded by passengers looking out for the pilot—a capital subject, I thought, for some clever pencil. The next morning when we reached Sandy Hook, I could not help comparing the coast scenery near us with some views I had seen on the Bosphorus.

"For the *first* time I am in America," I said to a Yankee fellow-passenger.

"Yes," he replied; "you are now, sir, in the land of the brave, the home of the free."

Mr. Harrison and myself were guests of the Hon. Mr. Dodge, President of the American Evangelical Alliance. On our arrival he conducted us to his country seat on the banks of the Hudson, near Tarryton.

We were in the midst of charming scenery, immortalised by Washington Irving; near the glen of "Sleepy Hollow," and the haunts of Ichabod Crane. By the little Dutch church in the neighbourhood lies a cemetery, where "the American Goldsmith" is buried.

We were driven to Sunnyside, where he lived and died, in an old-fashioned Dutch-looking house, with picturesque gables, bearing a seventeenth-century date. It is embosomed amidst trees which so overshadow the lawn and walks, that "Sunnyside," even when unclouded, can suffer nothing from the blaze of day. Miss Irving, niece of the author, and a friend of our host, welcomed us to this sylvan abode, and showed us her uncle's library, writing table, and shelves of books, just as he left them.

We should have been glad to remain longer at Mr. Dodge's villa, but were anxious to reach Niagara, as soon as possible; therefore, on the second morning after our arrival, Mr. Harrison, with Newman Hall, who had accompanied us to America, embarked on a steamer for the Catskills, on our way to the Falls. We arrived at the Mountain House in the evening, having, in our river voyage, been struck with the Hudson, as resembling in some parts, a succession of lakes full of Italian-like beauty. We spent a Sunday at our capacious resting-place, which could accommodate four or five hundred visitors, and engaged in united worship with Bishop Bedell, successor to Bishop McIlvaine, of Ohio. He preached in the morning, and at his request, I occupied the desk at night.

We did not reach Niagara till late on Monday, and heard the roar of the cataract some time before our arrival.

Niagara is a grand study, and we spent the greater part of four days over it—the first in taking general views, the other three in gathering up details. I sat down on the rocks, and wrote my impressions from point to point. From the suspension bridge, below the Falls, you have an inclined plane of troubled waters. From the south side of Goat Island, you have a still more striking view of the rapids, like an arm of the sea, two miles in width, and in front it dashes down the Horse Shoe Fall. Just at the edge it is a ridge of emerald, tinged, or rather lined, with white. Then it goes on in rows of streaks, white, white, white ; at the bottom, the flood vanishes in vapour. In the forenoon under sunshine the picture is crossed by a rainbow. Beyond the mist the river is a shifting floor of variegated marble. At a right angle with the Horse Shoe, the American Fall is seen in profile, from what is called, I think, "Prospect Park." The rapids below are finer than those above the Falls. Those below are hemmed in by rocks ; those above are bordered by open country on both sides. Further on, below the Falls, there is an enormous whirlpool.

Instead of a unity, I found Niagara manifold, varying as one wanders about the banks. The channel here is worthy of the stream. It is cut into precipitous cliffs, picturesque rocks, forests of trees, bridges, hotels and other houses. In photographs and engravings, there is often but a tame outline, with which the reality does not correspond. Of the upper and lower Rapids, I prefer the former in one respect; it gives good views of the foliage which fringes the water. Emphatically, one may use the word *beauty* in reference to the landscape as distinguished from the Rapids. Colours are charming—greens of all tints; at sunset streaks of pink, violet, lavender, lilac, along the edge of the Falls; azure tints in the river; sky with crimson and purple flushes at eventide.

At the expense of repetition, I will quote the words I find in my notebook written on a rocky bank:—
" Opposite, looking west, is the Canada side, skirted by thick trees, forming a continuous border—the Horse Shoe form of a rocky ledge, crossed by the sweep of water, would measure the third of a mile. It still resembles a ridge of emerald, tinged, or rather lined, with white. Then the flood plunges down, to rise again from the bottom in columns of vapour. In sunshine the whole is crossed by a wonderful rainbow. Then, afterwards, it appeared to me like an altar of frosted silver, spanning the end of a temple choir, sending up incense for ever and ever!

Looking down into the precipitous gulf, formed by the Canadian and American shores, one sees the river flowing on steadily like a shifting floor of variegated marble,—green, streaked with white. I shift my position, walking under the trees of Goat Island, about a quarter of a mile from the Horse Shoe, and sit upon a bit of tableland, forming what is called Lunar Island,—dividing into two unequal limbs the watery flood. At the bottom appears another rainbow. I shift again, walking up the Goat Island, and cross a bridge over Rapids, and then enter the grounds called (as just said) Prospect Park; and there one faces both cataracts — the American in profile, the Horse Shoe full face."

A suspension bridge crosses the whirling waters on which it makes one giddy to look down. Then occurs a turn, where a whirlpool is formed, and pieces of timber are swept round and round by enormous eddies. Four days I spent at these never-to-be-forgotten spots filled with marvels of Divine creation.

My visit to Montreal was very short, but we saw enough to indicate the city's prosperity; it underwent great reverses afterwards. We were invited to the handsome dwellings of several wealthy citizens, and witnessed much zeal in the cause of religion.

On our journey from Montreal to Boston we

passed through glorious scenery, some of it Swisslike. There were many tempting nooks furnished with hotels, winding roads leading up to forests on the hills, groups of white houses with green shutters, and a pretty church amidst them with a lofty spire. There is a wonderful charm about New England villages.

At Boston a cordial welcome was afforded by Dr. Dexter, who hospitably entertained us. My first impression, derived from what I saw of the city's less modern part, was that it had an English look; but on further acquaintance, after seeing its modern edifices, one receives the idea of a Continental capital. I was delighted with what delights everybody—the broad green common, adorned by goodly trees and goodly mansions. Some of the public buildings in Boston are very imposing: a Gothic church, built by Congregationalists, cost, I was told, £50,000; but since I was there I understand a much nobler Episcopalian edifice has been erected. On the Sunday morning I preached in a large Congregational church, where the music and singing were of a very superior kind, and the choir, I was told, cost a large annual sum. On the Sunday evening I went to a Baptist chapel, and, after sermon and prayers, a large number of the congregation adjourned to a schoolroom, where something like a Methodist love-feast was held. I met in the town with a nephew of Thomas Carlyle, who related to me that, while on a visit to England, he called on his uncle, and was told it was impossible to see him; Mrs. C. resisted as long as she could, but submitted at last. The nephew was admitted to his uncle's study, and the two relatives had a long talk to their mutual satisfaction.

Dr. Dexter planned an excursion to Andover, where we were received by the Principal of the College, the Venerable Dr. Park, a celebrated scholar and divine, who took me a drive round the neighbourhood, and pointed out the house of Harriet Beecher Stowe, and the homes of people described in her books. We had a delightful visit to a ladies' school, where Mr. Harrison and I received a cordial welcome. Our kind host took us to his residence several miles off, at New Bedford, and the next day conducted us to Harvard University, on the other side the Boston river. There we were entertained by Professor Abbot, who took care to show us a hall, built by a namesake of mine. Best of all my associations with Dr. Dexter and the neighbourhood was a most memorable day spent at New Plymouth where he pointed out the localities of the Pilgrim Fathers.

We proceeded to New Haven, where we found at the station, Dr. Porter, Principal of Yale University, waiting for us; we were conducted through leafy avenues to the college buildings, and there introduced to the famous American theologian, Dr. Bushnell, with other celebrities. The students then assembled, and listened to an elaborate speech by Dr. Dorner, the German scholar and divine, who happened to be there on a visit, having come as a delegate to the Alliance meetings. Yale College is a venerable institution, standing among the foremost Universities of the New World. The neighbourhood is interesting, and we should have been delighted, had time allowed, to explore the region where two of the regicides, Walley and Gough, concealed themselves for two or three years in a cave, to which they gave the name of Providence. One of them, Gough, suddenly appeared, when a Puritan congregation was attacked by Philip of Pokanoket, and delivered them out of his hands. He then disappeared like the twin brothers at the battle of Regillus.

Having had our glimpse of New England, we hastened to Philadelphia, to spend a quiet Sunday with a kind English friend, Mr. Yarnell. Philadelphia is magnificent, redolent of William Penn's memory, who amongst colonial founders, stands unique as a man of peace. He did not sweep away aboriginal savages with sword and shot, but entered into treaty with them, under the shadow of a spreading elm, which came to be held in great veneration. Views in the neighbourhood of Philadelphia, vie with noble monuments, visible on every side, of commercial civilisation and prosperity. The grand Masonic Temple had, when we were there, been recently opened; and it is amongst the finest structures in the city. But the Hall of Independence, architecturally unpretentious, has greater attractions for historic travellers. We were entertained in German Town, a charming suburb, by the Wissahickon—"fit haunt" for Shakespeare's fairies, Peas-blossom and the rest, flowing through tangled brakes, wealthy in wild flowers. Drives by the "wedded rivers" as Whittier calls them, the Schuylkill, and the Delaware—are enjoyments for high days and holidays. One view of the city I caught from a hill embosomed in trees. A long line of foliage from the tops of which rise cupolas and steeples, reminded me of Damascus, with its groves and gardens, mosques and minarets.

We saw something of private social life in German

Town. Several families in the neighbourhood were invited to spend an evening with us. It resembled a party on the Continent, where eating and drinking are not of much interest. The marked feature of the whole gathering was extreme yet tasteful simplicity. Some ladies were sumptuously dressed, and there, as in other places, appeared an eye for harmony of colours—a special American endowment, which struck me pleasantly. Manners were agreeable, and there was ease in conversation —a rare enjoyment. The ladies were self-possessed, and could hold their own, yet not rudely; and their kindliness indicated personal interest, which made their visitors feel at home.

We arrived at New York at the beginning of October, and were entertained by Mr. Dodge at his princely residence in Madison Avenue. Sir Charles Reed was guest there at the same time, and the arrangements for our reception betokened a cordial welcome.

In a "History of New York," it is stated that "when Henry Hudson discovered the river, now bearing his name, and Hendrick Christiansen, and Adam Block, followed up the discovery, the island of Manhattan was made the chief depôt of the trade, and Christiansen received the appointment of agent for the traffic in furs during the passage of the vessels to and from Holland. He immediately set about the construction of a small fort, with a few rude buildings, on the southern extremity of the island, thus laying the foundation of the future city."

"In May 1626, Peter Minuet arrived at New Netherlands, as Director-General, and immediately effected the purchase of the island of Manhattan, from the Indians for goods and trinkets to the value of sixty guilders or about twenty-four dollars." "In 1628 a church was organised with fifty communicants under the auspices of James Michaelius, a clergyman from Holland." From these feeble beginnings sprang the wharfs, the quays, the avenues, the squares, the warehouses, the stores, the halls, the libraries, the museums, the hospitals of New York. When shall we stop in the enumeration of riches belonging to this Queen of the West? Hence, too, we may say came the churches, the congregations, the colleges, the schools, the reformatories and the religious institutions, without number, which form the glory of that Western Metropolis. The first meeting of the Alliance Congress—for the expenses of which twenty thousand dollars had been subscribed—was held in the hall of the Young Men's Christian

Association. The hall contains fifteen hundred sittings, and was decorated with flags, flowers, and mottoes. It was crowded in every corner, and the spectacle from the platform was imposing, the audience being composed, to a large extent, of representatives from the States, and the principal nations of our Eastern Hemisphere.

Dr. Adams of New York, an eminent Presbyterian pastor, delivered an address of welcome. Elaborate yet unaffected, scholarly yet not scholastic, fervent yet not rhapsodical, fluent yet perfectly finished, pious without a particle of fanaticism,—it laid hold on people present, and made an impression talked of to this day. I have heard many a courteous speech at the opening of large assemblies, but never any thing like that, before or since.

The address of welcome was acknowledged in a hearty, but inferior style, by English, French, Dutch, and German delegates. "I am glad," said Professor Christlieb, the German, grasping the hand of Pastor Fisch, the Frenchman, "I am glad to see as the firstfruits of this gathering, that we Germans can clasp the hands of our French brethren."

The next morning we assembled in Steinway Hall. After prayer by Dr. Hodge of Princeton, Dr. Woolsey, Ex-President of Yale College, a distinguished student of International Law, took the chair. The Dean of Canterbury, Dr. Payne Smith, read a sympathetic letter from the English Primate, and immediately after prayer, he solemnly repeated the Apostles' Creed, in which the whole assembly followed in audible tones.

The Conference then began with the reading of papers, which, with addresses, were continued morning and evening at sectional meetings. The interest was kept up, attention never seeming to flag. When Sunday came, large churches were crowded to excess. The Holy Communion was administered in the afternoon, when Episcopal, Presbyterian, Baptist, Moravian, and Indian brethren took part in the service.

Besides the sectional conventions, an enormous general meeting was held in Brooklyn, when extempore addresses were delivered in free and easy style. But perhaps the most deeply affected audience was a crowded one in the Academy of Music the last Sunday night, for prayers and short addresses. A prima donna, I heard, was present: certainly there was one voice of pre-eminent sweetness and power in that vast congregation.

All the newspapers gave reports of the proceedings as fully as *The Times* does of our parliamentary debates. One afternoon two gentlemen, who had been clergymen, spent some time beforehand in preparing a report of what I meant to say in the evening. There was no other way, *they said*, of getting the report ready for the next morning. The interest taken in our proceedings by all classes greatly surprised me. Newspapers, representative of churches out of sympathy with our proceedings, noticed and criticised what went on: the secular press also took up the matter, and conveyed abundant information. What appeared in New York papers was transferred to others all over the States, and thus religious news of that week spread far and wide.

The whole report, published afterwards, was a curiosity for size and cheapness; but such voluminous accounts of a conference must not be taken to mean more than this—that Americans like to know whatever is going on, in every circle. It appeared to me that our transatlantic brethren are so fond of hearing public speakers, and of reading what they say, that they do not confine their thoughts to such discussions as are germane to their own convictions and tastes. They are curious to hear what anybody has to utter, if he speaks to the purpose, no matter what the topic may be. We should be mistaken, if we measured religious belief in New York by popular attention given to the Alliance.

The President, Dr. Woolsey, was a distinguished constitutional lawyer, consulted at times about international claims by European authorities; numerous professors of erudition and power, authors, orators, politicians, merchants, gathered round him in 1873; the European continent contributed such men as Dorner, Christlieb, and Krafft from Germany, Prochet from Genoa, Carrasco from Madrid, Bovet from Neuchatel, Stuart from Holland. Some of our own distinguished countrymen have been already mentioned. Ward Beecher delivered a wonderful oration in Dr. Adams' church on the subject of preaching. He was like a man stopping you in the street, and getting "hold of your button" so as to compel attention. I met him several times in America, and received acts of kindness, when his face was lighted up with an expression of rare beauty.

Nor were churches and halls the only "pleasant places." One evening Mr. Dodge had a reception to which eight hundred persons were invited, and at one moment, he told me six hundred were actually present. Introductions, handshakings, recognitions, questions, answers, observations and stories were incessant; whilst a band of musicians played at one end of a suite of apartments, it could not be heard at the other.

On Monday, all the delegates were conveyed by special train to Philadelphia. On the way we stopped at Princeton. Students of colleges assembled at the station, and uttered their characteristic cheers—in imitation of ascending and descending rockets—followed by such huzzahs as we do not hear in England. We marched in procession through the streets to the church, where a crowded congregation awaited our arrival.

We reached Philadelphia about three o'clock. There a long train of carriages awaited our arrival to convey delegates to the Hall of Independence. The city authorities represented by one of the judges, expressed a welcome, after which we were escorted to the Continental Hotel capable of containing the whole party. We all started next morning for Washington.

On the way we were delighted with surrounding scenery, especially when we came to Chesapeake Bay, into which the Susquehanna pours its waters. Woods were clothed with autumnal tints, crimson maples flashed their fires amidst manifold hues of decaying foliage; and the sunny prospect, as we skirted the bay, was beautiful beyond description. At the Baltimore station brethren from Washington invested us each with a white ribbon badge; then on we swept past homesteads, recently the abodes of slaves, many a hut serving as an original illustration for "Uncle Tom's Cabin."

We talked in the train with a black bishop, who entertained us with descriptions of negro excitability. He said coloured congregations would exclaim in church, as the preacher proceeded with his discourse, "That's true, Massa"; and a man once shouted, under the influence of what he heard, "Massa, that's like going up Jacob's ladder."

A distant view of the Capitol is not unlike that of St. Peter's at Rome, as seen from the Campagna. We saw a few city lions—the Capitol and Smithsonian Institute being chief; and we found this metropolis, not without form, for it is artistically laid out in thoroughfares radiating from the Capitol; but it is certainly "void," for nominal streets were there, but at that time without houses. We drove a long distance, across an open country, suggesting the idea of a city which *is not*, but only *about to be*. How it looks now, I do not know. Yellow dust was blowing in clouds, and lying in thick drifts on the steps of the Hall of Assembly.

General Grant carried in his face the signs of an indomitable will, and without any personal assumption behaved as one conscious of representative power. After my return home, Dr. Adams, who was then in England, told me that he acted as chaplain to the forces at the time of the great war, and rode by the General's side, when he reviewed the troops. As illustrative of his memory for little things, I may refer to the General's conversation with his old chaplain, when they met in England, and he alluded to the colour of the horse, the latter used to ride, informing him of the animal's death, which had just occurred. The General seems to have possessed the royal gift of not forgetting those to whom he had been once introduced. Let me add, he was proud of having commanded such an immense army as he did, and said to the Duke of Wellington—who repeated this to Dr. Stanley, my informant—" Your father was general in chief of only forty thousand men; I led as many as *half a million.*"

We visited a great number of institutions in New York—colleges, schools, hospitals, and reformatories. Colleges, architecturally, were not imposing; but the libraries and scientific apparatus possessed by some of them, were of a choice and costly kind·

I was told of one gentleman who had contributed £100,000 to educational objects. Schools are immense buildings; and at New York and Philadelphia it was a sight indeed, to behold pupils, gliding to their appointed places, and then upturning some eight hundred happy countenances towards the visitors come to see them. The examination of classes was most satisfactory, and the resources and adroitness of the teachers most admirable. Hospitals in the city are abundant, beyond what the necessities of the population seemed to require, and the reformatories afforded encouraging examples of discipline and improvement.

Parks and cemeteries are on a scale of such magnitude, and are so picturesquely laid out, that English visitors surveyed them with surprise. As to American scenery in general, justice had never been done to it.

We felt gulpy in taking leave of friends, and ending a visit so memorable.

The sea was calm, and the weather bright, as we steamed out on our voyage home, but a gale followed, and we had violent storms during several days. Serious accidents occurred in consequence, which gave a maimed appearance to some of the passengers. My dear friend Harrison had a serious fall. Waves rose many feet high, and they supplied a key to some of Turner's sea pictures, and also to Ruskin's eloquent language in describing the "truth of water"—the power, majesty, and deathfulness of the open, deep, illimitable sea.

A friendship I formed in America deserves a notice here, on account of the person's eminence and the obligations under which he laid me by his subsequent handsome gifts. Dr. Sprague had the largest collection of autographs in the world. The number was immense, amounting, I am told, to about 100,000. He was living at Flushing at the time I was in New York, and I had charge from a friend in England to call upon him. Though having never met him before, yet from previous knowledge of each other, we were at home, immediately after I had crossed his threshold. It is an American characteristic to treat as friend any one who has been known by kindly report beforehand, or who can present credentials of character. Dr. Sprague's wife and daughter received us at once as if we had belonged to the family. We crowded an immense deal of talk into a short space, and before we parted he made reference to his huge collection of autographs. As we had little time to spare, I had covenanted with my companion, Mr.

Harrison, that I would avoid that tempting topic, as it would detain us too long; but the ice being suddenly broken, there was no help, and I found myself plunged—I must say not unwillingly—into a subject which prudence had decidedly proscribed. Dr. Sprague found that I was one of the craft, but a minor member; and forthwith he profusely offered assistance, asking whether there were any letters of his countrymen I particularly desired to possess. What an overture! I modestly replied, I should be glad of a few lines written by Washington Irving. Before I left America there came a most interesting letter from Irving to his publisher, respecting a new edition of his works; and after my return to England, post after post brought most valuable contributions to my store of autographs. The very first included a letter signed by General Washington of historical value. It relates to the close of the War of Independence, and gives direction for cessation of hostilities immediately after the surrender of Lord Cornwallis, in 1781. Letters in the handwriting of Franklin, Jonathan Edwards, and a number of other celebrities, came to England from time to time, enriching my stores, almost to the period of Dr. Sprague's death. He was a popular preacher, a distinguished divine, a prolific author, and a man of widespread influence in the States.

In closing this account of American friends, I must say a few words about members of Harvard University. I had met with the Greek Professor at the Mountain House, on the Catskills, who spoke much of the principal, Dr. Peabody, for whom I felt a high respect. My friend, Mr. Harrison, and I were most courteously received by the Doctor at his residence, and were shown over the University buildings, especially that bearing the name of Stoughton, a Governor of Massachusetts. I was anxious to see the poet Longfellow, who resided in an old-fashioned house not far from the college. Unfortunately he was not at home, and I could not refrain from dropping him a line. I received the following reply :—

CAMBRIDGE, *October 7th*, 1873.

"MY DEAR SIR,

"I have this morning had the pleasure of receiving your friendly note, and hasten to say how much I regret that absence prevented me from seeing you when you were in Cambridge.

"We should have lived over again that bright summer afternoon at Mrs. Fuller Maitland's, which

I so well remember, and you would have told me of many friends whom I should like to hear of again.

"Perhaps I may still have the pleasure of seeing you before you return to England. If not, I beg you to present to Mr. and Mrs. Maitland my best regards and most cordial remembrance of their kindness and hospitality.

"With greatest esteem,
"I am, my dear sir,
"Yours truly,
"HENRY W. LONGFELLOW."

Mr. and Mrs. Fuller Maitland, members of a well-known old Nonconformist family, were members of my church at Kensington; and at their house I used to meet distinguished and interesting people. The occasion referred to in the foregoing letter made upon me a most pleasant impression. A large company had assembled to greet the American poet, and there was plenty of handshaking, which I feared would rather weary him, especially as so many of us were total strangers; but he assured me that I was quite mistaken, and that it gratified him much to be surrounded by so large a party, composed of those whom he regarded as English friends. Americans are in some respects more cosmopolitan and genial in new society, than Englishmen, and I was struck with this repeatedly in my transatlantic trip. I was quite affected with the kindness met with everywhere. Among those who showed special courtesy were some of the well-known Abbot family, and other professors at Yale, Andover, and Princeton, as well as at Harvard, and Mr. Winthrop, of Boston fame. Before I conclude this account of my American tour, one more incident remains to be mentioned. At some of the meetings in New York, I met with an intelligent and interesting Quaker. I found he was acquainted with Friends in England, and in the course of conversation mention was made of the Gurneys, when he informed me that Mrs. Gurney, widow of Joseph John Gurney, of Earlham, was residing in the vicinity of Burlington, in New Jersey. She was an American lady who became the wife of the Norwich philanthropist, and retired to her own country after her husband's death. Finding that I knew Mr. Gurney, his widow was informed of the circumstance, and presently I received a kind invitation to visit her at her own residence. My friend and I, after a pleasant journey, reached the outskirts of Burlington, and were welcomed by our hostess at a handsome house with picturesque surroundings. We had much conversation about Earlham, and I was shown into a comfortable library stocked with books, brought from the Hall which I had seen in my boyhood. She told me about a visit which Mr. Forster, father of the distinguished politician, had paid her, not very long before,—a visit speedily followed by his death, and interment in the neighbourhood. On the walls of the drawing-room I noticed a facsimile of the famous letter written to Mrs. Gurney, by President Lincoln, respecting the great war going on, in which the question of negro slavery was so inextricably involved. She and some other ladies had been favoured with a special interview on the subject of emancipation, and it was to this interview, and its associations that the facsimile referred. She asked, if I should like to have a copy of it, and then not being able at the moment to find what she sought, she took down the framed copy and presented it to me as a memorial of my visit. I carefully brought it to England, and as it is not known here, as it is in America, I subjoin the contents, showing the importance which Abraham Lincoln attached to the conversation of the zealous Quaker on the occasion mentioned.

"WASHINGTON, *Sept.* 4*th*, 1864.

"ELIZA P. GURNEY.

"MY ESTEEMED FRIEND,—I have not forgotten, probably never shall forget, the very impressive occasion when yourself and friends visited me on a Sabbath forenoon two years ago. Nor has your kind letter, written nearly a year later, ever been forgotten. In all, it has been your purpose to strengthen my reliance on God. I am much indebted to the good Christian people of the country for their constant prayers and consolations; and to no one of them more than to yourself. The purposes of the Almighty are perfect and must prevail, though we erring mortals may fail to accurately perceive them in advance. We hoped for a happy termination of this terrible war long before this, but God knows best and has ruled otherwise. We shall yet acknowledge His wisdom and our own error therein. Meanwhile we must work earnestly in the best light He gives us, trusting that so working, still conduces to the great end He ordains. Surely He intends some great good to follow this mighty convulsion, which no mortal could make, and no mortal could stay.

"Your people—the Friends—have had, and are

having, a very great trial. On principle and faith, opposed to both war and oppression, they can only practically oppose oppression by war. In this hard dilemma some have chosen one horn, and some the other. For those appealing to me on conscientious grounds, I have done, and shall do, the best I could, and can, in my own conscience under my oath to the laws. That you believe this I doubt not, and believing it, I shall still receive, for our country and myself, your earnest prayers to our Father in Heaven.

"Your sincere Friend,
"A. LINCOLN."

CHAPTER XI

1874—1875

IN the year 1874 I lost my old friend, Thomas Binney. His pre-eminent position amongst Dissenters was attested by copious notices in newspapers, and, by the scene at his funeral. That position arose from several causes—his character, abilities, pulpit popularity, and personal appearance, manifold and far-reaching sympathies, and a genial nature, characteristic of the best Englishmen. His influence in the Congregational denomination throughout the country was aided by the central position of the Weigh-House when London was different from what it is now;* by strangers from the provinces who flocked there as to a centre; by visits to various parts of the country at Nonconformist festivals; and by the transfer of so many members of his Church to other con-

---

* Written about 1883.

gregations throughout the land. Nor do I forget how his name came to be known, beyond that of any other of our ministers, throughout the British colonies, owing to his being the father and founder of the Colonial Missionary Society, and the guide and counsellor of many youths going to seek their fortune in America or the South Seas. Still further was his popularity owing to a visit he paid some years ago to Australia. Also, when I was in Canada, I often heard of a less public visit paid to that country at an earlier period.

Amongst the many subjects in which my friend felt interested, was that of improvement in conducting Nonconformist worship; he gave his views respecting it in an appendix to a work on Liturgies, by the Rev. E. H. Baird of New York. I refer to this subject particularly, because to a considerable extent I sympathised with him; not, however, in consequence of his arguments, but from previous convictions, which, during late years, have become stronger than ever. The authority for excluding all liturgical worship from our places of assembly, neither he nor I could ever understand. I see nothing in Scripture which ties a Christian down to this perverse one-sidedness. On the contrary, both methods are sanctioned in the Old and New Testaments. My experience since retiring from the pastorate has strongly confirmed my previous impressions. When leading public worship, as I did for so many years, my utterances of devotion were spontaneous, and I am sure imperfect; but what was obvious enough before, though sometimes overlooked, came home to my feelings when listening to words in public devotion, often unadapted to inspire or guide supplication and praise. Further, extempore words, though *free* to the speaker, are, to all intents and purposes, *a form* to the hearers; and if a form in extempore speech, when thoroughly suitable, be proper, why is not a form in written language? Since I have become deaf, and often cannot catch a brother's supplications, a form which I can *read* must obviously be preferable to one which I am unable to understand. Extempore public devotion, under many circumstances is of priceless value; but under some circumstances so is liturgical service. Attempts amongst Dissenters in the latter direction, I am aware, have in some instances failed, owing largely to prejudices handed down through past generations; until those prejudices melt away — some day perhaps they will — an alteration, such as to others like myself, seems quite hopeless.*

In the years 1874 and 1875, I took part in commemoration of two world-known Nonconformist celebrations.

The first was the unveiling of Bunyan's statue at Bedford. I went down with the Dean of Westminster, Lady Augusta Stanley, and Dr. Allon, who all did wisely and well the parts allotted them. Her Ladyship gracefully unveiled the bronze figure of the wonderful dreamer; and her husband uttered immediately afterwards the following effective words:—" The Mayor has called upon me to say a few words, and I shall obey him. The Mayor has done *his* work, the Duke of Bedford has done his," (he gave the statue,) "and now I ask you to do yours, in commemorating John Bunyan. Every one who has not read the 'Pilgrim's Progress,' if there be any such person, read it without delay; those who have read it a hundred times, read it for the hundred and first time. Follow out in your lives the lessons which the 'Pilgrim's Progress' teaches; and then you will

* I am glad that at Kensington, a liturgical element has been introduced, such as I should have approved, but could not accomplish, because I knew it would then be disapproved by many.

all of you be even better monuments of John Bunyan, than the magnificent statue which the Duke of Bedford has given you."

The Dean and Dr. Allon delivered elaborate addresses at the Corn Exchange, and it was allotted to me, to propose, after a public dinner, "The Memory of John Bunyan." The thought struck me, that his genius was equally imaginative and realistic. People rise from reading his dream, with impressions of character, as lively as those derived from perusing Shakespeare or Scott. They see in his delineations just such folks as walked the streets of Bedford, and plodded through Midland country lanes, two hundred years ago. I heard gentlemen at table say they thought Bunyan took his conceptions of scenery from neighbouring places. But I said I did not think so. He had never beheld hills like "the Delectable Mountain," nor a vale or plain like that of "Beulah." In fact, he took his scenery from Scripture, and gave it reality by allusions such as we employ, when touching on objects of every-day life. He was "Christian," "Evangelist," "Greatheart," all in one—a pilgrim to the Heavenly City and a preacher of the Gospel.

I may here add that two years afterwards brazen

doors were given to Bunyan meeting by the Duke, and were opened with due solemnities, the Mayor and Corporation attending on the occasion.

The unveiling of Baxter's statue at Kidderminster occurred in July 1875, when Dr. Stanley represented the Church of England at the request of the town authorities; and, at the same time, they requested me to speak on behalf of Nonconformity. It was a gala day; shops were shut, flags were hung out, people wore holiday clothes, and a procession of the Corporation, the Bishop, and the speakers marched to the spot where the statue was placed.

Soon after the Kidderminster celebration I visited a worthy friend of mine at Bridgenorth, the Rev. Daniel Evans. Whilst there I received a letter from Dr. Stanley saying that he had heard me mention a design I had of visiting Madeley. He said he found in his interleaved Bible, opposite Dan. iii. 19-27, the words "Fletcher of Madeley," and asked if I could discover at Madeley a key to this enigma, as it seemed to him. Mr. Evans and I had visited Madeley together, and in conversation recalled to mind an anecdote in Benson's "Life of Fletcher." A man threatened to burn his wife if she went to hear the vicar again. She went notwithstanding, and the preacher chose for his sermon one of the lessons for the day, instead of the text he had thought of previously. The lesson was in Daniel on the deliverance of Shadrach, Meshach, and Abednego from the fiery furnace. The man followed his wife at a distance to find out what it was in Fletcher's preaching that so attracted her. When the poor woman returned she found her husband on his knees praying by the side of the fire he had prepared for her martyrdom. I wrote to the Dean and told him the story, as recalled to my mind by my friend Daniel Evans. The Dean sent back his kind regards and thanks to *Daniel,* " who had discovered his dream and the interpretation thereof."

I have brought the Bunyan and Baxter celebrations together because of their similarity; and the Madeley incident because it became connected with the last of them.

In 1874, the year between the two celebrations, I resigned my charge at Kensington, when a meeting was held to present a testimonial, to which Archdeacon Sinclair contributed, and the Dean of Westminster, with other Churchmen, besides Nonconformist friends in large numbers, uttered loving words I can never forget.

The following report appeared in *The Times*:—

"DEAN STANLEY AND THE NONCONFORMISTS.

"On Thursday evening, April 15th, 1874, the Rev. J. Stoughton, D.D., an eminent Dissenting minister at Kensington, retired from the pastorate of his congregation there, after a connection with them extending over the long period of thirty-three years, during which he has had the reputation, while upholding the principles of Nonconformity, of maintaining the most kindly relations with the neighbouring clergy, and is understood to have enjoyed the respect of the whole community of Churchmen as well as Dissenters. The ceremony of last evening was held in Kensington Chapel, a handsome building in Allen Street, Kensington, where Dr. Stoughton has long ministered, and his congregation attended in great numbers on the occasion. Mr. Samuel Morley, M.P., acted as chairman, and there were present, among others, the Dean of Westminster, Sir Charles Reed, Sir Thomas Chambers, M.P., Mr. James Spicer, the Revs. W. H. Fremantle, M.A., J. Angus, D.D., W. M. Punshon, D.D., Donald Fraser, D.D.; F. J. Jobson, D.D., Henry Allon, D.D., Samuel Martin, and J. C. Harrison, the last-named of whom, on being called to address the meeting, took occasion to say that their reverend friend, Dr. Stoughton, though acquainted with every form of religious thought, had ever held fast to the Gospel; that, as a minister of religion, it had been quite a passion with him to be thoroughly fair and impartial; and that he had all along panted for union among all religious denominations. Later in the ceremony, the Dean of Westminster, having been called upon to speak, presented himself to the meeting, and was much cheered. He said there might perhaps be several reasons why he had been asked to address them. He could not plead the same long acquaintance as the previous speakers had claimed with their venerable pastor; but still, during the last few years of his acquaintance with him, he could truly say that there had been no occasion of joy or sorrow in his life on which he had not received some kind sympathy from him. There was another reason for his addressing the meeting. As a Churchman, and as a minister of the Church of England, he felt called on to express his gratitude towards one, not exactly of his communion, who had never once let fall from his lips a word of bitterness against the community to which the Dean belonged, and through whose heart he verily believed the destruction of Westminster Abbey would send a pang. He only trusted that when the twenty-first century arrived, and some future pastor of the chapel should write the history of Queen Victoria's reign, he would treat his communion with the same courtesy and appreciation as their present pastor had treated, alike, divergent ministers and pastors of the Church of the Commonwealth. He felt he had come there that evening not so much as a personal friend or as a minister of the Established Church, but rather as her representative of common friends through the writings of Dr. Stoughton and himself. He came there to express obligations which dear old friends of them both, who lived two hundred years ago, would have wished to express on an occasion such as that—Chillingworth, Jeremy Taylor, Sir Matthew Hale, and many more whom his friend had brought to one common platform. They had had before his time histories of the Puritans, where they heard of nothing but Puritans; they had also histories of the Church of England; but the work of Dr. Stoughton was the first that had brought those famous men together. There was, he knew, a charge brought against his friend and himself that they were not sufficiently good haters. However that might be, he was sure that Dr. Stoughton hated, as he did, party spirit, the want of candour, all untruthfulness, and insolent vulgarity, whether in Church or Nonconformity. All these the Dean hated with a detestation so complete that, if it were possible, he would be willing to curse them thirteen times a year. He could not part from that assembly or from that occasion without saying one word on the peculiar aspect of the farewell on which the previous speakers had so touchingly dwelt. Surely it was a transition of life which all of them might envy as they approached the term of their allotted existence, to be able to secure for themselves a margin of life and of comparative quiet before the great end came at last. There was a custom in old monasteries—he trusted it would not be altogether inappropriate to mention it at a meeting of Congregationalists—that when any of the ancient monks had served a term of thirty or forty years—he forgot which—they were then to be relieved altogether from their arduous labours; they were to be called by a gentle name which meant 'playfellow'; and one condition of their existence was that nothing that was disagreeable should ever be named in their company. Such to their friend Dr. Stoughton was the tranquil period through which he was now passing; and although they might still anticipate for him long years of active usefulness, whether by pen or by voice, there must be a delightful sense on his part in looking forward, having accomplished one period of his existence, to a more undisturbed time in which he might look back on what had been, and forward to what was to be to him and all alike. The Dean's speech, of which this is necessarily a summary, was repeatedly cheered during its delivery. A valedictory address, expressed in flattering terms, and reviewing the long connection between their pastor and the congregation, was afterwards presented to Dr. Stoughton by Mr. R. Freeman, on behalf of the Church and congregation, accompanied by the spontaneous gift of a purse containing £3000."

Besides others who were present on the occasion, as noticed in *The Times*, let me mention my excellent friend and neighbour the Rev. J. Philip Gell, formerly Vicar of St. John's, Notting Hill. He referred to the well-knit efforts of pastor and people, which had constituted the strength of the Church at Kensington, and remarked that it was little known how the force of public opinion acts and reacts on the life of a large permanent congregation. "The love which was thrilling that night was the Church's strength, and so long as that lived and flowed on the part of the people, and was sustained by the pastor's wisdom, so long would the Church live and prosper."

Dr. Morley Punshon, President of the Wesleyan Connexion, travelled from Leeds, where he had preached that morning. He trusted that the Church would be Divinely guided in choosing a successor. It was encouraging to witness such a presentation as that just made, the like of which many present had never seen before.

The years I spent at Kensington were very happy. I can say from experience that the life of a Congregational minister, in connection with a large and liberal Church—when full play is given to the social affections, elevated and purified by culture as well as religion—is an enviable lot, and calls for the devout gratitude of any one who has enjoyed it.

The friendships formed with many of my flock, a very few of whom are still living, have been amongst the choicest privileges afforded me by Divine Providence. Loving memories of them linger in my heart, amidst sweeping obliterations of names and faces incident to an age of fourscore and more, and those who survive me will, I trust, accept an acknowledgment of obligations deeply felt as these lines are written. I took special interest in some, now goodly matrons, who were school girls at Kensington in my time, and whose happy fortunes I have sympathetically followed through life. If they read these lines, they will understand the fatherly feeling with which they are written. Their parents, now at rest in the eternal home, were no small joy to me, and as they passed away, one after another, they left blanks not to be filled up in this world.

Two deceased friends I may here notice. At an early period in my Kensington pastorate, a gentleman called upon me in the vestry with a transfer to our Church from a communion he had joined in Manchester. At the time he was a rising engineer, and afterwards took part in the construction of railways over the Alps and in South America. He was a botanist, and came to possess a large garden and conservatory where he lived. He received the honour of knighthood, and as Sir James Brunlees became well known. He took a deep interest in our Congregational affairs, and after his change of residence from Addison Road, Kensington, still continued, with his family, to worship with us on Sundays. He was an intimate friend of John Bright, both of them being anglers; and I was entertained by stories of their success, as brethren of the rod. I often spent a few restful days at

Argyle Lodge, where he and his kind-hearted lady made me as much at home as I felt at my own fireside. She died suddenly, after my retirement, when she was visiting a friend. I was immediately summoned to meet and comfort the mourning family. Another friend—George Rawson, of Bristol, the gifted hymn-writer—also died after my retirement, leaving memories of intelligence, humour, and affection, which I shall fondly cherish as long as I live. His beloved wife, daughter of the Rev. John Clayton, one of my predecessors in the Kensington pastorate, died some years before at Bristol. The touching memory of her funeral, and of the company then present, passes before me as I write these lines.

When I wrote this chapter, I asked my dear daughter Georgie to give me some results of her own experience whilst visiting the poor. She returned the following notes:—

"Instances of unselfishness are sometimes very touching. I knew a Christian woman who suffered for years with weak sight, and had several operations on both eyes, so that she could only distinguish outlines of different objects. She heard of two little children, distant relations of her husband, being left orphans, and as she had no children of her own, she suggested that they should adopt these little girls, and lead them in early years to a knowledge of Christ. The husband was so touched at his wife's readiness, with failing sight, to take this burden upon herself that, though a common labourer, he was willing to incur the extra expense, and ever since that home has been one of the brightest I know.

"A poor woman expressed a strong desire that some one would speak to her sailor boy, who was wild and unmanageable. An opportunity occurred not long after, but the lad manifested great disgust at being talked to, and afterwards whenever I called he left the room. When about to start upon a voyage, I went to bid him 'Good-bye.' On leaving I said, 'The time may come when you will feel the need of a true friend ; remember that Christ is ready to receive you, for He has said, "Him that cometh unto Me I will in no wise cast out." These words may fill your heart with gladness some day.' I did not hear anything of him for a long time, but one evening I received a note saying he was lying ill in a hospital, and would I go and see him. I complied, and found he had never forgotten the Saviour's words which I had quoted. He resisted, he said, the voice calling him to forsake his sins and cleave to Christ till he could bear it no longer. At last he yielded, and the change produced in him was remarkable. During a long illness he manifested patience, unlike his old self, and the lad's cheerfulness and readiness to help his mother were very beautiful. He died in her arms, singing 'Safe in the arms of Jesus.'

"Many of the poor have seen days of prosperity, and have forgotten God; but, when adversity comes, like frightened children, they rush to the Father's arms. One man, possessing at one time over £20,000, with a hundred men under him, lost all. Then, when reduced to the greatest distress, he listened to the Divine voice.

"I remember that on Lord Chichester's library table there always stood a large card, with the words:

'Lord Jesus, make Thyself to me
A living, bright reality.'

"And such words unite the rich and the poor. One of the poorest women I ever met, had a strong realisation of Christ's constant presence; and it so beautified her life, that all who entered her humble home felt such a prayer had been answered in her experience. I never talk to her but my mind is carried back to the Stanmer library."

At the end of this chapter, which closes my Kensington ministry, I venture to speak of my methods of preaching.

The main object of my ministrations was the illustration of God's Holy Word. Archbishop Whately preferred " to set his watch by the sun "; and, therefore, tested the results of his own thinking, and other teachers, by a comparison of them with the decisions of Scripture. When Scripture was plain, the subject on which it pronounced a distinct judgment was regarded as fixed for ever. That method it was my desire habitually to pursue. I made it my aim, not only to interpret the meaning of a particular verse taken by itself, but to catch, and fix in my mind, the *drift* of Apostolic thought in particular instances. It has been said, irreverently, that some expositors, when persecuted in one verse, flee to another, and the connection between the several parts of a paragraph is overlooked and lost.

It was my desire to look at long *trains of thought* in the writings of St. Paul as a sacred landscape, in which here and there a verse occurs as a lofty hill, which serves as a commanding point for surveying a landscape of thought round about. A single verse is often a key to an entire paragraph.

It was my habit to go over now and then a large extent of Scripture—doctrinal, biographical, historical. " Stars of the East, or Prophets and Apostles," formed a series of personal sketches in the Old and New

Testaments, afterwards published by the Religious Tract Society. Another course, called " Lights of the World," were illustrations of character, drawn from records of Christian experience and action, such as " William Tyndale, or Labour and Patience "; " Richard Hooker, or a Soul in Love with God's Law and Holy Order "; and " Robert Leighton, or the Peacefulness of Faith."

Besides such methods I did not scruple to lay under contribution to the pulpit, condensed summaries of Puritan works, such as Baxter's " Now or Never "; also I may mention that a course of Sermons on " Pilgrim's Progress " excited much interest, and three or four of these I repeated at the close of my pastorate.

As to the real value of a sermon, form must never be confounded with substance. It is vain to vote the mantle into majesty. A royal robe depends for effect on the richness of the material, not on the adjustment of its folds. Toller's " Sermons " * so eulogised by Robert Hall, depend for their impressiveness, not on a careful selection of words—in this respect they are open to criticism—but upon the intrinsic majesty of such thoughts as they express.

There is an obvious contrast between French and

* With a short Memoir by Robert Hall.

English preachers in this respect. They are more attentive to form than we are. I have witnessed effects in Parisian, and in Italian churches as well, produced by modes of delivery, such as I never saw in our own country. Young preachers in England might make their sermons more effective than they are, by greater attention paid to a mode of delivery.

Let me add a word or two as to preparation from week to week. At the beginning of a week I chose subjects for the following Sunday; and then gathered up from day to day, in reading and talking, arguments and illustrations suggested by books, scenery and conversation. One's mind may be brought to such a state as to gather together what is valuable and useful from time to time, as the magnet attracts to itself grains of precious metal over which it sweeps. And, let it not be forgotten, we may sometimes *build* up a sermon by adding one thought to another; and at other times *plant* a sermon through an idea which takes root and grows into a goodly tree. My method then was, on a Saturday evening, to *review* and revise what I had prepared, to criticise its substance and arrangement, and alter it in matter and form, so that on Sunday morning it could be poured out to the people in freshness and force.

On week-night services, I sometimes took up

Church history, or archæological illustrations of the Bible. Bible-classes, of course, were held ; but in the latter part of my Kensington pastorate, I was greatly helped in this, as in other respects by my worthy friend, the Rev. J. Alden Davies, who was for a few years my assistant minister.*

* In what I have ventured to say about pulpit preparation I have hoped to help my younger ministerial brethren.

CHAPTER XII

1875—1879

IN my last chapter I brought together two celebrations—one in honour of John Bunyan, the other in honour of Richard Baxter. Another celebration now claims attention, not of an English Nonconformist, but of a Protestant Reformer, whose fame covers the world—Martin Luther. English commemorations of his character and work were held late in 1875 and early in 1876.

Before I mention any particulars respecting the Luther celebration, I repeat what I have said elsewhere :

"There is no other man of a similar order whose fame touches so many topographical points, and sweeps over so wide a surface. The local reminiscences of Shakespeare and Milton, even taken together, are few, and cluster round a metropolis, a provincial town, and two or three villages. But how many cities, castles, and houses there are in Germany scattered far and wide which may be said to have Martin Luther for their presiding genius! Guide-books call attention to some spot where he went, some fortress or tenement which gave him shelter, some church in which he preached, some locality which his name has made famous; and there are scenes and houses unmentioned in guide-books, over which lingers the spell of his memory. One comes across mementoes of Charles V. in divers directions; but even they are fewer, less interesting, and less honoured than those of the monk who gave the emperor so much anxiety, and who by his devotion, and energy accomplished the reformation of the Teutonic Church. Certainly no king, no kaiser, can vie with him as to the place he occupies in the thoughts of his own people, and indeed of the whole Christian world." *

Washington Irving concludes his essay on "Shakespeare and Stratford-on-Avon," by remarking it would have cheered "the spirit of the youthful bard that his name should become the glory of his birthplace, that his ashes should be guarded as a most precious treasure, and that its lessening

* "Homes and Haunts of Martin Luther," p. 4.

spire, on which his eyes were fixed in tearful contemplation, should one day become the beacon towering amidst the gentle landscape to guide the literary pilgrim of every nation to his tomb."

It is no depreciation of Shakespeare's genius to say that above his aspirations after fame, whatever they might be, rose the aims and desires of Luther — a man absorbed in zeal for the salvation of souls, and for the glory of his Saviour; but it would have filled him with wonder, could he have foreseen the place he was to occupy in the history of the world, and how the double tower of the Stadt Kirche, in which he preached, would become a beacon to guide tens of thousands from both hemispheres to the Augustinian monastery, where he lived, and to the Schloss Kirche, where he lies buried.

The Luther Commemoration in England was enthusiastic.

Soon after I left Kensington an immense assembly gathered in Exeter Hall, to take up points in Luther's character and work. If I remember rightly, I dwelt on that occasion at some length on his domestic life, often assailed by his opponents, but held in admiration by Protestants all over the world. In lectures and addresses, delivered at Norwich, Peterborough, Bedford, and elsewhere, I dwelt on his manifold excellences and achievements, at Leipzig, at Worms, in the Wartburg, and his Wittenberg home. My remarks accorded with those I have now introduced.

After the close of my pastorate in Kensington, Ealing became my home. The professorships at New College were continued. Sundays were spent in preaching the Gospel. Literary studies were pursued to a larger extent than they had been when pastoral duty claimed chief attention.

In 1876 I was grieved by the death of Lady Augusta Stanley, for she manifested towards me kindness which could not fail to inspire my warmest gratitude. I never knew any other person who had so much dignity and sweetness of demeanour, one who, with many-sided sympathy, could make her numerous guests feel how sincere were her friendly demonstrations. It often surprised me, as it did others, how she paid marked attention to all her guests, however numerous they might be. Her tact was admirable. Nobody could leave the Deanery with the idea of having been neglected.

Her "At Homes" were extraordinarily popular, for every one was sure of meeting with notabilities of Church and State, literature and science. Her husband was in full sympathy with her in all these respects.

She was intimately acquainted with foreign celebrities, and her conversation about them was of much interest. She and her mother, Lady Elgin, spent some days in Lamartine's house at Paris, when violent mobs, during the Revolution, assembled in front of the residence. The President behaved bravely, but expressed fear lest any insult should be offered to English ladies under his roof. Mother and daughter, if I remember right, had been offered refuge by the President when the utmost peril filled the French capital. Lady Augusta related interesting anecdotes of Lamartine; and I gathered that he habitually indicated no small confidence in himself, feeling that he was the greatest man in France, as no doubt, at the time, he really was.

Her Ladyship and the Dean were well acquainted with M. Guizot, and gave interesting accounts of that distinguished statesman, and of his habits and studies after retirement from public life. I happened once, when talking of Earl Russell, to make the remark, that I had heard of his cold manner to political acquaintances. Her countenance lighted up, and she spoke with enthusiasm of what he was in the bosom of his family, and the circle of intimate friends. Bishop Thirlwall was a great favourite with her, and she related interesting anecdotes of that distinguished man, indicating a warm heart, in union with a keen intellect.

Lady Augusta's visit to St. Petersburg with the Dean, at the marriage of the Duke of Edinburgh, proved too much for her strength, and at Paris in the following autumn serious illness set in. From time to time amendment and relapse excited hope and fear, until all prospect of recovery vanished. She spoke of friends, sent kind messages, and talked calmly and with humble confidence of the other world, saying, "Think of me as near, only in another room. 'In my Father's house are many mansions.'" I had a touching note from the Dean asking me to be a pall-bearer at the funeral. All chosen for that office indicated causes, classes, and places in which she felt an interest. Religion, literature, and philanthropy, the neighbourhood in which she lived, and Scotland—each had a representative.

The assembly of mourners in the Jerusalem Chamber; the spectacle in the Abbey; the procession up the nave whilst the Queen occupied a little gallery not far from the western door; the calm submission of the bereaved husband, as he sat by the coffin; the solemn entrance into Henry VII.'s

Chapel; the ray of sunlight falling on the coffin as it sank into the vault; and especially the words, "I heard a voice from Heaven," sung by choristers invisible at the moment, as if music came from the Upper Temple—these incidents can never be forgotten.

It was by royal command that this lady, descended from the royal Bruce, was buried in a chapel reserved for royal persons; and immediately after the interment wreaths from the Queen and her children were strewn over the grave. The three benedictions—the Mosaic, the Pauline, and the Ecclesiastical—which the deceased loved to hear were pronounced, at the close of the service, by the Dean from a desk in the nave. She had said to him, "Think of me as you repeat the holy words." He did, when she was gone as when she was living.

The Dean sometimes referred to his visit to St. Petersburg in company with her ladyship, and spoke of his having before him, as he tied the nuptial knot on that memorable occasion, no less than four princes, each of whom was expectant of a crown—the Prince of Wales, the Crown Prince of Prussia, the Crown Prince of the Netherlands, and the Czarevitch; and he also mentioned this circumstance—that after the wedding party had passed in state through a magnificent hall, where no provision for a banquet could be seen, within an hour and a half they sat down to a feast of sumptuous splendour, reminding him of Belshazzar's, not in point of excess, but in point of regal display. The fact was, the side-tables had been concealed behind screens and drapery. The middle one had in that space of time been fixed and adorned.

I may here mention that one day, during a visit to the Deanery, I had much conversation with Miss Stanley, the Dean's sister, an agreeable companion, who freely indulged in some common recollections of dear old Norwich, and some friends whom we had both known. She told me a great deal about her good father, the Bishop, dwelling with admiration upon his exceedingly simple habits, and his determination never to give at the Palace *grand dinners*, but only such as combined hospitality with Christian unostentation.

Two or three days previous to Lady Augusta's funeral, I breakfasted at Lambeth, when Archbishop Tait, amongst other things, spoke of his desire for some union with Protestant Dissenters as far as it was possible; and this led to proceedings which, as they have not been reported in any fulness, may be recorded here.

It was a delicate question who should first move in the matter. The Archbishop wished to invite brethren to Lambeth, but what reason was to be assigned for taking such a step? At length it was arranged that some communication should be made to him, indicative of a disposition on the part of Nonconformists to confer with Episcopalian brethren. On such a ground the Archbishop considered he might bring together bishops, ready to join in a conference. I undertook to prepare a letter and get it signed, so that Dr. Tait might feel he had sure footing for what might follow. It was based on a recognition of pleasure felt by Nonconformists, in consequence of passages in his recent charges touching religious union. The letter went on to express willingness to meet brethren for consultation respecting co-operation in religious service so far as it might be possible and wise. It was signed by well-known ministers, and was acknowledged by the Archbishop under the term of "memorial," an expression which, if I remember rightly, had not been employed by us.

Four Nonconformist ministers accordingly went down to Lambeth to converse on the subject.

Previous to this interview, it was my conviction that to discuss the subject of *union* by itself was by no means desirable, as it might raise questions which would defeat the end in view. In harmony with this, the following opinion was expressed by a friendly prelate :—" Such a neutral subject as the progress of irreligious thought, would do well as a basis for a friendly meeting."

In a note received from the Archbishop before we met, he said, " I beg leave to assure you that all the bishops whom I have consulted agree in the extreme importance of this movement, and in an earnest desire that by proper preliminary arrangements your proposal for a conference may be brought to a satisfactory result." The proposal for a conference, I think, did not *originate* with me, though I quite approved of it, and was glad the Archbishop had kindly arranged for its being held.

I subjoin the following record, received from Lambeth, respecting a conference which the ministers named held with the Archbishop beforehand :—

" May 24th, 1876 : The Archbishop of Canterbury saw the Rev. Dr. Stoughton, the Rev. Dr. Angus, the Rev. Newman Hall, and the Rev. Dr. Aveling.

" The gentlemen present having heard from the Archbishop what had passed with the bishops who met at the Ecclesiastical Commission, it was the opinion of those present that there was ample room for united efforts to stem growing infidelity and ungodliness.

"1. Therefore that a united conference as to the best means of attempting to spread the knowledge of the answers to materialistic and atheistic sophistries might be attended with very beneficial results.

"2. That such a conference might with great advantage consider the lamentable ignorance and indifference as to religion which prevails amongst masses of the community, and the best modes of meeting these evils.

"3. That such a conference might also with advantage consider what efforts are needed to rouse the classes above the artisan class to a greater appreciation of the realities of religion.

"4. That it would be desirable that at such a conference those present should come prepared to state their experience as to the difficulties to be met, and the proposed remedies. It was agreed that a day after the first week in July would be suitable for such a conference.

"The result of this was reported by the Archbishop to an informal meeting of certain bishops at the Room of the House of Lords: present, the

Archbishop of York, the Bishops of London, Winchester, St. Asaph, Llandaff, Gloucester and Bristol, and Carlisle; and Monday, July 4th, at twelve noon, was fixed for our gathering."

We assembled accordingly on July 4th, and there were present besides the Primate, the Bishops of London, Winchester, Peterborough, Gloucester, Bath and Wells, Drs. Allon, Raleigh, Punshon, Rigg, Aveling, Angus, Cumming, Robertson of Edinburgh (an old schoolmate of Dr. Tait); the Revs. J. C. Harrison, Newman Hall, Josiah Viney, and several others whom I cannot call to mind as, unfortunately, I have not kept a list.

The Archbishop presided, read the Scriptures, and offered prayer. He opened the proceedings by an appropriate address, and then requested me to give some account of the steps which had led to our meeting together. I could not help referring to some remarkable gatherings in the Jerusalem Chamber, March 1640-1, convened by Dr. Williams, at that time Bishop of Lincoln, and also Dean of Westminster, when several other dignitaries met certain Presbyterian divines. "This," I remarked, "was done by order of the House of Lords, with a view to settling points of difference between ecclesiastical parties of that day. A scheme of comprehension was contemplated. It came to nothing, though the intercourse seems to have been pleasant, and they were hospitably entertained by the convener." "This was the last course of all public Episcopal treatments," said the witty Thomas Fuller, who added: "The guests may now soon put up their knives, seeing, soon after, the voider was called for, which took away all bishops' lands." I emphasised the fact that we had assembled for a very different purpose, not to discuss any plan of comprehension, but to see how parties, remaining ecclesiastically as we were, could, notwithstanding, *unite* in defence of our common faith against those who opposed it.

"We have a common cause," it was added; "and let us aim at extending the influence of our common Christianity—this would bring us into spiritual and practical fellowship, the most enduring of all bonds." The Bishop of Bath and Wells followed and spoke on the specific point—how we should meet doubts and difficulties in reference to religion. The Bishop of Peterborough discussed the subject generally, with great eloquence and force. The Bishops of London and Winchester made practical suggestions as to guarding Christians against scepticism, and rousing people at large from indifference and neglect. Drs. Rigg, Angus, and others, combatted infidel objections and enforced attention to the subject before us. A spirit of harmony pervaded the meeting.

We broke up the morning conference at two o'clock, and then lunched together; reassembling at three o'clock, when the Bishop of Gloucester, Dr. Punshon, and several besides, resumed the conversation. No representatives of the press were present, and no report, that I am aware of, was taken and preserved. We wished to prevent the controversial treatment of what took place. Two of those who were there, together with myself, received and complied with a request to prepare some brief statement for *The Times*, on the character and purpose of our meeting. Of course, the whole matter was criticised afterwards, chiefly however in private. I do not remember that it was taken up controversially in religious periodicals. To correct some misapprehensions—expressed in a Dissenting newspaper—I, at the request of an esteemed brother, wrote a short letter of explanation.

When we separated, gratification was expressed by those who were present. Some Nonconformists did not enter into the movement; others did, and that most heartily. From several Episcopalian friends we received assurances of approval and sympathy. It issued in no united action ; no fresh organisation had, as far as I know, ever been intended. The purpose designed was accomplished by interchanging thought, collecting information, and encouraging one another in ministerial work.

For Archbishop Tait I had great respect and affection. He was singularly kind and conversable, without affecting any official superiority. Under his grave countenance, and habitually serious demeanour, as one who lived ever " in his Great Taskmaster's eye," there were veins of cheerfulness and humour in his familiar intercourse—I felt deeply, his gentle sympathy, expressed in a letter of condolence, on my dear wife's death ; and the last time we talked together, being interrupted by another person, he broke off in the opening of what seemed an amusing tale. He appreciated the relative position of Church and Dissent, better than any other dignitary I have met with. He would say that Nonconformists had their traditions, organisations, endowments, and influence, which gave them a status they were not likely to surrender by bringing over what belonged to them, into an Episcopalian organisation. A fraternal *modus vivendi*, he regarded as the object to be aimed at, not an absorption of Dissenting bodies into the Establishment. He, no doubt, would have preferred to see *One Great Church* in England, under a moderate Episcopacy; but he seemed to cherish little hope of any such object being accomplished.

On a former page allusion was made to Mr. Bagster, of Polyglot fame. In the year (1877) his venerable wife, at the age of 100 *within a few hours*, died at Old Windsor; and her accumulated years attracted the notice of Her Majesty, who honoured her with a visit just before her decease I called at the cottage in which she expired, after the royal visitor had been there, and there heard the particulars of the interview. Her Majesty I was informed, brought with her the Princess Beatrice; and, on their entrance into the bedroom, where the old lady was lying, she at once expressed her gratitude for the signal favour bestowed by her Sovereign, saying that "she was looking forward to her own speedy dismissal to the immediate presence of the Saviour, where she hoped hereafter to meet Her Majesty." Pleasant conversation followed, in which Mrs. B., at the Queen's request, related her memories of George III., Queen Charlotte, and the Royal Family, as they used to walk on the Castle terrace, in the presence of a large number of loyal spectators. The Queen manifested interest in particulars respecting the good old lady, related by her daughter; and in consequence of the report she gave on her return home, Prince Leopold, as I was told soon afterwards, paid a visit to Old Windsor, and wished for a rehearsal of what had been communicated by his Royal Mother. Repeated gracious inquiries from the Castle followed. At the funeral service a note was put into my hands, written by the Duchess of Roxburgh to Miss Bagster, tenderly touching on that lady's sorrow, for her late bereavement; and concluding with the words: "The Queen begs you to convey to all the members of your venerable mother's family, the assurance of Her Majesty's condolence." This note was read to the mourners.

In 1877 I made two pilgrimages which left memorable impressions. All my life I have been an enthusiastic shrine-seeker, loving to trace out spots sanctified by footsteps of heroic and holy men. I heartily adopt the words of Dr. Martineau, "No material interests, no common welfare, can so bind a community together, and make it strong of heart, as a history of rights maintained and virtues uncorrupted and freedom won; and one legend of conscience is worth more to a country than hidden gold and fertile plains."

At different periods I have visited the birthplaces of Shakespeare and of Raleigh, of Cromwell and of Wesley; the homes of Knox, Hampden, Milton, Baxter, and Howard; the haunts of Johnson, Goldsmith, Watts, and Cowper; the graves of Bunyan, Burns, Scott, and Chalmers have all had attractions for me.

The pilgrimages I made in 1877 were the following:—

The first to the Vosges district in France, searching for Ban de la Roche, the scene of Oberlin's labours, and the resting place of his remains.* From Strassburg my daughter and I went to Mutzig, situated amidst a theatre of red sandstone hills mantled with woods and vineyards. Then from Mutzig we proceeded to Fouday, through valley after valley, if not exactly picturesque, yet really pictorial, and finally approached the parish of the model pastor. In the heart of the village of Ban de la Roche, are the church hallowed by his preaching, and the grave where he sleeps. Three broad slabs lie on the green turf, side by

---

* Since my visit to Ban de la Roche I discovered that, in a part of the country not far off, an Irish missionary, Columbanus, in the sixth century laboured for the temporal, as well as the spiritual, welfare of the people. See Wolf's "Country of the Vosges," p. 214.

side, the middle one inscribed with the words, "Il fut 60 ans père de ce canton.—'La Mémoire du juste sera en benediction.'" An iron cross bears the name "Papa Oberlin." We were surprised to find the spot, though highly situated, so rich in beauty as summer waned; an afternoon sun warming the crisp air, and lighting up objects with varied tints. At Walderbach, a Swiss-like village, full of cottages and fruit trees, we found the parsonage house in which the good man lived and died. We were welcomed by the present clergyman's wife, whom we had met before, without knowing her. The good lady took us over the rooms associated with her husband's predecessor. There was the study where he worked, and the bedroom in which he slept. Some of his furniture is preserved, with a collection of toys he made for children, and a large jar full of still fragrant rose leaves, a few of which were gratefully accepted as a memento of the visit.

The other pilgrimage was in England to Broad Oak, Shropshire, where Philip Henry resided and where his son Matthew was born. It stands where the Wrexham Road is intersected by a lane leading to Whitwell Church. It is a small farmhouse, part of a larger one, with heavy beams, and a broad chimney corner, like what one sees in Anne Hathaway's cottage near Stratford-on-Avon. When in its primitive state, it must have been spacious, for, says the famous Puritan, "I have room for twelve friends in my beds, a hundred in my barn, and a thousand in my heart." Here he resembled "Abraham sitting at his tent door, in quest of opportunities to do good. If he met with any poor near his house, and gave them alms in money, he would, besides, bid them go to his door for relief. He was very tender and compassionate towards poor strangers, and travellers, though his candour and charity were often imposed upon by cheats and pretenders."

The mention of Broad Oak occurs repeatedly in the Life of the father, written by his affectionate son. The latter tells of his father's removal to Broad Oak, and the providences concerning him there, of "the rebukes he lay under at Broad Oak," and of the last nine years of his life, in "liberty and enlargement at Broad Oak." At a time when ministerial engagements were by no means so numerous and diversified as they are at present; when habits of home study, quiet visitation of the flock, and catechising the children, rather than preaching on public occasions, attending large meetings, and travelling to and fro along the length and breadth of the land, distinguished both town and country clergymen; when those who were connected with the Established Church, and had no restraints put upon their activity, spent what would be now considered very retired and monotonous lives; what must have been the secluded and stationary position of an ejected minister between the Restoration and the Revolution! No wonder, then, that almost every incident and effort belonging to Philip Henry's career belonged to the farm at Broad Oak, where he lived and died, and wrote and suffered, and walked and taught, bringing up his children, and receiving his friends, and paying visits to his neighbours, under the shadow of the umbrageous trees which gave a name to his pleasant homestead.

I drove over to the house, or rather that part of it which still remains, a part of the kitchen, as I suppose, in which the good man used to preach. The people of the house showed me some relics—the pulpit cushion, and, I think, the pulpit itself, or some portion of it; also some buttons which belonged to Philip Henry's coat.

At Whitwell is a chapel containing Philip Henry's

monument, which once stood in the parish edifice of Whitchurch.

At the end of the Whitwell epitaph are the words, "In dormitorium hic juxta positum demisit June 24, Anno Dom. MDCXCVI, Ætatis LXV." Was it in imitation of this, that the words were introduced in Matthew Henry's monument in Holy Trinity Church, Chester, "Confectum corpus huic dormitorio commisit 22 die Junii, 1714, Anno ætat 52"?

Dr. Howson, Dean of Chester, who was staying with me at Crewe Hall when this visit was arranged, intended to be my companion, for he was a great admirer of the Henrys; but illness prevented him.

In 1877 I was invited by Dr. Stanley to deliver a missionary lecture in Westminster Abbey, one of a series he had arranged, in which some friends of his, not clergymen in the Establishment, took part.

In 1877 I gave a lecture in the room of the Society of Arts on the prospects and perils of modern civilisation. One of the audience was a native gentleman attached to the Chinese Embassy —a very intelligent person, speaking English well, and showing by his conversation how clearly he grasped points of the address he had just heard. It was a singular circumstance that a representative of the largest empire of the world —which not long ago counted all other nations as barbarous—should listen to a barbarian as he represented the good and *evil* of European civilisation.

Just before Christmas (1877) two or three days were spent at the Deanery of Westminster, and on the Sunday afternoon Dr. Stanley walked with me on the terrace of the Parliamentary Houses, where we had some interesting talk. He pointed to the palatial edifice at our back as we looked across the river, and said, "This is the palace of the nation"; turning attention to St. Thomas' Hospital, he remarked, "That is the palace of the poor"; and next, looking towards Lambeth, he added, "There is the palace of the Church." We discussed the state and prospects of the Establishment, and he, as a staunch advocate for its continuance, propounded schemes of reform, which, looking at the state of parties, seemed to me quite impracticable. He was filled with an idea of comprehension, if not within wide Episcopalian limits, then by a State union of different denominations—for example, thus: He would have been glad to see a Presbyterian Moderator, a

Congregational Chairman, and a Wesleyan President sitting in the House of Lords on a bench with the bishops. He further thought that, as Charles II. was willing to have Nonconformist chaplains, after the Restoration, so an English sovereign might now, without any impropriety, do the same; and if the Uniformity Act were modified so as to allow a Dissenting minister to enter a pulpit of the Establishment, there would be no legal bar in the way. My friend had the widest sympathies possible, and union, with him, was a passion.

In some respects I have a feeling like the Dean's, but I hold theological and ecclesiastical principles such as he did not adopt. One fundamental difference between us was that he overlooked the exercise of Church *discipline*, to which I attach great importance. The study of State organisations has convinced me that the "union of Church and State" creates insuperable barriers in the way of ecclesiastical discipline. If the Church be linked to the State, so that a subject of the State becomes thereby legally entitled to membership and communion,—that forms a strong bar to a faithful correction of moral misconduct and fundamental disbeliefs. It was a great difficulty under the Commonwealth. The devoted and holy Thomas Wilson, Bishop of Sodor and Man, found it so in carrying on his diocese. He said in his famous "Ecclesiastical Constitutions" that his desire was "We may not stand charged with the scandals which wicked men bring upon religion, when they are admitted to, and reputed members of, Christ's Church; and that we may, by all laudable means, promote the conversion of sinners, and oblige men to submit to the discipline of the Gospel." But for myself, let me say I have not found any difficulty in the maintenance of discipline in Congregational Churches. Whatever might be the basis of Dr. Stanley's far-reaching comprehension, it appears to me there might be a much broader range of religious sympathy and co-operation between distinct religious bodies connected with the maintenance of well-accentuated beliefs, and the exercise of ecclesiastical discipline.

In the early part of the following year I visited Edinburgh to lecture for the Philosophical Society of that city. My subject was "The Great Rebellion"; and I made a double attempt, first, to vindicate the Parliament policy as against the despotic unconstitutionalism of the infatuated monarch; and secondly, to criticise the proceedings of some eminent men on the Puritan and popular side. The society invited me to lecture again, when different historical ground was taken, and a sketch was presented of English and Scotch life in the days of Queen Anne.

My old friend, and large-hearted host, the Rev. George D. Cullen, favoured me with the company at dinner, of Dr. Goold, Moderator of the Free Church; Dr. Hanna, son-in-law to Dr. Chalmers; Dr. Alexander, and others—and we had earnest talk about topics of the day. Scotch and English elements of thought, blended so as to bring diversities into view, without any portion of the acrimony common to polemical debate. True blue Presbyterianism rose in contrast with milder colours of Ecclesiasticism. There was no want of thrust or repartee, but we kept the unity of the spirit in the bond of peace. Edinburgh society is of the choicest kind. Some of the best talkers may be found on the other side the border; and memories of celebrities in Auld Reekie, are amongst the most pleasant of my life. On the occasion just noticed, my friend Mr. Cullen took me over to St. Andrews; and there Principal Tulloch did the honours of ciceroneship to perfection. In the evening we dined at the house of Professor Swann, where further social enjoyments of a high university order were found to be in store.

During this visit to Scotland a curious fact was related to me by the librarian of the University. Drummond of Hawthornden bequeathed books to the library of that institution, and in the catalogue appeared an item of " MSS. respecting Mary Queen of Scots."

These MSS. were long missing, and inquiries about them were made in vain. Not very long before my visit, the librarian received a communication from some one who said he had, in his possession, papers belonging to the University ; and on receiving a reply to his letter, he forwarded them. They turned out to be the missing treasure. How came this about ? As well as I can remember it appeared that a librarian of the last century put one day into his coat pocket these very MSS., and took them home for examination. He suddenly died. His clothes were sent to a relative, and amongst them, the coat containing the documents now mentioned. For a century afterwards they remained forgotten, and then came to light. The possessor, finding they belonged to Edinburgh University, wrote to the librarian as stated above, and restored them to their proper place. The recovered property was shown to me. It included original papers published some time ago, and others not previously known; but, if I may venture to say so, after a brief inspection, they did not promise to be of so much service as was hoped, in throwing fresh light on the mysteries of poor Mary's career.

The seventh General Conference of the Evangelical Alliance was held in Basle, September 1st 1879.

There was a large gathering of delegates from Germany, France, Austria, Italy, Spain, Holland, America and England. The president was M. C. Sarasin, Councillor of State, who is said to have descended from a Moorish ancestor settled in the canton. He showed himself to be acquainted with English literature.

"Let me remind our English friends," he said, "of the words their great poet puts in the mouth of Richard II.:

> 'Look not to the ground
> Ye favourites of a king! Are we not high?
> High be our thoughts.'

"Let us cherish high thoughts, my friends! Are we not the servants of a King, of the King of kings, and Lord of lords? And is it not His work we are carrying on?

> 'Die sach' ist dein, Herr Jesu Christ,
> Die sach' an der wir stehen.'
> (The cause is Thine, Lord Jesus Christ,
> The cause for which we stand.)

"Thus let our work be done, our testimony be given, our efforts be united, in the same joyful steadfast spirit, with the same buoyancy, with which the Apostle, with chained hands, appealed to his flock at Philippi, 'Rejoice in the Lord always, and again I say, rejoice.'"

These were animating words, and awakened an enthusiastic response, when uttered in the old church of St. Martin, where Æcolampadius first preached the doctrines of the Reformation.

I give the following *resumé* of some remarks I made at the Basle Alliance meeting.

The Times reported:

"Dr. Stoughton contrasted the gathering of peoples in that assembly, representative of all nations, with a meeting held in Basle four hundred and fifty years ago. Christendom was then in a very divided state, for the spirit of religious inquiry was breaking out, and the great moot-point was, in all theological controversy, 'Where lies the ultimate authority for religious beliefs —in Popes, in Councils, or in the Word of God?' They met that day in times of a somewhat different character, but of still deeper and wider agitation, for the question now was, not only whether the Church or the Bible was the final test of truth, but also whether reason or revelation should be our guide as to the highest of all subjects which could affect the present and future interests of the human family. But how vast the difference between that famous Council at Basle and the Evangelical Alliance Conference of this day! Under what different aspects was union regarded by the two assemblies! The one aimed at uniformity, at a precise and definitely-expressed agreement of opinion, in relation to theological and ecclesiastical points, which might be enforced on all Christendom by pains and penalties,—even death, to a recreant brother. The other seeks to promote unity, holding, after the experience of ages, that uniformity was impossible, and that true unity could not only be attained, but was compatible with a hearty, loving, sympathetic Christian fellowship throughout the family of the redeemed. He then contrasted the appearance of the two meetings, traced out the history of the followers of John Huss, and, in a long and exceedingly able and interesting historical review of the history of the Reformation, showed that Protestant England was not only indebted to Basle for men but for principles; and, identifying the two with the work of Calvin at Geneva and John Knox in Scotland, he contended that the outcome of those early struggles was not only religious freedom in Europe, but, mainly through the Puritans of England, the religious life and progress of America. Their simple reliance now, as then, was the Gospel of Christ, and freedom to preach and practise its heaven-born truths."

I have a great delight in all genuine Christian union, but my conception of it is by no means confined to the cultivation of love and sympathy with those, who in all, or in most, respects concur with me. There is an admirable passage in Julius Hare's preface to the third volume of Arnold's "Rome." "We are so bound and shackled, by all manner of prejudices, national, party, ecclesiastical, individual, that we can hardly move a limb freely; and we are so fenced and penned in, that few can look over their neighbour's land, or up to any piece of sky, except to *that which is just over their heads.*" I took an active part in the early history of the Evangelical Alliance, and I rejoice in those points of agreement which are expressed in its Evangelical faith; but I have never liked its exclusion of some good people from its fellowship, on the ground of differences in relation to ecclesiastical ordinances. I would look kindly over "my neighbour's land," and towards "pieces of sky" which are not "just over my head."

I can scarcely bring myself to speak of the sorrow which befell me in November 1879. My beloved wife then died, and was interred in Hanwell Cemetery, which pertains to the parish of Kensington. The beautiful words in Proverbs are inscribed on her gravestone: "Her children arise up, and call her blessed; her husband also, and he praiseth her." Some time ago I read in the Life of my American friend, Dr. Hodge, the following passage respecting the deceased companion of *his* life. I can truly appropriate it to my departed loved one. "A humble worshipper of Christ, she lived in love and died in faith. Trustful woman, delightful companion, ardent friend, devoted wife, self-sacrificing mother, we lay you gently here, our best beloved, to gather strength and beauty for the coming of the Lord."

My dearest friend Joshua Harrison, who was to her as a brother, preached a funeral sermon, in which he said, "The strength of her life was her faith in the Son of God. Her path, though the sun shone brightly upon it, was often a thorny one. Her own health was liable to frequent interruptions, and her heart was pierced again and again by the loss of children, whom she loved better than herself. Oh, the unmurmuring resignation with which seven several times, she saw her dear ones carried to the grave! Oh, the courage with which she bore the shock! She never wavered in the conviction, 'He loved me and gave Himself for me,' but felt that these sad sorrows must be only the obscurer manifestations of His love. And hence she could write, 'Here we shall never be exempt from trial and sorrow, but when we reach that changeless home above, there will be no need of sanctifying us there. All that is needful to make us meet for that holy place must be done here; and oh, how much pruning and purging, how much of grace and strength we need to help us to walk more closely with Him.'

"She has reached that changeless abode now, and has left all sorrow behind. Long, long had she been waiting, but the message came so suddenly at last, that, without knowing she was dying, she found herself at home. The words discovered in her desk, which by copying she had made her own, received sweet and exact fulfilment:

'The way is long, my Father, and my soul
Longs for the rest and quiet of the goal;

While yet I journey through this weary land,
Keep me from wandering ; Father, take my hand,
    Quickly and straight,
    Lead to Heaven's gate
      Thy child.

' The way is long, my child, but it shall be
Not one step longer than is best for thee,
And thou shalt know, at last, when thou shalt stand
Close by the gate, how I did take thy hand,
    And quick and straight,
    Lead to Heaven's gate
      My child.' "

CHAPTER XIII

1879—1883

NEED was felt for some change after my sad bereavement; so in March, 1880, my daughter and I started for Italy. We tarried on our way a week at Cannes with my friend, Mr. Prust, of Northampton, an old fellow-student, who had a villa in the Riviera. I greatly enjoyed the climate and scenery, and felt soothed by walks and drives on the shores, through the cork groves, and round about to more distant places of interest. Old affections sprang up anew between my friend and myself as we talked of auld lang syne. Nothing could exceed the kindness shown by him and his two interesting nieces.

I met with some old acquaintances at Mentone; amongst the rest, with a gentleman well known in the political and religious world and closely connected with Lord Palmerston. He gave me much information as to what he apprehended was the state of thought and feeling amongst the upper class in reference to Christianity. There seemed to be a large amount of light-hearted, thoughtless scepticism on the part of young people; girls catching from their brothers doubts as to God and Christ and eternity—doubts circulated in conversation and in periodicals. The facts indicated did not strike me as deep and earnest, but as froth on the surface of common talk; not, however, to be passed over as a trifling phenomenon, for if those who occupy superior stations in the world have their faith shaken as to natural and revealed religion, it forebodes mischief to wider circles round them. My informant was inclined to believe that outspoken doubt and disbelief was less to be dreaded than concealed enmity. Moreover, that whilst there was much to excite concern in literature and social intercourse of the present day, there was also an increase in the higher as well as lower walks of thorough-going Christian experience and practice. In my own limited acquaintance I have been cheered to find instances of what appeared genuine piety where I little expected them; works of benevolence going on nowadays amongst all classes are surely tokens for good, which ought to fill us with thankfulness. We are all tempted to confine ourselves to one side of the world and Church picture before us; but we shall not get at the whole truth by shutting one eye and keeping the other wide open.

Leaving Cannes, we travelled by the Cornice Railway to Genoa, and there renewed acquaintance with churches, palaces, and picture galleries, seen years before. Then tarrying at Spezzia, we saw some new specimens of Italian scenery and life. Pisa and Florence were again visited, cities in which I loved to linger; and at the end of about ten days we reached Rome.

I had an introduction to Cardinal Howard, who sent me an invitation to visit him. I was met by a Monseignor friend of his, with whom I had a good deal of conversation. We discussed several topics, and then touched upon the relations in which Catholics and Protestants stood to one another. He considered there was improvement in this respect, more social intercourse existing between them than was once the case.

Pio Nono had a Jewish friend, who became a convert. Seeing him one day depressed, "the holy father," as this Monseignor called him, asked what was the cause.

"I have just lost my father, who died a Jew, and

I am greatly concerned about the state of his soul."

"But was he a good Jew, devout and acting up to the light he had?"

"Yes," was the reply.

Then came the Pope's rejoinder, "I will pray for him; and do you pray for him, and I doubt not that God will have mercy on him."

These were his words as well as I can remember. The drift of the story and its application were intended to show that the deceased pontiff did not despair of a Jew's salvation. He did not look upon those outside the Roman pale as beyond the reach of God's mercy, though needing purification in a future state.

Whilst we were talking the Cardinal came in. The reception he gave me was singularly cordial, and we had a good deal of friendly chat relative to the Stanley family. The favours I asked he granted at once; one was a special introduction to the chief librarian at the Vatican, and the seeing more of its treasures than I had done when I visited the library many years before. He took me into his library, well furnished with books, in handsome bindings, and we had some talk about Thomas Aquinas, in whose writings I took an interest. He recommended to me some little books of analysis and comment. He also procured a papal permission for my daughter to see St. Peter's Crypt, which is closed to ladies generally, on all days of the year except one. The Cardinal arranged with one of the Vatican librarians that I should have special facilities for seeing historical documents; and afterwards, on my reaching the Vatican by appointment, I was received by an officer, who accompanied me into one of the magnificent galleries, which I had seen years before, to find then all book-cases closed. Now some of them were opened, and I was permitted to take down any volumes I liked; and I at once luxuriated in the inspection of charming Aldine editions of patristic and other authors—the paper as white, and the printing as fresh, as when they were produced four centuries ago.

I was surprised to find that provision was made for the use of printed books, and certain MSS., by readers, admitted after the fashion in our British Museum. There are catalogues, giving titles and press-marks; and, by writing for what you want upon slips of paper, and handing them to an attendant, as in the British Museum, you attain the volumes desired, which you can use at desks provided for the purpose. A catalogue of much greater compass than exists at present, I was informed, is in progress; but the Cardinal told me, it might be a long time before it was finished, adding, that Rome is the Eternal City in more senses than one. He encouraged me to believe that even the archives of the Holy See might be accessible; but, far short of that, MSS. which I wrote for, and examined, were sufficient to convince me that there is abundant materials for extensive research, beyond what was formerly possible. Besides, in the vast Library of the Dominicans—who once had their monastery at Sopra Minerva—a library which is now open to the public, under certain regulations, there are the archives of the Roman Inquisition; the historical use which now can be made of them, appears in many numbers of *La Rivista Christiana*, in which I found many valuable extracts. Much interesting information respecting early Italian confessors may be found in those Inquisitionary records.

I saw several Protestant brethren in Rome; and, besides preaching in the Presbyterian Church twice, was invited to address a large meeting of Italians, through the medium of the Rev. Mr. Piggott, who was my kind interpreter. I took occasion to lament that Italian Protestants, whilst not by any means numerous, were broken up into so many parties; said that it would be far better if they would work together; and if that were impossible, it was at least desirable and easy, not to interfere with each other's proceedings, by opposition or uncivil criticism. Judging from a response on the part of an Italian, I was glad to find my remarks were not deemed offensive; but I am afraid they did no real good.

Whilst in Rome at this time I tried to turn my visit to some account by restudying its Christian antiquities. Christian art in its early state is a subject illustrated by the Catacombs. The rude paintings and sculptures familiar to every Roman visitor, familiar by means of books to thousands who have never seen the originals, are historical and symbolic. Noah and the Ark, Abraham offering up Isaac, Moses receiving the law, Jonah and the whale, Daniel and the lions, the three Hebrews in the furnace—these have a Christian meaning, and point typically to truths respecting Christ's redemption. Subterranean Rome, it has been well said by a French author, is "*a living book*, palpable, everlasting," and there are written on its pages, in hieroglyphic ways, truths which are held by all true Christians, whether Protestant or Catholic. The Agape or love-feast, a ship emblematic of the Church, the cross, the fish, the dove, and other well-known signs of Christ and His salvation, occur over and over again. Also there are historical pictures of the Nativity, and of Peter denying his Master. Portraits also are found of Christ, of Peter, of Paul. The Virgin Mary is seen by the side of her husband, whilst the Holy Child, like an Italian bambino, lies in His cradle, an ox licking His feet; close by, the Magi are watching stars in the east. No picture or image of the Virgin, in solitary magnificence, at all resembling the Madonnas of a later period, so far as I can make out, has been discovered in the Catacombs. The contrast between the early attempts and the later achievements of Roman Christian art in doctrinal significance, as well as in imaginative conception and technical skill, is obvious and striking. To pass from the former to the latter requires an immense stride; to go from examining early representations of gospel facts and principles, to look round churches and galleries rich in the works of modern Catholic artists, is to exchange worlds. The difference in religious meaning is as great as the difference in artistic merit.

During this visit to Rome some remarkable religious meetings were conducted by Dr. A. N. Somerville, of Glasgow, who in other parts of Italy the same spring, held revivalistic Protestant services. Those at Rome occurred on a spot, to reach which many citizens had to cross a bridge with a toll bar on it. Notwithstanding, on the evening when we attended, I should think about eight hundred people were present. The preacher could not speak Italian, and what he said was translated into that language, by a native Protestant. Everything was skilfully managed, and the effect appeared on the whole, solemn and impressive. Congregations after the same methods had been previously gathered in Florence, where the addresses, according to report, had produced considerable impression. Sankey's hymns, translated into Italian, were sung at Rome, with Sankey's tunes; how far solid evangelical results followed I could not ascertain.

We made, at this time, two excursions which I must notice. One was very short: only as far as Ostia, where there are still some Roman remains. The present town is not worth notice, but the ancient city, Hare says in his "Days near Rome," is like Pompeii. I cannot quite agree with him. The deep ruts of Roman chariot wheels; fragments here and there of Roman pottery, human bones, coloured marbles, and a few architectural relics, are of interest; but what attracted me to the spot was the memory of Augustine, who, in his "Confessions," paints such a touching picture of his mother Monica's illness and death. Thoughts of that interview, as related by the converted son, were the only charm of our visit, and the hour or two we were compelled to spend in the place, for the refreshment of our coachman and his horse, were most dreary. The long, long gossip going on between a priest and the mistress of the little farm, betokened the intense idleness and vulgarity of both,—typical, I fear, of the whole neighbourhood.

Another expedition we made was of a very different kind. We engaged a carriage to the charming haunts of Tivoli, where picturesque objects in the town and its vicinity, and the stupendous waterfall with manifold associations, clustering round the immediate neighbourhood, created memorable delight. Next day we drove to Subiaco, along an interesting road rich in memories of old Roman rural life. My daughter wrote in her journal :—

"It was a glorious morning, the sun was shining brightly, and in the cool spring air, our three pretty little black horses dashed along the road at a good pace, so that we soon found ourselves winding in and out amongst the Sabine Hills. We climbed up a steep ascent, only to go dashing down on the other side. The retreating hills, rising here and there to a great height, were clothed with trees, some of a sombre colour, some fresh with the bright hue of early spring, with here and there a cluster of silver olives, making a delightful variety of colour; whilst, at our feet, the roadside was beautiful with anemones, cyclamen, honeysuckle, and saxifrage; and, lower still, ran the refreshing river Arno."

Not far from Subiaco there is a deep gorge with sloping sides of rock and foliage, reaching down to the river Arno, bordered by chestnut trees, amidst which, here and there, rises a tall cypress. The brow of the hill on the side nearest Subiaco, is crowned by a far-famed monastery in which, very different from what it is now, the great St. Benedict, founder of a monastery which bears his name, spent his early days and prepared for his great life work, which began at Monte Cassino, on the road from Rome to Naples.

We left Subiaco for Olevano, and were benighted on our way, as the horses toiled up hill after hill. We reached Olevano late at night, and caused quite a commotion in the narrow street, by our inquiries after the hotel, where we were to pass the night, and which, ignorantly, we had passed by, at the hill-top which overlooks the town. There, to our delight, we met with a most enjoyable reception, as the house is a favourite resort for artists; and though we blundered into a room, already occupied by guests, we were permitted to remain, and listen to charming stories of the place and its surroundings. After tarrying a few hours next morning, we had to hasten our departure, that we might catch a train on the railway from Naples to Rome.

After leaving Rome on our way to England, we halted some days at Venice, and revived old recollections. I went over points of interest in a visit years before, and new pictorial and architectural pleasures were enjoyed. We proceeded to Bologna, and crossed the beautiful Lago di Garda, spent a day or two at Trent, where special services were being held for young people, and hosts of "shining ones" in white, crowded the churches.

In 1881 I visited Italy again, especially for the purpose of carrying on researches commenced just before. The journey was rapid. Reaching Turin, accompanied by my dear daughter, I began my work by searching out localities which I could easily identify. In other places I picked up illustrations I desired; for, when the mind is bent on a particular inquiry, it is wonderful how it draws cognate matters to itself. We made an excursion to Pavia, and, on the way, stopped at the beautiful monastery of Certosa. Pavia, situated on the river Ticino, with a covered bridge, is interesting, from its antiquities and history. The churches are specimens of Lombardic architecture, and in the Duomo one was startled to find the tomb of Augustine, Bishop of Hippo, whose remains were transferred from Africa to this city. They were there at the time of our visit, his monument being full of magnificence and beauty, in general form and particular details. Since I was at Pavia, the body has been restored to its original resting-place. Pavia connects itself with the philosopher, Boetius, by a popular tradition that he was imprisoned in a tower belonging to the city. Piacenza and Bologna during this journey afforded gleanings which helped me to realise important events occurring there at the time of the Reformation; but it was in Florence that I did most work, and spent more than a week from day to day tracking Savonarola's footsteps through the streets, from San Marco to the Palazzo Vecchio, and back again, not forgetting his visit to Lorenzo di Medici at his villa in Careggi, with views of rich woodlands and grassy fields. But my chief employment was in the public library, searching out and deciphering original documents, connected with his trial. According to one account Savonarola underwent an examination, first by words, then by threats, then by torture; and on the second day of his imprisonment was put on the rack. The account of the trial which I gathered from original sources, was in harmony with that of Villari in his life of the martyr. There are two letters appended, one addressed to the Pope respecting *la vita buono* of the sufferer, and another by a large number of Florentine citizens. I was especially interested in Savonarola's Bible, which he used to carry under his arm. It is entitled "Biblia integra," the type beautifully clear, the date 1491. It contains some of his prophecies in MS. Signor Guicciardini has contributed a large collection of Savonarola's works to this Magliabecchian Library, as it is called, and the catalogue of them runs over sixty pages.

After leaving Florence, we visited the Waldensian valleys, of which I have given some account in my "Footprints of Italian Reformers," and I may here add, that I agree fully with Professor Comba in his opinion, that the Waldenses, properly speaking, do not appear in history earlier than the twelfth century, and then they are seen scattered over the South of France at Metz, and in the Netherlands — their origin being ascribed by their enemies to Peter Waldo of Lyons, who does not appear to have visited the valleys. I found the good people in the valleys opposed to the results of Professor Comba's researches. An intelligent daughter of a Waldensian minister said, "We do not believe in them at all here." After studying the subject, let me add, I do.

In 1881 my dear friend Dr. Stanley died, after so short an illness that I had no opportunity of seeing him in his last hours. His funeral was an event of national interest.

He had much of the mind which distinguished "that disciple whom Jesus loved." His singular sweetness of disposition was partly natural, for he was a gentle, quiet boy, winning many hearts; but it was gracious and spiritual also, a result of sincere discipleship to the Divine Master. I often felt surprised at his extraordinary amount of forbearance under most unjust and cruel attacks. I once alluded to the need of patience amidst such trials, instancing Archbishop Tillotson, who left behind him a bundle of scurrilous letters, labelled with the words, "May God forgive the writers as I do." I learned from my friend that once he was accused of infidelity by an anonymous correspondent; and on another occasion, after the figures of Moses, David, Paul, and Peter had been placed in the choir of the Abbey, he received a note beginning with a charge of idolatry. Our Broad Church Dean, and the prelate of the Revolution were ecclesiastically and socially much alike. As to theology the former told me there is much in the teaching of Scripture which transcends human conception, much which, running along lines of mystery, he felt himself unable to follow; but, at the same time, he would remark, there is much more that is plain, which "a wayfaring man, though a fool," may receive and "not err therein." To these plain things, he said, he desired to cleave; these plain things he endeavoured to preach. The main difference between others and himself was that certain Evangelical principles were plainer to them than to him.

His interest in Bible study was intense, especially with regard to historical and biographical subjects; and it was well said, that whilst some critics seemed to delight in destroying certain parts, his delight was to build them up into a grand whole. His habit was to maintain truth, so far as he saw it, rather than to attack and overthrow error; and his gift of felicitously adapting events and passages of Holy Writ to passing incidents and characters, was truly wonderful; especially when an opportunity occurred for weaving sacred associations round the walls of his beloved Abbey. Nor did he fail to turn his skill in this respect to admirable account, when preaching in America.

Dr. Stanley's amiableness never betrayed a suspicion of weakness in his character. Indeed he had a side almost stern in some of its appearances; and he fought against what he deemed evil, with great vehemence; and stood up very boldly, I know, against unprincipled people, declaring that he would not meet them, except in the presence of witnesses.

To see him at his best was to be with him alone, when he gave full sway to his thoughts and feelings, expressing them with greater freedom than I ever heard him do in company. The most enjoyable time was late in the evening, after guests had retired; especially when he conducted me to my bedroom, candlestick in hand, and tarried for a good while chatting about subjects and persons of interest to us both.

Not long before his death, I spent a night at Westminster, when we talked about Oliver Cromwell. With much pathos he read aloud Carlyle's description of the Lord Protector's last hours; and, some time before this, he told me that he had been engaged in endeavouring to ascertain what became of the hero's remains after indignities done to them at the Restoration.

Soon after the Dean's death, I received from Mrs. Drummond, his executrix, a note accompanied by the picture it referred to. "In a memorandum left by our dear Dean, he desired a photograph of him, which used to stand in the drawing-room, should be sent to you, in remembrance of a sincere friendship."

With regard to the composition of historical works he was in the habit of employing such information as he could gather from friends.

Oxford men have told me, that he used to lay under contribution whatever he could learn from other people's researches. For these, however, he was always ready to make ample returns.

Dr. Stanley told me that he was in the habit of looking at some historical characters through the medium of living people, who appeared to him, in one way or other, to resemble them. Excellencies and frailties on the part of deceased individuals, thus came out more vividly before him. It struck me as a considerable help to a realisation of what departed persons *might* be ; but it requires to be carefully employed, lest from resemblances which are real, we infer other things which are imaginary.

His taste was comprehensive. He loved everything which related to English history, especially where it touched his own dear Abbey. Conformity and Nonconformity he sometimes sought to harmonise in surprising ways.

I may add here that there was in the Abbey a monument to Dr. Watts in a dilapidated condition, when I suggested a plan for its restoration. The plan was adopted, and in consequence the monument was for a time removed. During its absence I received a note containing a playful allusion to the circumstance :—

"If some strong Nonconformist should wander through the Abbey this week, he may go away with the impression that in a fit of sudden intolerance the Dean had torn down the monument of Isaac Watts. I assure you that the gaping and vacant chasm in the wall might well suggest such an interpretation. I hope, however, in a few days the restored angel and the mended harp of your sweet psalmist will dispel any hopes that may be awakened in High Churchmen or suspicions in Nonconformists."

I was informed not long after the Dean's death, that a gentleman in Kent had in his possession what was said to be Oliver Cromwell's skull. A friend of mine procured from that gentleman an invitation to see the relic. A large, handsome box was placed on a table, and out of it was taken, wrapped up in silk, a man's skull. The lower part of the face was gone, leaving the upper jawbone entire, or nearly so ; and within the mouth we saw the shrivelled remains of a tongue, while some of the skin on the upper part of the face was still preserved. What astonished me was the quantity of hair adhering to the scalp ; and also the following circumstances pertaining to the relic. The inside, carefully examined by a medical companion, plainly appeared to have been embalmed ; signs of this were attached to the surface. Moreover, part of a spike penetrated the upper bone, showing that once the skull must have been exposed in a way common enough, when men, put to death for political crimes, had their heads set up in conspicuous places. Finally the head had been severed from the body, not by a sharp axe, but by a knife which had hacked and torn the skin. These peculiarities pointed to one who, having received honourable burial, was afterwards beheaded with a blunt instrument, and then treated as a traitor, by having his head exhibited like those fixed on the top of Temple Bar. These peculiarities pertained to Oliver Cromwell; and to no one else. Documents are preserved together with the relic. They state that the relic remained publicly exposed for a long time, till one night a gale of wind blew it down; that a soldier on sentry picked it up and took it home, and then became alarmed at finding there was search made after it by public authorities. He concealed it down to the time of his death; and when danger was over, the secret was divulged. The skull was afterwards exhibited as a source of profit, and an account of the exhibition appears among papers preserved in the box. After being withdrawn from public view, it was privately sold to an ancestor of the gentleman possessing it at the time of my visit. There is a story afloat, that Cromwell was not buried in Westminster, another corpse being substituted for public interment, and, therefore, that the body hanged at Tyburn was not his! This story is not to be trusted.

In the August following Dean Stanley's death, I made, with my friend Harrison and some of my family, a tour in Germany. We were delighted with the Bavarian Highlands and the Bader See.

We visited Oberammergau, and heard much about the Passion Play, and were conducted to the place of performance, by persons who had taken part in it. They gave us interesting information. The priest of the place is no bigot. He insisted that a Protestant, who had died in the village, should be interred in consecrated ground, for which, we are told, he received a rebuke from Rome. The drive we had from Partenkirchen to Mittenwald called forth exclamations of great delight.

In the following winter I mixed with members of various denominations, some widely separated from others. This led me to think a good deal about consistency. I noted down at the time considerations of this kind. Everybody admits the palpable truism, "Truth is true, and falsehood is false," and some deduce from that the corollary: "Then stick to the true, and eschew the false altogether. Countenance what you believe, by consorting exclusively with such as believe as you do."

But, it must be remembered, systems are complex, and cannot be fairly dealt with in the fashion recommended by some. In many cases, what is condemned as a whole, contains seeds of another sort. There are estimable people who are not accustomed to analyse what they condemn, and cannot see what of truth may be found in the midst of error. To look alone at one side of a system, which, after all, has much of truth, may involve us in error. Thinking of Divine sovereignty, if not connected with human responsibility, may land us in Antinomianism; to dwell upon responsibility by itself, may make us Pelagians.

In the summer of 1882, I went down to Rodborough, in Gloucestershire, to visit my friend, Sir S. Marling, just made baronet, and to preach, I think, for the seventh time, on behalf of the Sunday Schools. The Countess of Huntingdon, George Whitefield, and Rowland Hill had all been in some way connected with the chapel.

On the occasion now mentioned, there was a large gathering of day and Sunday scholars, a picture worthy of Wilkie's pencil. Sir Samuel and his lady were encircled by guests old and young, receiving from them demonstrations of affection in loud huzzas.

Soon after my return from Italy I attended meetings connected with Wesleyan Methodism, when my friend Mr. McArthur, (afterwards knighted), was Lord Mayor of London. He invited me at different times to meet a large number of ministers of his own and other communions, and at such times he manifested the catholic spirit by which he was eminently distinguished. I think it was once in his mayoralty that the archbishops and bishops dined at the Mansion House table, when toasts were proposed, to which the Archbishop of Canterbury had to respond. Afterwards Nonconformists were honoured in the common way, and it fell to my lot to reply in a few words. The Archbishop had, in a good-natured style, referred to the cares and troubles of his right reverend brethren, and himself. Alluding to what he had said, I ventured to remark I was quite content with my humbler position, and had no aspirations after a seat on the Episcopal Bench. Further, I pleaded, as I always do, for catholic union, and remarked that I strove to be a Christian first; next, a patriotic religious Englishman; and thirdly, a devout Dissenter, adding that I should be ashamed of my Nonconformity, if that were so obstreperous, as to quarrel with the subordinate place I assigned to it.

At the close of the year 1882 Dr. Tait, Archbishop of Canterbury, died. With him I had the pleasure of being acquainted soon after his appointment to the See of London. Our relations afterwards were very friendly. I was kindly invited to share in the pleasure of his Lambeth hospitality; and at a time of deep domestic sorrow he was one of the very first to express affectionate sympathy in a letter of condolence. I found him always very kind, and he impressed me with the conviction that in his judgment of Conformity and Nonconformity, and of the relative duties of Churchmen and Dissenters, he took much more sensible views than most of his brethren. He did not seem to anticipate, as at all probable, the comprehension of all, or most, English Christians within the pale of one community; since each denomination has its principles, its traditions, and its trust property, and is not likely to merge its peculiarities in the adoption of others. A wise, liberal, Christian *modus vivendi* was the object of his desire. I attended his funeral, and met in his residence at Addiscombe, a large number of clergymen, and men of different opinions, drawn together by a common regard for his eminent moral and religious worth. The trees were bare, the ground was covered with snow, and the long procession walked through the park, the winter sun brightening the scene. The whole struck me as very solemn, and in harmony with the occasion that had brought us together.

My journeys abroad were approaching an end when in 1882 my daughter and I spent a few weeks in Switzerland, on the shores of the Genevan lake, and in its neighbourhood. One memorable expedition we made was to Grenoble and the Grande Chartreuse. The monastery was difficult of access early in this century, but now there are well-appointed vehicles for conveying tourists from the railway to the gates of this romantic retreat. The ascent as far as Laurent du Pont is up a road lined with acacias, bordering barley fields, commanding glimpses of a magnificent valley, with bosky dells, cut in twain by the river Isere. The gorge to the right increases in grandeur as one ascends. Purple rocks rise from depths of massy verdure, sublimity succeeds beauty, and, after reaching a broad mountain-girdled plain, one arrives at a halting place called Laurent du Pont. Thence the road becomes more steep, winding along ledges of rock, whence, through openings, one looks down on pine woods, and sees the stream fighting its way, like our contested passage through this troublesome world. We reached a thick forest at the top of the pass, and came to the monastery—a pile of buildings sheltered on green uplands. There were before us long walls, square towers, and steep roofs, dappled with dormer windows; here and there was a slender spire. The buildings stand 4268 feet above the level of the sea, and one of the corridors is 660 feet long. The original foundation dates far back; but little of what one now sees is older than the seventeenth century. The founder was the famous Bruno, who, with six companions, retreated to this spot so secluded and desolate. *Chartre* signifies a prison, but it also expresses what we mean by the word *charter*. The buildings have been seven times destroyed, but in the seventeenth century the convent reached its meridian glory.

No sooner had we entered the penetralia of the building, than we saw notices requesting visitors not to smoke, nor loiter, nor speak loudly; and in the distance were monks with white cloaks and cowls, gliding about like ghosts from the other world. Pictures of Carthusian convents were hanging on the corridor walls; and the Chapter House exhibited badly painted portraits of past generals. Following our guide, we entered a vaulted cloister, with windows on one side and doors on the other, bearing texts of Scripture, such as "Narrow is the way which leadeth unto life," and "Whosoever he be of you that forsaketh not all that he hath cannot be My disciple." Stations of the Cross are hung upon the walls; through a window are caught glimpses of a green garden, bright and cheery amidst sombre appearances all round. The dormitories have each a cupboard-like bed, a little reading desk, a stove, directions for novices, a statuette of the Virgin, and a crucifix. There are workshops fitted up with lathes, and a small chapel with an altar cloth, covered with skulls and crossbones. Inscriptions such as "Vanity of vanities, all is vanity," expressed the characteristic feeling of the inmates. The library is handsome, well fitted up, with beautifully bound books.

Visitors are not admitted to the monastic chapel; but from a tribune they are permitted to look down on the ante-chapel, and witness matins at the appointed hour. The brotherhood are remarkable for industry, being graziers of cattle, and manufacturers of liqueurs.

The clock struck six just after we left the monastery, and a calm summer evening shone on the old walls, the green pastures, and the climbing woods. The pass, as we descended, struck us as almost equal to the Via Mala in grandeur, united with beauties which the other scene can scarcely boast. Road-making, tree-felling, saw-mills, iron works, distilleries, cement manufactories, told of widespread industry. The old monastery lay behind; modern enterprise stood out before.

We were rapidly driven through Laurent du Pont, as the star-studded sky, streaked by the Milky Way, overarched the region. We noticed glow-worms in the hedges, brought out by advancing night, and presently the wide vale at the foot of the descending road seemed dusted with bright-looking objects like glow-worms; but they turned out to be the lamps of Voirons, where we took the train for Grenoble, and finished a day of remarkable interest.

CHAPTER XIV

1883—1885

AT this period I was engaged in the preparation of "The Spanish Reformers," and to give vividness to the work, with regard to local scenery and circumstances, I resolved in March 1883 to visit the Peninsula, where I might gather what was possible for the accomplishment of my purpose.

My daughter was my companion, and had been studying Spanish to render me assistance. We travelled through France on our way to the north-east of Spain.

We halted at Lyons: in the neighbourhood of it persecution occurred in the second century; but unlike what obtained in Spain three hundred years ago, it was not the persecution of one class of Christians by another, but the persecution of the Church by a heathen world. We find embedded in the Ecclesiastical History by Eusebius a document giving an account of sufferings by believers at that time who were in the neighbourhood of Lyons. Vienne, with its glass houses and metal foundries, coalpits and smoke, is now passed by travellers, without any interest; but in the second century it took precedence of Lyons, and had a flourishing Church, a member of which—Blandina, a maiden slave—suffered death as the penalty of her faith.*

We tarried a night at Lyons, drove round the city, saw the cathedral and other buildings, and ascended a hill on which stands the church of Notre Dame de Fourvières, covered and crowded with ex-votive offerings, in return for miraculous cures by the Virgin. From the elevation views are caught of extensive scenery. Thence we proceeded to Arles, rich in Roman remains, including a magnificent amphitheatre. The cathedral of St. Trophimus said to have been one of St. Paul's disciples, is an interesting specimen of twelfth or thirteenth century architecture. Thence we proceeded to Narbonne, a quaint old town, of importance in Roman times, with ramparts still of some interest, and quaint streets, through which we had an evening's ramble. The cathedral of St. Just is an unfinished edifice of

* Eusebius, "Eccl. Hist.," V. 1, 2.

the thirteenth century, with some good tracery in the windows. The city is distant from the sea only about eight miles. Thence we proceeded to Perpignan, and, entering Spain, reached our destination at Figueras, where we were kindly welcomed by our friends,* who are engaged in evangelistic work amongst Roman Catholic Spaniards.

Figueras is a considerable town, which greatly interested us. It was the day before Good Friday that we arrived, and we were much amused by a number of boys with wooden mallets vehemently beating the pavement, which was explained to us as a custom indicative of hatred to the Jews for having crucified our Lord; what the Jews had to do with Figueras I could not make out. In the evening there was a procession through the streets of a truly magnificent description. It consisted of the gentry in the town, attired in antique Spanish costumes, and presented an imposing spectacle. Ladies personated the Virgin Mary and other Scripture characters, and numerous candles carried by attendants made a splendid illumination. On the following day, Good Friday, we had a drive into the country, where we saw and heard of what went on in the way of missionary work conducted by our zealous

* Pastor and Madame Rodriguez.

friends. In the evening we visited a neighbouring church which was illuminated, and crowded with people engaged in religious service. After this, we saw in the streets a long procession, including penitents, who were fettered with chains.

From Figueras we travelled to Barcelona, a city rich in commercial enterprise and wealth, the streets crowded with people and enlivened by carriages of grandees and wealthy merchants, as well as by vehicles employed in humble traffic. The cathedral is a noble edifice, in which we attended Divine worship on Easter Sunday. A priest with difficulty made his way through a densely-crowded congregation to the altar steps, where he knelt and prayed, and then mounted a temporary pulpit. As soon as he opened his lips, all eyes were turned towards him. His voice was marvellous and his attitudes were graceful; sometimes he was persuasive, then indignant, always earnest; women wept, tears ran down men's cheeks. The sermon was on our Lord's resurrection. He insisted on our duty to remember Christ—"the Way, the Truth, and the Life"; and he showed the effect of this on the hearts and lives of believers. He dwelt on the duty of repentance, and urged people to come to Christ. In a touching manner he referred to his own experience, and exhorted the congregation to believe, pray, and obey the Gospel; saying over and over again, "*Haber fè, fè, fè*"—"Have faith, faith, faith."

I met with signs of Protestant work going on in Barcelona, and a gentleman residing there at the time, told me of what the British and Foreign Bible Society was doing in Spain. He gave it, as his opinion, that it exceeded other instrumentalities in the efficiency of its service. I find it stated by a Spanish author, that Barcelona abounds in mendicancy, and I have, as I write, a woodcut before me representing a pitiable crowd of beggars at one of the cathedral doors.*

Next to Barcelona, we visited Tarragona, travelling there by rail. Tarragona is situated on an eminence commanding a fine view of the Mediterranean, and I was much interested in the architecture of the cathedral, a building of the eleventh century, fully described by Street in his work on "The Gothic Architecture of Spain."

Whilst tarrying at Tarragona, I made an excursion to Poblet, rarely visited by English, though frequented by French and German travellers. This place is distinguished by monastic remains of extraordinary magnificence. You wander

* De Aniccio, "L'Espagne traduit de Italien."

amongst courts, cloisters, and dormitories, through stately halls, which once boasted of a magnificent library rich in MSS.; through a palace appropriated for the use of royal and noble visitants; and through a stately church with a nave of seven bays. The architectural grandeur of the whole is amazing; I was surprised to learn that it is so rarely seen by our countrymen. Kings and nobles were brought there for interment, and in that respect it vies with our Westminster Abbey. At Poblet shattered tombs may still be seen; and few, if any, but Spaniards of purest blood, were permitted to sleep within the monastic walls. A marble slab may be seen covering the remains of an Englishman, described in the Spanish guide book as "Felipe de, Marquése de Malbursi y de Cacharloch," etc. Wharton was the English name of this well-known personage, who was made Knight of the Garter by James II. He had become a Roman Catholic, but his father was a distinguished English Nonconformist.

Our next destination was Valencia, to which city we travelled by rail, enchanted as we approached it, by beautiful scenery which one does not find abundant in Spain. Augustus Hare breaks out rather rapturously respecting his approach: "Day broke in time to show us the first vision of tall palms, with their feathery foliage, rising black against one of Tennyson's 'daffodil skies,' which above, still deep blue, was filled with stars." The groves and gardens appeared to me very beautiful; and the soil is so fertile, that lucerne is sown fifteen times in the course of a year. Valencia has battlemented walls; and its arched gate, the Puerta de Sarranos, reminds one of old English barbicans. It is an Oriental kind of place, and has charmingly arched entrances for light—*agimes*, —*i.e.*, openings by which the sun enters. The city is full of memories, connected with the Cid, which I have not space to introduce; but I may mention that precursors of the Reformation entered the city in 1350,—under the name of Beghards, who figure rather prominently in the religious history of that period.

The Cathedral of Valencia is a noble edifice, and has one magnificent entrance of richly decorated Gothic. There is, in the Colegio del Patriarca, a ceremony every week on Friday, which attracts a number of people. It consists in letting down an altar piece by concealed machinery; and then, by withdrawing a curtain, there is disclosed a large picture of our Saviour on the Cross. Those who assemble to witness this ceremony, are required to appear in mourning. I explored the city from end to end, and found it by no means so uninteresting as some represent it.

We started in the evening for Cordova, a long distance; but as it was accomplished in darkness, I noticed nothing by the way, except stoppages at stations and a change of trains. We crossed the Sierra Morena, which, in some places, at least, must be very magnificent, if one may judge from an engraving of tall rocks facing each other, leaving scarcely room for muleteers to pass between. The approach to Cordova is inviting, and the Moorish city is beheld amidst a fertile region, across which runs the Guadalquivir.

We had been invited to take up our abode with an exemplary Scotch missionary in the city. The sojourn was in a quiet street at a comfortable dwelling, with an open space in the middle of the residence, planted with shrubs. Upon this we looked down from windows in our apartments. One room on the ground floor is sufficiently large to receive a congregation of about fifty people. We were there on a Sunday and attended worship in the evening.

The Mosque of Cordova, now a cathedral, is one

of the most wonderful buildings in the world. The surrounding walls are from thirty to sixty feet high. The courtyard measures 430 feet by 210. Once there were nineteen entrance gates, now there is but one. Formerly there were inside the mosque 1200 monolithic columns, now there are only 850. What is the *coro*, or choir, of the cathedral, was erected in the sixteenth century, after the Mohammedan mosque had become a Catholic church. We had pleasant walks and drives in the neighbourhood.

The next celebrated place in our route was the far-famed Granada, of which expectations were highly raised, without any disappointment. We wandered about the Alhambra for several days. The Hall of the Lions, the Hall of the Ambassadors, and the Hall of the Abencerrages,—with their arches and columns, courts and colonnades, fountains and flowers,—kept us spel-bound day by day. We read Washington Irving on the fascinating spots which he describes so vividly. We could but bow to his relentless fidelity, where he assures us that, after examining Arabic authorities and letters, written by Boabdil's contemporaries, he was convinced, that the whole collection is fictitious with a few grains of truth at the bottom.

The fame of the Alhambra swallows up all which is wonderful in Granada, but, the city retains much besides worthy of a traveller's attention. The prospect you have of the place, the plain, and the surrounding hills, is magnificent; and the cathedral, commenced in 1529, after the defeat and banishment of the Moors, is a building of architectural interest. It contains the Capella Real, with the tomb of Ferdinand and Isabella; also of Philip the Handsome, and his wife Juana, "Crazy Jane," as she was called, mother of the famous Charles V. The granddaughter tells us: "She committed her soul to God and gave thanks to Him, that, at length, He delivered her from all her sorrows." In connection with the cathedral, we meet with Fernando de Talavera, better known by Spaniards than by Englishmen. Though he remained a Roman Catholic, he deviated from the common opinions and usages of his age. The Carthusians have a monastery outside the city, and on visiting it, I found pictures of English priests, reported to have been martyrs at the period of the Reformation. No doubt their sufferings are exaggerated on the monastic walls, but it is a fact, beyond reasonable doubt, that there were Roman Catholics put to death by English Protestants.

We started one morning from Granada for Seville,

and, on crossing the Vega by the railway, we saw a good barley crop in the month of April. At Bobadillo, we got on the Seville line, and found the country improve as we came near to the city on the banks of the Guadalquivir. There, instead of antique and uncomfortable *fondas*, travellers meet with spacious and well-furnished hotels. We tarried several days in the city.

The cathedral, of course, was the first object of interest; and, as soon as possible, we repaired to it, and received an overpowering impression, as we looked above, beneath, around. Above there is the magnificent roof, spanning the breadth of the temple; beneath there lies a large slab covering the remains, not, as sometimes supposed, of Columbus, who discovered America, but of Fernando, his son. In Holy Week an immense Greek cross, carved in wood, is raised over the spot, and lighted up so as to produce an indescribable effect. The *coro*, or choir, is as grand, though in another way, as the nave which leads up to it. In an upper part of the edifice there are preserved MSS. and other memorials of unrivalled Spanish discoveries, and they were freely shown to us. We went to the Museum, and feasted on Murillo's pictures. We were also taken by a friend to see another work of the same artist, since presented, I am told, to the Pope.

Seville was headquarters of the Protestant cause. The Reformation did not penetrate much below the hidalgo class. It left the masses almost untouched. In Seville stood the Inquisition prison, till it was removed to a palace in the Calle san Mario. "Here," says Mr. Wiffen in 1842, "while gazing on the edifice with feelings of awe, I recalled to remembrance those martyrs for the truth, and, at the same time, I listened with painful interest to the narration made to me by a Spanish gentleman, of an attack on those very premises at a recent period by an infuriated populace, who suffered but few of the friars confined there for political offences, to escape with life. The building having taken fire some perished in the flames, while others fell by the hands of the assassins." The tables were turned just then, priests were in prison for political crimes, as heretics had been incarcerated in the sixteenth century.

Old Venetian political policy was carried out against Protestantism, and the Inquisition office, with opened ears, listened for whisperings of heresy. Horrors went on in secret places. I cannot relate them, but they may be found in what is written by Limborch and Llorente. A few miles from Seville is the monastery of San Isidore—the cradle of the Spanish Reformation—and I visited the building with deep interest. The chapel remains in tolerable repair, and is used as a parish church. The chapter-house, sacristy and cloisters are preserved. Ancient pictures hang on the walls, and old embroidered vestments are shown to visitors. Bibles and Protestant books were of old secretly brought within the walls, and monks began to read them.

I have described Seville Cathedral and its treasures at some length in my volume on "Spanish Reformers, their Memories and Dwelling Places." I cannot repeat here what has been said there. But let me say, the city is full of interest to travellers, hotels are comfortable, shops are well stocked with curiosities, manufactories are hives of industry, and pictures by great masters are found in churches and private houses. I was enchanted with some of the Murillos, and would advise every traveller to visit the Sala de Murillo in Seville.

I should have been glad to have prolonged my stay, and to have revisited spots full of historic interest. But I had much before me to see and study in the interior and north of Spain; therefore, though unwillingly, we took the train one night for Madrid, making that a starting point for other explorations.

I may mention that during our stay at Madrid we were entertained in a curious straggling house, occupied by Dr. Fliedner, a minister, who acted as chaplain to the German Embassy. The house, it is said, was occupied by the famous Escovedo, secretary to the still more famous Don Juan of Austria; and one night as he was returning home six ruffians waylaid him, between eight and nine o'clock, and inflicted on him wounds, of which he died in half an hour. Peres, a great villain who hated Don Juan, is said to have obtained the sanction of Philip II. for this abominable deed, prompted by the discovery of an amour between Escovedo and the Princess of Eboli. It is a horrible story of crime and vice, common in the secret annals of Spain.

In Madrid I had the privilege of using the public library, and found there a large collection of English and French, as well as Spanish, literature. I am sorry to say, that on the shelves, many volumes in our language appeared, written by "advanced thinkers," tending to the diffusion of anti-Christian principles. And, in the windows of booksellers I noticed works for sale of the same description. The Bible Society I found at work within limits marked by law, and I attended one evening a Spanish congregation gathered by Protestant agency, and had the privilege of addressing those present, through the medium of an interpreter. I met with specimens of Spanish superstition which were very degrading. In one case I saw papers, with a figure of the Virgin's shoe printed upon them, sold to ignorant people as a sacred charm.

The Plaza at Madrid is a magnificent square, encompassed by a line of handsome buildings with a garden, fountains, and an equestrian statue of Philip III. in the middle. Here some of the *autos* were held in the seventeenth century, and in 1869 excavations were made, where incontestable proofs of burnings appeared in bones, charred wood, chain links, nails and rivets discovered in the soil. Dr. Manning, in his "Spanish Pictures," wrote soon after the discovery: "I visited the spot, and much as I had heard of the horrors of the Quemadore, I was not prepared for the sight I beheld; layer above layer, like the strata of a geological model, were these silent, but most eloquent witnesses of the murderous cruelty of Rome."

I may here add that I saw other mementoes of the Spanish Inquisition in underground vaults connected with a house occupied by the Rev. Mr. Jameson, a Presbyterian clergyman at work in Madrid. I found recesses walled up, which it was said had been cells in the days of persecution.

Of course, I visited the immense picture-gallery

in Madrid; but the size and number of rooms with multitudes of paintings on the walls, were so bewildering, as to make only a confused impression on my mind. Spanish art has not the charm for me which it has for many. Velasquez and Murillo, of course, are pre-eminent. The latter stands first of all in my estimation. No one, who has seen only the dirty beggar boys at Dulwich, can have any conception of Murillo's merits. It is in Seville, however, that he must be studied, if any one would see him at his best. I found no Murillo in Madrid which charmed me like those it was my privilege to enjoy in the Capital of the South. There is a good chapter on Velasquez and Murillo in Sir E. Head's "Handbook of Painting—Spanish School."

"Velasquez and Murillo are preferred, and preferred with reason, to all the others, as the most original and characteristic of their school. These two great painters are remarkable for having lived in the same time, in the same school, painted for the same people and of the same age, and yet to have formed two styles so different and opposite that the most unlearned can scarcely mistake them, Murillo being all softness, while Velasquez is all sparkle and vivacity." *

---

* "Life of Wilkie," p. 472.

A curious story is told of a picture by Velasquez—the portrait of Adrian Pulido Pareja. Philip IV. coming, as usual, to see the artist at work, started when he saw this portrait, and addressing himself to it, exclaimed: "What, art thou still here? Did I not send thee off? How is it thou art not gone?" But seeing the figure did not salute him, the King discovered his mistake, and, turning to Velasquez, said: "I assure you I was deceived."

We visited the Escorial some distance from Madrid. Philip II. is buried there. Its situation is wild and desolate—a vast expanse of undulations, scarcely to be called mountainous, except in the distance, where snow-streaked sierras send cutting blasts over the slate roofs and against the grey stone walls. The building itself looks like a manufactory, at best like spacious barracks; one may think it something between a prison and a convent, or rather a combination of the two; at any rate its cold, stern, repulsive exterior is a fair type of the builder's character and influence. The only objects of much interest, and they are in truth most melancholy, one finds in the monkish apartments, the monastic chapel, and the costly sepulchre of the founder and his family. A long and narrow room is shown with brick floor and leathern chairs, where he dined. Next to it is another, only separated by folding doors, from which, when open, the despot borrowed the light by which he wrote his despatches. In this room is a plain oak table, with three brass ink bottles on one side, and a velvet writing-case in the middle; these, with the leather-bottomed chair on which he sat, are carefully preserved. From this room you pass into a third, low and dark, a mere cell, whence through an opening in the wall, the altar of the monastery chapel may be seen; there he spent his last hours, after being, like his prototype Herod, smitten by an angel of the Lord, and eaten up of worms; no death could be more horrible. That chapel is an enormous marble building, most costly, most dreary, and into one corner of the *coro* he would sometimes steal, to perform his devotions with the Jeronymite brotherhood. The sepulchre under the high altar is reached by a slippery marble staircase; and round the sides of the vault are placed sarcophagi, one above another; Charles V. occupies the topmost position, Philip being placed under his father. The dismalness of the spot is unrelieved by any emblem or suggestion of Christian hope: not even such a ray falls over it as that which lighted up the mind of the heathen Cicero, when he spoke of meeting in the future life an assembly of noble souls.

Toledo is about forty miles from Madrid, and is easily reached by rail. Scenery on the way is uninteresting till you get near the city, when, crossing the bridge over the Tagus, you are reminded of the rocky seat on which sits Durham Cathedral. Winding through narrow streets of the city and past Moorish-looking entrances into courts, called *patios*, I thought Toledo was a sort of album, with ornamented leaves on one side, and romantic legends on the other. At the foot of St. Martin's bridge lies a cave, where Roderic, the last of the Goths, saw the lady whose seduction caused the Moorish invasion; which invasion robbed the monarch of his crown. The cathedral is grand indeed. The cloisters are full of rich tracery, elegant pilasters crowned with statuettes, and open windows adorned by elaborate tracery. The interior is worthy of its surroundings and its approach; and I was deeply interested in the Mozarabic chapel. There is preserved a thin folio, bearing the name of the chapel, and containing a Latin service, used there every day. With it is connected an absurd tradition, the story and meaning of which are disputed by archæologists. With the cathedral you have connected the name of Bartolomo Carranza, called the Black Friar, whose long story is entwined round the Council of Trent, and with Philip of Spain, who married the English Queen Mary. He attended Charles V. on his deathbed, and was accused of heresy; and yet the Pope raised for him a monument in commemoration of his virtues. It is said Carranza believed in the doctrine of Justification by Faith; and his history from beginning to end appears to me a hopeless puzzle.*

In Toledo is the "Square Market," as it is called; and here occurred bullfights and burnings, —one of the latter in 1560, when Philip II. was present.

We returned from Toledo to Madrid and leaving the capital, a week or so afterwards, travelled to Valladolid. The chief, indeed the only, architectural monument in Valladolid is found in the combined edifices of San Pablo's Church, and San Gregorio's College. The facade of the former is an elaborate example of Gothic flamboyant; but the gateway of the latter with its heraldic ornaments,

---

* I have gone into this story in my "Spanish Reformers." p. 185.

coats of arms, statues in niches, and numerous figures, has a bewildering effect. Columbus and Cervantes both resided in this city; the former died in the Calle de Colon, the latter wrote the first part of "Don Quixote" in the Calle de Rastro.

Ford, in his voluminous "Guide to Spain," at the beginning of a notice respecting Valladolid, says: "In the first street, above the bridge, is the site of the old Inquisition, the Court of Chancery, and the prison"; adding the remark: "The great Chancery or Court of Appeal for the north of Spain was moved to the present building by Ferdinand and Isabella. The inscribed motto, '*Jura fidem ac pœnam reddit sua munera cunctus*'—seems rather strong, to all who know what Spanish *justitia* is, let alone Chancery in general."

Incipient stages of reformation come before us in this city. One sees in imagination "The Calle del Doctor Cazalla," of Jewish extraction, a man of renown for his Protestant work, born in 1510; he had been Court preacher and champion of orthodoxy, until he came under the influence of German reformers. But he seems by no means to have been a Martin Luther, for, when he was accused of dogmatising in a Valladolid conventicle, he solemnly denied the fact, and said he had not *indoctrinated* other people with his own views. His end was not heroic. After being dislocated on the rack, he recanted with a hope of life, but he found no escape. The night before his execution, when acquainted with the final sentence, the poor man said, " I must prepare to die in the grace of God, for it is impossible for me to add to what I have said, without falsehood." We learn that, after all, he did not break with Rome, but received absolution ; and then, instead of being burnt, he was strangled. His house was pulled down, the spot strewn with salt, and a column placed where the building had stood. An inscription upon it stated : " Lutheran heretics assembled here in conventicle against the Catholic faith and the Roman Church." A namesake, Francesco de Vibero Cazalla, more valiant for the truth, remained constant to the last. Another martyr behaved heroically, only lamenting that his wife abjured, and he saw her dressed as a penitent. But we are told the husband's look never departed from her eyes. In my " Spanish Reformers " I have given a detailed account of several sufferers for the truth at Valladolid.

Of the cathedral, Street, in his work on " Spanish

Architecture," says: "Nothing could ever cure the hideous unsightliness of the exterior"; and he adds: "The side elevation remains as Herrera, the architect, designed it, and is really valuable as *a warning.*" The author describes Sta. Maria l'Antigua, close to the cathedral, as the most attractive church in Valladolid. He says of the city: "It was too rich and prosperous, during an age of much work, and little taste, to have left mediæval architecture of any real value; yet as a modern city it is, in parts, gay and attractive; being, after Madrid, the most important city of the north of Spain." From what I saw of the place, I can endorse this opinion.

We reached Burgos, after a short journey, and found the town much less interesting and agreeable than Valladolid, but the cathedral is incomparably superior. The picture of its facade, doors, windows, and towers, is vividly imprinted on my memory.

We were now approaching the border of France, and I had memories revived of a first dip into Spain, years before. Though the land be still the same and the skies the same, different feelings arise from departure out of a country, compared with one's entrance into it. We reached a new and very comfortable hotel at San Sebastian, and there I revived recollections of curiosity and interest, felt years before, when I first crossed the border and became acquainted with the costumes, the manners and customs of Spanish life.

CHAPTER XV

1885

THIS year I paid my third and last visit to Rome. A comparison of the city and neighbourhood as they were during my first visit with what now appeared, was very striking. Formerly it retained much of the appearance it had in the previous century. There were narrow streets, bad pavements, old-fashioned houses; monks and friars of different orders, white, black, grey, thronging thoroughfares; cardinals' coaches with liveried servants, in gay coats and cocked hats; the Pope, driving down the Corso, whilst the whole population watched him with reverence on bended knees: now these old sights had vanished; comparatively few ecclesiastics could be recognised by their costumes; only companies of boys, in red or blue collegiate garb, attracted attention by contrast with other people. At Easter in the olden time the ceremonies at St. Peter's were gorgeous, the illumination of the dome brilliant, the fireworks in the Piazza del Popolo unrivalled : now Mass on Easter Sunday was far from imposing, there was no feet washing, no dinner to poor pilgrims, no *Miserere* in the Sistine chapel, no blaze of candles in the Pauline. The Forum had formerly lines of trees, groups of cattle, peasants in rural costume; now marble sculptures had been brought to light. The neighbourhood of St. John Lateran had been waste and void; now it was covered with modern houses. What a change in the Fontana, outside Rome, the traditional site of St. Paul's martyrdom. The monastery, when I had seen it before was desolate, now it was surrounded by abundant vegetation; the culture of the eucalyptus plant being the secret of this transformation.

Hare laments, in the following strain, changes which had occurred in the city and were to be regretted :—

"The baths of Caracalla, stripped of all their verdure and shrubs, and deprived alike of the tufted foliage amid which Shelley wrote, and of the flowery carpet which so greatly enhanced their lonely solemnity, are now a series of bare featureless walls standing in a gravelly waste, and possess no more attraction than the ruins of a London warehouse. The Coliseum, no longer 'a garlanded ring,' is bereaved of everything which made it so lovely and so picturesque; while botanists must for ever deplore the incomparable and strangely unique 'Flora of the Coliseum,' which Signor Rosa has caused to be carefully annihilated; even the roots of the shrubs having been extracted by the firemen, though, in pulling them out, more of the building has come down than five hundred years of time would have injured. In the Basilica of Constantine, the whole of the beautiful covering of shrubs with which nature had protected the vast arches, has been removed, and the rain soaking into the unprotected upper surface, will soon bring them down. Nor has the work of the destroyer been confined to the Pagan antiquities, the early Christian porches of S. Prassede and S. Pudenziana, with their valuable terra-cotta ornaments, have been so smeared with paint and yellow-wash as to be irrecognisable; many smaller but precious Christian antiquities, such as the lion of the Santi Apostoli, have disappeared altogether. And in return for these destructions and abductions Rome has been given—what? Quantities of hideous false rock-work painted brown in all the public gardens; a Swiss cottage and a clock which goes by water forced in amidst the statues and sarcophagi of the Pincio; and the having the passages of the Capitol painted all over with the most flaring scarlet and blue, so as utterly to destroy the repose and splendour of its ancient statues."

We visited a very old house in the Ghetto, where at the time services were held by a company of Jewish converts. Rude, uncomfortable and mean, the place looked to any one accustomed to modern churches; yet that dreary apartment, up a flight of stairs, was typical of places for Christian worship in the imperial city of the second century. Few fashionable people know the existence of the room I mention, and attendants shyly ascend the dirty steps, wishing to be unobserved; just so, no doubt, it was with some of the companies in the second century who in Rome " sang praises to Jesus as to God." In the reigns of Trajan, Hadrian, Antoninus Pius, and Marcus Aurelius, little was known about the Gospel by the higher ranks. Emperors, consuls, magistrates, marched along the streets in haughty indifference, or with contemptuous hate towards the new superstition.

Much inquiry has arisen as to where Paul lived during his captivity in Rome. A local tradition affirms that in a subterranean church dedicated to the Virgin Mary, which you pass going down the Corso, you have the very "hired house," where for two years the Apostle lived. In the crypt-like place, there is nothing which looks like a human dwelling; and the tradition itself, in a city where such traditions abound, is of little if any value. A house in the Ghetto, extremely ancient, was pointed out to me by Dr. Philip, a Jewish missionary, as the probable spot; but his idea seems to have had nothing to rest upon, except that this old building is in the Jews' quarter. What is fatal to the identification of the "hired house" in either of these spots is that the New Testament indicates it as connected with lodgings occupied by the Pretorian guard. The "soldier that kept him" would not be far away from comrades; and soldiers in general would be accommodated in the Pretorian camp, of which traces exist near the Porta Pia—a long distance from the Corso and the Ghetto.

My third visit to Rome was the close of my foreign travels. A word more in reference to them. Most frequently on my way to other countries, I passed through France to Paris, either by Calais and Amiens, or by Havre and Rouen. Let me refer for a moment to the cathedral at Amiens, one of the wonders of the world — the largest place of worship I know, except Cologne Cathedral, St. Peter's at Rome, and St. Sophia at Constantinople. It takes away one's breath to look up at its rich clerestory, and its roof, 140 feet high, half as high again as that of Westminster Abbey. Rouen has architectural beauty, and an historical interest beyond other French cities. The Church of St. Ouen surpasses the cathedral, and the Palais de Justice is a beautiful specimen of Civic Gothic. But associations of what happened in that city, during the fifteenth century, surpass its material monuments. Poor Joan of Arc—most touching example of self-delusion and self-sacrifice the world ever saw—how she absorbs interest as one stands in the Place de Pucelle, where she was burnt, the victim of French ingratitude and English revenge! Paris is so well known by everybody that no notice need be taken of it here.

We now return to Great Britain.

In the autumn of 1885 the Evangelical Alliance met at Edinburgh and Glasgow, and in the latter city I was entertained by the Lord Provost, Sir William and Lady Collins, and met there, Admiral Sir W. King Hall and his lady, with whom a pleasant friendship sprang up, and I accepted an invitation to visit them at their home, but his death soon afterwards deprived me of the anticipated pleasure. They appeared to me spiritually minded people; their society with that of our excellent host and hostess filled me with great pleasure. At the meeting I lamented, as I am accustomed to do, our numerous ecclesiastical divisions. "Here we are as Christians connected with denominational churches, and we may be compared to persons living in an island city, where we have our own municipal regulations, where some are in what may be called Episcopalian Square, some occupying Methodist Terrace, some residing in Congregational Road, and some liking to live by the waterside. Whilst these differences exist amongst us in this world, surely it sometimes crosses our minds that they are distinctions of a very temporary nature. The things which are seen are temporal, but the things not seen are eternal. We are looking away from what is familiar to what is now rare indeed —perfect unity."

I have long found it to be one of the sorrows incident to old age to lament the loss of attached friends. In this respect I was much tried in the year 1886, for I had then to deplore the death of Lord Chichester, who became acquainted with me through the medium of the Evangelical

Alliance about twenty years before. Of late he was unable to attend meetings, but our intercourse in private continued and increased as years rolled on. Descendant of Sir John Pelham, who figured in the French wars, described by Froissart, and an immediate relative of a well-known political family of the same name in the last century,—the Earl became an earnest Christian and an active philanthropist for more than half a century. Possessed of wide and varied information respecting men and things, and being eminently genial and altogether free from ostentation, his society could not but be agreeable and instructive. It was a treat to hear him recount incidents and conversations of former days. At different times he brought within view George IV., William IV., the Duke of Wellington, leaders of the Whig party, and other magnates. He told me that when approaching his majority his father proposed that he should enter the House of Commons, and the Duke of Newcastle promised him a seat for Newark. Before an election arrived the father of young Lord Pelham died, and the son became a peer. It is remarkable that the seat intended for him in the Lower House was next occupied by the now famous William Ewart Gladstone. "The Grand Old Man," in conversation with my friend not long before his death, speculated, in his characteristic way, upon possible consequences to each, had the seat been accepted by young Lord Pelham. With the Hare family, the Osbornes of the ducal house of Leeds, the Rev. F. D. Maurice, and other distinguished persons, the Earl had been intimate, and could tell many a story about them. Though a thorough Evangelical, and zealous for all the great truths of Christianity, he was singularly free from prejudice against people of different views. He could appreciate goodness wherever it was to be found.

The Prince Regent, with old Queen Charlotte, paid a visit to Stanmer, the family seat, near Brighton, when the Earl was a boy, and an amusing picture in one of the rooms exhibits his Royal Highness in dandy fashion—his diminutive mother wearing a wonderful bonnet, the former earl acting as cicerone, and his eldest boy riding on a smart pony. The Stanmer Pelhams are descended, on the female side, from Oliver Cromwell, and have in their possession the Lord Protector's Bible in four volumes, a miniature of him, which, I think, belonged to Lady Falconbridge, and a portrait of His Highness's mother. It is curious to find these Commonwealth relics associated with mementoes in the family arms,—I refer to the buckle and strap of Sir John Pelham, who assisted in taking King John of France prisoner at the battle of Poitiers. In addition to these memorials, mention may be made of a fine copy in the library of Walton's "Polyglot," with the rare preface containing a reference to Oliver Cromwell.

Soon after the death of Lord Chichester I lost another friend, Mr. Cheetham, M.P. His daughters were educated at Kensington, and hence an intimacy sprang up between us, cultivated by visits to Eastwood, near Staleybridge, where he resided. He was a shrewd, energetic man, and figured conspicuously in the Anti-Corn Law League. His command of the Lancashire dialect, and his knowledge of Lancashire life, made him an amusing companion, and Lord John Russell would sometimes engage him in characteristic recitals, greatly to his lordship's diversion. Mr. Cheetham had in early life known much of the Moravians, and ever retained a deep interest in that remarkable community, though to the end of life he remained a constant member of the Congregational communion. I have long been of Dr. Johnson's mind: "If a man does not make new acquaintances as he advances through life, he will soon find himself left alone. A man, sir, should keep *his friendships in constant repair.*" On that principle I have habitually sought to make up for losses from bereavement.

Here let me add a few lines respecting the Archbishop of York, Dr. Magee, previously Bishop of Peterborough.

I first met him at Norwich where we took part in a Bible Meeting, and in the course of my remarks I spoke of "sinking ecclesiastical differences" on such an occasion. Dr. Magee, then Dean of Cork, made an amusing reference to this, and repeated it with kindness and humour the next day, as we travelled together by rail to London. We talked incessantly and at the end he pressed me to visit him at Cork. Several years passed without our meeting, and then at a funeral service in Westminster Abbey, he kindly accosted me, saying, that as I had not been to see him at Cork, I must go and see him at Peterborough, where, not long before, he had been appointed bishop. Several visits followed, which I greatly enjoyed. My impression of him as a brilliant talker, which I received on our journey from Norwich to London, was now increased, and nothing could exceed his hospitality and that of his amiable wife and daughters. We had several drives; and one day we sat down together in a picturesque churchyard to discuss ecclesiastical questions, where, as he said, the associations and "*genius loci*" were on his side. I forget altogether what passed between us, beyond a series of *pros* and *cons*, and can only say that we finished as we began—he a Churchman, I a Nonconformist, but both good friends. Once when I was at Peterborough I heard him preach in the Cathedral for the Bible Society, on the jubilee of the auxiliary, when he took for his text two passages: "Is not this the carpenter's son?" "The Word was made flesh, and dwelt among us, and we beheld His glory, the glory as of the only begotten of the Father, full of grace and truth." He admirably brought out the Divine and human sides of our blessed Lord's personality and then presented this as being in harmony with the Divine and human elements in Holy Writ. As is well known, he did not use a MS. in the pulpit; nor, as he told me, was he in the habit of *writing* his sermons beforehand. He seems to have had the gift of mental composition, and also of expressing himself extemporaneously in felicitous diction and with quiet ease. Nor was he at all verbose, as many fluent speakers are.

He could tell a story as few people can, sparkling with humour, and distinct in point. I remember two he told of Dean Mansel. Taking a lady round St. Paul's, she paused to look at a figure of Neptune with his *trident*, remarking that she was shocked at seeing in a church such heathen mythology. "Why," rejoined the Dean, "that looks more like *Tridentine* theology." At a public dinner, after a toast to Reform—the word on the paper had an *e* at the end—"Reform," the Dean remarked, "often ended in an *émeute.*"

As I was preparing for my journey in Spain I met the Bishop at the Athenæum, when he told me he was doing the same, and proposed we should go together, adding that he could help me with his knowledge of Spanish. I had heard him speak of his residence in Spain when he was a boy, and I should have been delighted to fall in with his plan, but found it quite impossible beforehand with regard to time. However, we agreed to inquire after each other at consular offices, as we passed from place to place; but I found I was always too late, or too soon. When I called at an hotel in Madrid, where he had been staying, I learned he had just left for the railway; and after our return, he told me his daughter saw me in the street as they were hurrying to catch a train.

How many remarkable facts have been related within the last few years respecting old English houses and estates! During a visit to Lord Ebury, at Moor Park, he told me the mansion he occupied had been in the hands of many distinguished families; and that reminds one of what is said in the Eastern tale: "Call it not a palace but a caravanserai." It belonged to the Abbot of St. Albans; to Neville, Archbishop of York; to Henry VII.; to De Vere, Earl of Oxford; to Cardinal Wolsey; to Lucy, Countess of Bedford; to Sir John Franklin; to the Earl of Ossory, who sold it to the Duke of Monmouth, whose Duchess sold it to Mr. Styles, of South Sea Bubble notoriety, to be afterwards purchased by Lord Anson. After changing owners again and again, it was secured by the Marquis of Westminster for his son. Lord Ebury informed me it had never remained in the same family more than two generations. There runs a curious story of the Lady of the Earl of Monmouth, who possessed the estate in the seventeenth century,—that her ladyship protested against the intention of James I., to put his son Prince Charles "into iron boots, to strengthen his joints and sinews"; for he seemed to have been physically as a boy what he was, in some respects, morally as a man—very *weak-kneed.*

In the course of my recollections, I have had much to say of foreign tours, and also of journeys in different parts of England for various religious purposes; but, in drawing my personal narrative to a close, I am constrained to add a few lines, respecting visits to friends in my own county, where I have enjoyed welcome rests amidst ministerial toils.

One spot, long years ago, where I was wont to seek recreation was Letheringsett Hall, near Holt, in my native county, Norfolk. There still lives Mr. Cozens-Hardy, whom I knew as a boy, about five years old, in days when we worshipped in Calvert Street Chapel, Norwich. He married a lady whom I recollect as a girl, and who was long the light of his dwelling, well known to numerous guests. They hospitably entertained me in many of my summer holidays, and drove me round the neighbourhood called "The Garden of Norfolk." Respecting his beloved wife, let me quote words which I wrote for a short family memorial of her: "My last two or three visits found her weak and frail, but yet a good deal of her old buoyancy would come back as we sat chatting round the fire. She seemed to have a quiet faith in the blessed Gospel, but with some shadows of doubt and fear respecting herself. No bold, self-asserting professions, as is the case with some, but a genuine sympathy in reference to the fundamental truths of the Gospel, which form the resting-place of all true believers. She seemed to know more of the Valley of Humiliation than of the Land of Beulah; not often climbing the Delectable Mountains, but by no means a prisoner in Doubting Castle." Her good husband has for many years been the main supporter of the Methodist Society in Holt, and his son, the eminent Q.C., has been for many years a member of the Congregational Church at Kensington. The large-hearted Mr. Colman, M.P. for Norwich, married Mr. Cozens-Hardy's eldest daughter, and in their hospitable homes at Carrow and Corton I have spent many a happy day.

I may add here that amongst delightful sojourns in English homes, I gratefully reckon Stanley Park, the residence of Sir Samuel Marling; a marine villa at Dawlish, belonging to Sir Thomas Lea, Bart., also his home at Kidderminster; the beautiful Quinta on the Welsh border, belonging to Colonel Barnes; and the marine residence of Miss Cheetham, one of my interesting school-girls at Kensington.

During the later portion of my residence in Kensington, there was a considerable increase of Roman Catholics residing in the neighbourhood. When I first went to it, a small place of worship sufficed to meet their wants, but before I left, a large church was built near the Vicarage, and another in the high road, partly hidden by buildings in front. After the formation of a Westminster Archiepiscopal see, the last-named edifice became a pro-cathedral, where Cardinal Manning sometimes officiated. As I did not hear of numerous conversions, in the neighbourhood, to the Romish faith, I was curious to know whence the increase arose, and one day I had a long conversation on the subject with Monsignor Capel. He informed me that it was owing largely to an increase in the number of priests who had come to reside in the place, and who attracted many retired people who were desirous of opportunities for confession and spiritual advice.

Hence, I gathered that the increase of Catholics in the neighbourhood did not arise from local conversions; this explained what had been a matter of wonder. The Monsignor was very sociable and communicative, and gave much information about Romanism, its usages and dignitaries. He had a great deal to say about the political relations of distinguished Catholics at that time. How far all his reports were to be trusted I cannot say.

Certainly there was much activity amongst

Hammersmith Catholics. Within a few doors of my house there was a sisterhood active in collecting whatever they could of money, garments, and other benefits for the poor, and on the edge of Brook Green rose a handsome church, in which special revival services were held. I attended one of these, and heard a priest make earnest religious appeals to careless sinners.

There was a nunnery not far off, and from the abbess, through the medium of a relative, I received an invitation to witness the ceremony of taking the veil. As a spectacle, there was something about it pathetic and touching, but as an act of worship the whole struck me as altogether out of harmony with primitive Christianity. The relative who conveyed to me the invitation was the daughter of a Dissenting minister, a girl highly imaginative and poetical, who made some little stir in earlier life by a book entitled "From Oxford to Rome," by "One that made the Journey." She told me of a complimentary note on the subject from a High Church politician; and I found that she had been thrown a good deal in the way of Oxford "perverts," as they were called. She became a decided convert, and related to me much of what she saw amongst her new friends. By her severe penances she broke down her health until she died, but not in the religion she had recently embraced. The faith of her childhood, in its simplicity, returned in her last days. I do not know that she made a formal renunciation of what she had lately embraced, but she desired no priestly ministrations, and fell back upon her Bible, and the truths she had accepted in former days. She joined in her father's prayers by her bedside, and so went home to rest for ever with her Saviour, whom she loved amidst all her aberrations of controversial thought.

Soon after my resignation I paid a summer visit to my friend Mr. George Moore, of Whitehall, Cumberland, the well-known merchant prince. There I met Lord Justice Lush, his lady and daughter, Dr. Moffat, Canon Battersby, and Mr. Smithies, the "Workman's Friend." One day we had Bible readings in a baronial-looking hall; another day we had outdoor recreations for the villagers, when a select party dined at the mansion. In the evenings we were taken to places in the neighbourhood to attend Bible meetings. On Sunday we went to church in the morning and to chapel in the evening. Our host was in all his glory.

With the good judge I had much conversation, and heard something of his early life story. He had been on the point of settling in America when he was young, and went there more than once before he finally made a home in his own country. He was a beautiful character, an example of Christian politeness, general intelligence, and professional learning.

In closing notices of towns to which I have paid ministerial visits, let me mention Hastings, in which, from circumstances to be mentioned, I feel more than ordinary interest. I do not speak of the decisive battle on the field of Senlac, which ended the line of Saxon sovereigns and gave to England a Norman king, but of personal memories, somewhat unique in their connection. There was, many years ago, a venerable Dissenting minister in the town whose congregation was small, and it was thought by London friends and others, that a new and larger chapel should be built, and efforts made to revive the cause. I was invited to preach at the dedication of that building, and at the close of the sermon found my old fellow-student, the Rev. James Griffin, was present. He had just before, owing to impaired health, resigned an important pastorate at Manchester, and, as he seemed to be recovering strength, I suggested that this new chapel at Hastings might be a suitable sphere for resuming his ministry. The congregation invited him to become pastor, and he faithfully and successfully for many years discharged the duties of that office. It became after a time necessary to erect a still larger edifice, and, in connection with the opening services, I was for a second time invited to preach to the people. Mr. Griffin soon afterwards engaged in the erection of another chapel outside the town, and when the time for opening it approached he invited me to undertake that service. Thus a threefold cord of interest attached me to Nonconformist friends at Hastings. Moreover, repeated visits on the part of my dear wife and children increased my interest in the town, and the hospitality of my friends I remember with gratitude. My dear friend James Griffin still lives, adorning the doctrine he has successfully preached for more than half a century.

The autumnal meeting of the Congregational Union was in 1886 held at Norwich. My friend, the Rev. Edward White, was chairman, and I was invited to read in the old Meeting House, where I worshipped in my youth, a paper on the early history of Norfolk Congregationalism. There was a large gathering of ministers and other friends in the city, and, as in other cities and towns, Episcopalians received Nonconformists as their guests. It was my privilege to be entertained by the Bishop, with whom I had become acquainted while sojourning under the roof of his brother, Lord Chichester, at Stanmer Park. I was received and treated with the greatest kindness and comfort, and found this Episcopal home a beautiful example of Christian simplicity and devotion.

The Mayor of the city received members of the Union and other friends in St. Andrew's Hall on the Monday evening; and one afternoon Mr. Colman, M.P. for Norwich, had a large garden-party in his pleasure grounds.

I availed myself of opportunities during the week for rambling about scenes of my boyhood, amidst many changes in architecture, manners and customs, including habits of religious life. The trade of the city had flowed into new channels; old families such as I knew in my boyhood were no more. New faces I saw everywhere, and pensive thoughts were naturally suggested when one traversed memories of seventy years. How different had been my lot from what it might have been! Church and Dissent did not stand in the same relations to each other as they had done once. There was more mutual charity, more, I believe and trust, of real religion. Certainly, Evangelicalism had made way in the Establishment, and was not regarded as it had been in days gone by.

I took a ramble outside the old city, and called on young friends; and so caught glimpses touching borders of auld lang syne.

It fell to my lot to occupy a bedroom in the palace exactly to my taste. It is described by Blomefield in his "History of Norwich." Lined with carved wainscot brought from the demolished abbey of St. Bennet in the Holm, retaining still the arms of that abbey—of the Veres, and others, particularly those of Sir John Fastolff, their great benefactor. There were also busts of heroes and remarkable men and women, "brought hither by Bishop Rugg." The place recalled images of old, and stories which had interested me in youth; if they did not people my dreams, they coloured my meditations.

My "Recollections of a Long Life" began with a notice of being born in Norwich; and as the last visit to my birthplace was at the time now indicated, I think it is a fitting point for terminating my narrative.

CHAPTER XVI

IN completing this volume I propose to take a survey of what I have seen and noticed, amongst distinct religious denominations, during seventy years.

I. To begin with the Church of England. I remember hearing a sermon by the late Bishop of Manchester, at the reopening of Chester Cathedral, when, in no measured terms, he dwelt upon ecclesiastical abuses, as they existed during the last century, and the earliest part of the present. He exposed the nepotism of bishops, the worldliness of clergymen, and the indifference of Church-people to religion in general. About the same time another prelate privately told me that things in his diocese, when he was first consecrated, had reached such a point as made it wonderful how the Establishment had survived. He complained of the limited power diocesans had at command, to repress existing evils, and gave an instance, how in his own case he had spent a large sum without any effect for the removal of a clergyman who had dishonoured his profession. About the facts charged against the delinquent there could be no doubt, but proceedings failed through technical objections. I remember when I was a youth there were scandals in the diocese of Norwich, publicly known, yet legally unassailable. Plurality and non-residence were notorious. Preaching was neglected to a shameful degree; in one case fifteen churches were served by three incumbents. Livings had to be sequestered through clerical insolvency or scandalous misconduct. Bishop Stanley wrought a great reformation in these respects, much to the dismay of delinquents, much to the satisfaction of parishioners. I remember him perfectly well. Of slight figure, with white hair, he tripped along the streets of Norwich on a Sunday, to one church after another without giving beforehand notice of his movements, but surprising rector or curate at the close of the service by rising to pronounce the benediction. He was as unremitting and efficient in his clerical position, as he had before been in his naval duties. The magistrates' seat prepared Ambrose for his episcopate at Milan: the deck of a ship prepared Edward Stanley to rule the diocese of Norwich.

The typical High Church clergyman of my early days was a person perfunctorily discharging his duties, living on civil terms with his parishioners, known in the parish by clerical costume, reading prayers in a surplice, and preaching in a black gown, visiting the best society in the neighbourhood, kind to the poor, and looking upon Dissenters as a rather suspicious class.

But a great change took place in 1832. Earnest men, as we have seen, arose at Oxford, who devoted themselves to the study of certain Anglo-Catholic divines and Greek and Latin fathers. Some of them introduced ritualistic practices, older than the Reformation. The change under Henry VIII. and Elizabeth was approved by them no further than as it wiped away stains from the face of popery. I recollect a High Church layman telling me he liked an ornate service, but that he was left far behind by the newly advanced party. I have myself witnessed ceremonies in Anglican churches so nearly approaching the Romanistic that only a practised eye could discern the difference. There were, however, men of another order, who had a liking for Anglo-Catholic theology, but eschewed revived ceremonialism; and I have heard a High Churchman in Westminster Abbey preach such a sermon on the necessity of the Holy Spirit for the salvation of souls as, with a few expressions, a Methodist might have delivered. He pronounced a glowing eulogium on John Wesley. On one side this clergyman appeared a warm-hearted Evangelical, on the other, he was a staunch High Churchman.

When I think of Evangelicals early in this century, they present a different class from men of the type just described. As a boy in Norwich I heard Simeon of Cambridge, and Legh Richmond of Turvey; and I remember them at this moment as they appeared in the autumn of that year to advocate the British and Foreign Bible Society. The former of the two does not come to my recollection so vividly as the latter; him I can now see, with his pleasant face, and large spectacles, mounting, with a lame foot, the pulpit stairs of St. Lawrence's Church—attired, not in a white surplice, but in a black gown: nothing priestly in his appearance and manner. His sermon was on behalf of the Society for Promoting Christianity among Jews. He took for his text, "For thy servants take pleasure in her stones and favour the dust thereof." With a soft, winning voice, and "a sweet reasonableness" he discoursed on the interest, which all Christians should feel in building up the Church of God, especially with stones gathered from ruins of the House of Israel. In St. Andrew's Hall he spoke on behalf of the Bible Society, and related a conversation he had on the subject with the Emperor Alexander of Russia, when he visited England after the Napoleonic wars. He also told touching stories of what the Word of God could do for people amidst sins and sorrows. As to Charles Simeon, whom I heard, he did not penetrate like dew, but came down with hailstones and coals of fire.

At a later period Episcopalians bestirred themselves in many parts of the country, and from end to end, in building and other efforts for church extension, and I recollect Dean Alford told me how surprised the Church Commissioners were at the liberal response given to challenges for aiding ecclesiastical objects.

In 1865 the old Act of Uniformity was modified so as to relieve the consciences of such as scrupled to declare unfeigned consent to everything contained in the Prayer-Book. *Now* the requirement was an assent to the Articles, the Common Prayer, and the Ordering of Bishops, Priests, and Deacons, and a declaration that the doctrine of the Establishment was agreeable to the Word of God. In 1867 a commission was appointed to regulate public worship, the result of which was unsatisfactory.

In former pages of this volume I have noticed devoted and exemplary Churchmen through whom my own soul has been nourished and stimulated. It would be ungrateful not to recognise, on these pages, spiritual benefit I have derived from sermons preached and books written by living Churchmen.

Before I close this section of reminiscences touching the Church of England it will be interesting to notice an accession to it of a remarkable person who had previously been a Dissenter. Her name, now so extensively known, was Sarah Martin. My old friend Mr. Walford often alluded to her in his conversations, and in his Autobiography, written in a series of letters published by his direction, he gives the following narrative :—

"This young woman, during my residence in Yarmouth, supported by her needle both herself and, I think, also an aged grandmother, with whom she lived at Caister, near Yarmouth. When I first knew her she was, I imagine, about twenty years of age. She introduced herself to me as one who had been as inconsiderate and negligent of religion, as she was ignorant of the nature of genuine Christianity. By some means, which I do not now remember, she was induced to come to the New Meeting, where she heard one or more discourses from me, which, she assured me, had produced very deep impressions upon her, and entirely changed the character of her mind and conduct. She subsequently became a member of the Church of which I was the pastor, and was most diligent and attentive to the public and private meetings of the Church. I found her to possess great energy of mind, by the exercise of which she very soon became well informed in the truths and duties of Christianity, and ardently disposed to do any good that was compatible with her station in life. Her affection for me was such that it is not too much to say of her, as St. Paul did of his converts among the Galatians, that, if it had been possible, they would have plucked out their own eyes and have given them to him (Gal. iv. 15). Her regard for me, and the ministry I exercised, continued unalterable through the several years in which I resided in Yarmouth, after my acquaintance with her commenced. I afterwards saw her several times during occasional visits which I made to that place, when I found that she still retained an affectionate remembrance of me."

She was in humble circumstances, and earned a scanty income by the use of her needle; but she coupled with it extraordinary efforts for the good of others, and this disposed some ladies, members of the Established Church, to contribute to her support. This enabled her to devote more time to her charitable work, and at length she was so absorbed in it that she became a kind of missionary to the inmates of the workhouse and the prisoners in Yarmouth gaol. She read and explained the Scriptures to them, and in devotional service, she carried on for their spiritual welfare, she employed parts of the Church Prayer-Book. Gradually, I infer, she became attached to those who helped her, and this association led to her becoming a member of the Establishment. After her death a commemorative window was placed in Yarmouth parish church, and at its reopening, after a costly restoration, Bishop Wilberforce pronounced an eloquent eulogium on Sarah Martin's character. Some intimate Nonconformist friends of mine remained attached to her, and showed me numerous MSS. in her handwriting.

I now return to the ranks of Dissent and proceed to notice—

II. English Presbyterianism. A word on its earlier history will here be appropriate. The Presbyterians of the sixteenth and seventeenth centuries were orthodox. After the Restoration many of them adhered to the Westminster Confession, but a departure from it, in some instances, appeared in the century after. Arian and Socinian opinions began to obtain, but those who held them claimed connection with the Presbyterians of the Commonwealth, on the ground that they followed such worthies in the exercise of religious freedom and the rights of conscience. Their forefathers had repudiated the Prayer-Book, and now they, their sons in the cause of religious freedom, renounced the Westminster Confession. For the most part they remained steadfast in believing New Testament miracles. The Rev. Mr. Madge, a noted English Presbyterian, sixty or seventy years ago, said to me once, he could not understand how a man could be called a Christian who did not believe in our Lord's resurrection.

During the reign of William IV. the two most prominent English Presbyterians of the old school were the Rev. Mr. Aspland and Mr. Madge. The latter I knew well. Mr. Aspland was an eloquent speaker, and exerted himself conspicuously in the cause of Unitarianism, with which he identified the interests of religious freedom. His son, in writing his father's life, pourtrays that gentleman's religious connections, social virtues, and decision of character;

but does not conceal his warmth of temper, and dislike to certain eminent Trinitarians. Mr. Madge, before he became minister of Essex Street, London, was for some years settled in my native city, and presided over a wealthy congregation, in which were several distinguished literary and artistic people. The Martineaus, the Aldersons, the Starks, and other distinguished families, were of the number. They worshipped in the Octagon Chapel, as it was called from its architecture, and for a number of years the building was the most distinguished Nonconformist place of worship in the eastern capital. It was rather sumptuously fitted up in my boyish days, and the attendants were not wont to mix much with other Dissenters. If there were any fault in this, I dare say it was shared on both sides.

Returning to the English Presbyterians at large, but especially as they existed in London, I must speak of a trust established by Dr. Williams, of the last century. He was orthodox, but the administration of funds bequeathed by him came into the hands of those Presbyterians who deviated from his doctrinal views, but still retained the Presbyterian name by which he was known. Though Unitarians in opinion, they by no means confined their charity to Unitarian ministers and chapels; and still the "Williams' Scholarships" are enjoyed by students preparing for orthodox ministrations amongst Independents. Dr. Martineau was for some time an administrator of the trust, but strongly objected to the exclusion of orthodox ministers from its administration.

During the last century there were Presbyterians in England holding decidedly Evangelical views, and of late there have been numerous congregations gathered, which, in their unity, form what is called "The Presbyterian Church in England." Scotch brethren of great renown — Dr. James Hamilton, Dr. Young, and Dr. Archer—I had the privilege of numbering amongst personal friends, and they were held in honour by all Evangelical Churchmen and Nonconformists.

III. Another large section of brethren were Baptists, distinguished by certain *doctrinal* and *disciplinary* views;—the former as Particular or Calvinistic, on the one hand, and General or Arminian on the other;—the latter as Open communionists and Strict communionists. Open communionists admit to the Lord's table those who have not been baptised by immersion; Strict communionists confine the Lord's Supper to those who have been immersed. Such distinctions are now fading away. Calvinists and Arminians are comprehended in the same union, and Strict communionists are comparatively few.

Robert Hall, the advocate of Open communion, I never saw: he died when I was young. Joseph Kinghorn, his opponent, a distinguished Hebrew scholar, I knew well, as he lived in Norwich during my boyhood. William Brock, who succeeded him, and afterwards became minister of Bloomsbury Chapel, London, entered the ministry about the same time as I did, and we regarded each other with warm affection. Dr. Cox and Dr. Steane were widely known in the religious world, and with both of them I entered into a fellowship of work and worship at the opening of chapels and on other public occasions. John Howard Hinton was another Baptist brother, of whom I saw much when he was at Reading and I was at Windsor. He was more original, more metaphysical, more scientific, and more excitable than others whom I have mentioned, perhaps of a higher intellectual order, and still greater depth of religious emotion. Mr. Spurgeon, who has so recently left the world, and whose influence and fame extended further than any other Nonconformist in modern times, I greatly respected and admired; and though I did not share his intimacy, I saw something of him in my own home, and a little more in his, where he had a magnificent library, and received his numerous friends with cordiality. His popularity amongst aristocratic people was, for a little time, much greater than is generally supposed, for I was informed by a lady of distinction that for some weeks in his early career he was a leading topic of conversation in upper circles.

IV. I now turn to the Quaker community. Well do I remember meetings at the Goldencroft, Norwich, where, at the upper end, sat men and women called Public Friends. My mother, born in 1770, told me of yearly meetings held in our old city, when sometimes Friends from America attended: and so great was the number of visitors that it raised the market price of provisions. Some ladies who came from the other side of the Atlantic wore dresses with open skirts and green aprons. No bows of ribbon were seen, while bonnets of black and of lead-coloured silk crowned the heads of young and old. What Charles Lamb says in his "Elia" corresponds with what I recollect, and what my mother used to tell me, how "troops of the shining ones" were seen walking the streets, on their way to the house of worship, where their silence was more eloquent than speech. I have read with sympathy "The Life of John Woolman," written by himself, and so warmly recommended by the essayist. "Get," says Charles Lamb, "the writings of John Woolman by heart, and love the early Quakers."

A very serious diversion in theological opinion existed among American Friends early in this century, and it is because an effect of it appeared in England that it is noticed here. A French Friend—the well-known Stephen Grellet—travelling in the States, makes this entry in his journal, under date 1822:—"We proceeded to Long Island, where I attended all the meetings, but here my soul's distress exceeded all I had known during the preceding months, though my baptism had been deep. I found that the greatest part of the members of our Society and many of the ministers and elders, are carried away by the principle which Elias Hicks has so assiduously propagated among them. He now speaks out boldly, disguising his sentiments no longer; he seeks to invalidate the Holy Scriptures, and sets up man's reason as his only guide, openly denying the divinity of Christ. I have had many expostulations with him in which I have most tenderly pleaded with him, but all has been in vain."* From what I have read in American literature

---

* "Memoirs of Stephen Grellet," vol. ii., 130.

touching what is known as the Hicksite controversy, it appears to me plainly indicative of a denial among many American Friends, that Jesus Christ, in the orthodox sense of the term, was Divine, and that He did not make any atonement for sin. Hicks appears to have been a thorough mystic, unintelligible to common-sense people. At all events he converted many to his views; and these views were caught up by some Friends in this country. To what extent exactly they were adopted in England I cannot say: but they created alarm amongst many Friends on this side the Atlantic. Great sorrow at the abandonment of Evangelical doctrines led to secessions from Quakerism on the part of excellent people who had been born and bred in the community. Some of them resided, at the time I speak of, on the borders of Wales, others in the county of York. They became Congregationalists, and in tours on behalf of the London Missionary Society, I was received hospitably in their homes, and had gratifying opportunities of witnessing their beautiful Christian life.

Joseph John Gurney, of Earlham, felt seriously concerned respecting the American defection, in a community to which he had been attached from childhood. He had studied in the University of Oxford, had cultivated friendships in other denominations, was a good classic and Biblical scholar, and also an author of theological works. Mr. Gurney was "concerned" about the effect of Hicksite opinion on American and English Friends, and therefore took up his pen and wrote in reply to the leader who had done so much mischief.

Mr. Gurney, like his sister Mrs. Fry, undertook journeys for preaching the Gospel, and once he visited Windsor for that purpose. I was unwell at the time, but he called and talked by my bedside, and commended me to God in prayer. Several Quaker families at that period were living at Staines and Uxbridge; with them I had much intercourse, especially when we were joined in the advocacy of Slave Emancipation. The community, in both towns now named, was considerable for numbers and for wealth.

Friends now dress, speak and act much like other people. Conforming to common custom, they still eschew all extravagances of fashion. They no longer forfeit membership by "marrying out of Society." "The Right Honourable John Bright" (how shocked George Fox would have been at the title!) told me once, that relaxation in strictness as to unimportant points, had checked a decline in numbers going on before.

V. Methodism, of course, brings to my mind a long train of early associations. Not merely names, but living forms, of noted preachers belonging to the second decade of this century come back to my recollection.

Calvert Street Chapel was opened about 1812, and Dr. Coke preached.

I cannot say that I remember his sermon; but, as noticed already, I distinctly recollect seeing the odd-looking, diminutive man, standing on a table talking in the committee room of Bethel Hospital,* adorned by paintings of foundress and governors. Dr. Coke energetically addressed on the occasion a number of people, who had been invited by my grandfather, to hear the noted advocate of Methodist missions. Many years afterwards I mentioned the circumstance to a gentleman, who at the time took care of the patients, when he fetched an old committee book, in which this gathering was noticed, with a minute expressing the displeasure of the Governors at such a liberty being taken, and forbidding anything of the kind in future. The Wesleyan congregations in Norwich were then very large, and *local* preachers—uncultivated men in humble life—

* See page 2.

frequently occupied the pulpit in the afternoon service at Calvert Street, and, remember, delivered animated discourses likely to do their hearers good.

Dr. Jabez Bunting was a very influential man among the Methodists when I was young. For many years he was regarded as ruler of the Connexion,—exerting a despotic sway over the whole body. Such general conclusions oftentimes are not fairly drawn from existing facts, and how far widely extended opinion in the case now noticed, is justifiable I cannot undertake to say. To me he was very agreeable, and for him I had great respect. William Bunting, his son, was of a different stamp from his father, and though a skilful critic, he had not his father's gift of authority and rule.

Before the middle of the century came Dr. Newton, to open a second chapel, in the upper part of Norwich; his magnificent voice and careful diction produced a powerful effect. I met him in after-life at Windsor, when he told me that he was accustomed to leave his home on Monday morning in the Manchester circuit, and travel by coach to the other end of England,—perhaps cross over to Ireland,—and then get back, at the end of the week, ready for preaching the next day. He said he weekly delivered five or six sermons, making them "on the wheels" as he went along. He seemed a stranger to physical fatigue.

During my Windsor ministry I became acquainted with a noted Wesleyan, who was not an itinerant, but a local, preacher. He went by the name of "Billy Dawson," and was eminently gifted with humour and pathos. I heard him preach, and listened to his platform speeches. He was not only naturally eloquent, but histrionic too; in speeches and sermons he acted while he spoke. He made you realise what he described. It is said that George Whitefield, when preaching to sailors, described a storm at sea so vividly that some of them shouted, "Take to the long boat." Dawson had a like power of realising what he described. He would, at a missionary meeting, make a telescope of his resolution, and putting it to one of his eyes, describe what he saw in imagination,—perhaps a picture of the millennium drawn from Isaiah's prophecies. I was young, just come from college, at the time I speak of, and made a speech in which I used some words which were not so plain as they might have been. After the meeting he spoke to me kindly, suggesting equivalent terms in plain Saxon. It was a good lesson for an unfledged bird.

When I was a member of the Wesleyan Society, I attended class according to rule, and I found the practice beneficial, inasmuch as it was a constant spur to self-examination. The primitive agape, revived amongst the Methodists, exists under the name of love-feast, at which, together with eating bread and drinking water as an expression of fellowship, men and women are accustomed voluntarily to rise, and give some account of their religious experience for edification to others. These addresses I found often interesting and useful. By such means, a habit of spiritual intercommunication amongst Methodists is kept alive; beneficial in some cases no doubt, but liable to abuse in others, as most good things are. I am constrained to relate how this habit on the bright side manifested itself on a private occasion during a meeting of Conference in London. Dr. Jobson, an eminent Wesleyan, invited a party of friends to his house. He kindly included me in the number, and I found at his hospitable board the President for the year, and some ex-presidents. Together with them, Drs. Binney, Raleigh, Allon, and Donald Fraser were present. Our host was a thorough Methodist, and very comprehensive in his sympathies, for he had mixed with different denominations. He had many friends in the Establishment, and in early life had studied under an eminent Roman Catholic architect, at whose house he met bishops and priests of that communion. On the occasion I refer to, he in an easy way initiated a conversation which I can never forget. He appealed to his guests, one by one, for some account of their religious life. All readily responded; and this is most remarkable,—all who spoke attributed to Methodism spiritual influence of a decisive kind. To use Wesleyan phraseology, most of them had been "brought to God" through Methodist instrumentality. Dr. Osborne was present, and made some remarks, at the close of which, with choked utterance, he repeated the verse—

> "And if our fellowship below,
> In Jesus be so sweet,
> What heights of rapture shall we know,
> When round the throne we meet?"

The Norwich Methodists were chiefly humble folks with a sprinkling of some in better circumstances; their habits were very simple and they looked upon some who made money as becoming "worldly," or at least, as exposed to temptation. At that time, however, such as possessed social comforts could not be justly charged with conformity to the course of this world; and over their little gatherings in one another's houses there was shed a religious atmosphere such as was breathed in class and love-feast. Early in the century on a Sunday, between afternoon and evening service, there might be a large tea-party, where the preacher, a class-leader, and other members of Society would talk and pray and sing, till it was time to go to evening service at chapel. This communion seems to me now as I think of it such as is described in Malachi : " Then they that feared the Lord spake often one to another, and the Lord hearkened and heard it ; and a book of remembrance was written before Him for them that feared the Lord and that thought upon His name ; and they shall be Mine, saith the Lord of hosts, in that day when I make up My jewels, and I will spare them as a man spareth his own son that serveth him."

Worldly prosperity has since fallen to the lot of not a few Methodists, and the usual temptations surrounding wealth have tested their character ; but I am thankful to say, amongst those whom I have visited, I have found beautiful instances of adherence to religious principles. I may mention a friend already noticed, Sir William McArthur, K.C.M.G. When Lord Mayor of London he continued his previous Wesleyan duties; and whilst bountiful in his hospitality eschewed usages of a fashionable kind. In his year of office the Œcumenical Conference was held, and during its meetings repeated Mansion House invitations were given to friends in sympathy with Evangelical religion. I attended his funeral, and in his residence on Notting Hill a large number of mourners assembled, and we had a short devotional service together, very touching, tender, and beautiful.

My personal recollections of Methodism, which roll back more than seventy years ago, linger round Yarmouth and Norwich. At Yarmouth I used to worship on a Sunday in a curious old-fashioned square chapel, with galleries on the four sides. There was a deep one opposite the two entrance doors, and attached to the front of that gallery was a pulpit—by what means, as a boy, I never could make out. The preacher ascended from behind by a staircase, invisible to the congregation, and then from the top of the staircase descended by two or three steps into a curiously shaped pulpit. I distinctly recollect the venerable Joseph Benson, then a patriarch, who had been associated with Methodists in John Wesley's time. I think I see him now, of slender frame, venerable aspect, and wearing a coat of dark purple. Of course I have no recollection of what he said, but he was regarded as a saintly man in those days. In the autumn Yarmouth was frequented by a number of mariners from the north—coblemen they were called—who had come to fish for herrings off the Yarmouth coast. They were staunch Methodists, and used to hold a prayer-meeting after the general service. How those men used to pray with stentorian voice, which called forth loud "Amens" from voices all over the chapel!

In Calvert Street, Norwich, there used to be special services on Christmas-day. After a prayer-meeting at six o'clock in the morning there was preaching at seven o'clock, when hymns appropriate to the season were sung, accompanied by violins and wind instruments of different kinds. I did not fail, between five and six o'clock, to rise and cross the city in order to be in good time for these services. They usually commenced with the hymn—

> "Christians, awake, salute the happy morn
> Whereon the Saviour of mankind was born;
> Rise to adore the mystery of love,
> Which hosts of angels chanted from above;
> With them the joyful tidings first begun
> Of God incarnate and the Virgin's son.

> "Then to the watchful shepherds it was told,
> Who heard the angelic herald's voice: 'Behold,
> I bring good tidings of a Saviour's birth,
> To you and all the nations upon earth:
> This day hath God fulfilled His promised word,
> This day is born a Saviour, Christ the Lord.'"

With the Methodist chapel in Calvert Street my earliest religious thoughts are connected. Watch-nights and love-feasts, are sacred in my recollection.

VI. Respecting the Congregationalist denomination, of which I have spoken already, let me add that in 1877 I was requested by Dr. Schaff, of New York, to give my impression of prevalent beliefs amongst us. I replied as follows : " Looking at the principles of Congregationalism, which involve the repudiation of all human authority in matters of religion, it is impossible to believe that persons holding those principles can consistently regard any ecclesiastical creed or symbol in the same way as Catholics, whether Roman or Anglican, regard the creeds of the ancient Church. There is a strong feeling against the use of such documents for the purpose of defining limits of religious communion, or for the purpose of checking the exercise of free inquiry ; and there is also a widespread conviction that it is impossible to reduce the expression of Christian belief to a series of logical propositions, so as to preserve and represent the full spirit of Gospel truth." (See Schaff's "Creeds of Christendom," p. 833.)

No doubt there may be heard in some circles loose conversation, seeming to indicate such a repugnance to creeds as would imply a dislike to all formal definitions of Christian doctrine; but I apprehend the prevailing sentiment relative to this subject among our ministers and churches does not go beyond the point just indicated. Many of them consider that while creeds are objectionable as tests, and imperfect as confessions, they may have a certain value as manifestoes of conviction, on the part of different communities.

Some people write and talk on the subject of present opinion, with a positiveness which only omniscience could warrant. No mortal can know what is going on in the minds of thousands, touching momentous subjects; yet such knowledge is requisite for the confident conclusions of certain critics. We may speak decidedly of what is commonly taught in a community, yet this should be done with qualifications and no farther.

Silence on momentous points may prove a loss as to the full wealth of theology; but I am thankful for gain at the present day in richer views than formerly of our Lord's character, and the bearing of it upon life and conduct. Let me add, however, if *Redemption* in all its fulness be not prominent in pulpit ministrations, power will be gone. Some suppose we are making theological advance, and that discoveries are opening akin to those in physical science; but people who have more carefully surveyed the wide field, and more observantly studied the history of religious thought, discover that much as seen at first sight, is chiefly a falling back upon what was old and forgotten.

In closing what I have to say of modern Congregationalists, I venture to notice deceased ministers whom it has been a privilege to number amongst my friends.

I knew but slightly the Rev. William Jay of Bath. He has been incidentally noticed in these pages already, for he was old when I was young. He rose from a lowly rank in life to be regarded as teacher and companion by the intellectual and noble. Mrs. Hannah More valued his ministrations and cultivated his society. Wilberforce used to attend his chapel when staying at Bath; and an Indian ruler, when in England, went to hear him at Surrey Chapel, and expressed great admiration of the sermon.

The next to be mentioned is John Angell James of Birmingham. I remember perfectly well the first sermon I heard him preach when I was a student. The text was: "Our conversation (or citizenship) is in heaven." His voice was richly toned—a genuine birth gift improved by culture. He introduced the following illustration: A pilgrim in the Middle Ages, on his way to Jerusalem, passed through Constantinople. A friend took him from street to street, pausing to point out attractions, in magnificent buildings, and the rich scenery of the Golden Horn. He wondered the traveller was not enchanted. The latter replied: "Yes, all very fine, *but it is not the Holy City.*" The application was obvious and well enforced.

Dr. Raffles of Liverpool—noticed already as one of my companions to Rome—and Dr. Hamilton of Leeds, well known throughout England, won the affections of their people by sympathetic intercourse, and interested them by eloquent instructions and appeals. The former enunciated his carefully prepared periods with a voice naturally musical, the latter delivered his thoughts in condensed sentences, which reminded one of a person taking very short steps. There was an intellectual power in the sermons of the last-named, not indicated in those of the former.

John Alexander of Norwich I cannot pass by without notice. Like David, he was a youth with ruddy countenance. His speech throughout a sermon fell gentle as a snowflake, without any coldness of touch. He read much, and made good use of what he read. The charm of his private life and conversation exceeded the effect of his public ministry, though that was great.

I must mention another name. John Harris was for some years a secluded pastor at Epsom, little known. He wrote "The Great Teacher," but though far above the common level of such literature, it made little impression, compared with its merits. A prize was offered for an essay on Covetousness and Christian Liberality. Harris won the prize, and printed the essay. The effect was instantaneous.

The book sold edition after edition, and the author's name became generally familiar. Requests for his services were universal. He was everywhere talked about, and when he preached places were crowded. His popularity lasted as long as he lived, but he died when he was fifty-four. He was unassuming, kind-hearted, generous to poor ministers, genial in conversation, and beloved by all who knew him.

Another brother must be mentioned—Baldwin Brown—of superior intellectual type, well educated, an extensive reader, and one who delighted in a large circle of sympathetic friends. He gathered round him a good congregation, composed chiefly of thoughtful people, who became assimilated to his characteristic teachings. He wore himself out by incessant study and pulpit service.

I must not pass by David Thomas of Bristol, my fellow-student and friend through life, whose elevated and genial character won from a wide circle warm attachment, and whose unique pulpit power captivated all capable of sympathising with one so thoughtful and so good.

Nor can I omit Alexander Raleigh, my successor for a short period at Kensington, who fulfilled a ministry dear to many who listened with delight to his characteristic teaching.

The last name I mention is that of Samuel Martin, minister at Westminster Chapel. He had gifts of a peculiar description, which marked him off, and made him stand by himself, both as minister and man. His appearance, voice, manner, habits, were all his own. He *lived* for his Church, in whose interests he was thoroughly absorbed. No one not intimately acquainted with him could have an adequate idea how he loved his flock, and lived for their welfare week by week. I. had reverent affection for him as a saintly man, and I witnessed evidence amongst his large circle, in town and country, how he watched for souls as one that must give an account. His congregation during Parliament months included several

M.P.'s, whom he gathered together for patriotic prayer.

His neighbour, Dr. Stanley, had a reverent regard for Mr. Martin, and I know that the Dean and Lady Augusta went to Westminster Chapel to hear his voice and worship with his people. He spoke to me of him in terms of strong affection, also telling me of a brother clergyman who, after a visit to his sick chamber, pronounced him one of the most saintly men he had ever seen.

www.ingramcontent.com/pod-product-compliance
Lightning Source LLC
Chambersburg PA
CBHW051743300426
44115CB00007B/673